yakking
around the
world

Also by Simon Hughes

From Minor to Major
A Lot of Hard Yakka

yakking around the world

A Cricketer's Quest for Love and Utopia

Simon Hughes

SIMON & SCHUSTER
A VIACOM COMPANY

First published in Great Britain by Simon & Schuster UK Ltd, 2000
A Viacom company

1 3 5 7 9 10 8 6 4 2

Simon & Schuster UK Ltd
Africa House
64–78 Kingsway
London WC2B 6AH

Simon & Schuster Australia
Sydney

A CIP catalogue record for this book is available
from the British Library

Hardback ISBN 0-684-86637-4
Trade paperback ISBN 0-743-20833-1

Typeset in Palatino by SX Composing DTP, Rayleigh, Essex
Printed and bound in Great Britain by
Butler & Tanner Ltd, Frome and London

Some names and characteristics of people in this book
have been changed to protect their privacy.

To Callum and my Mum, who saved all my letters

Contents

Athletes when sluggish are revitalised by love making, the
voice is restored from being gruff and husky
Pliny the Elder c. AD 79

London .

1.

Sad

I've been playing away all my life.

In Colombo and Cape Town, Coogee and Cottesloe, Barbados and Bangladesh, Durban and Delhi, Wanneroo and Woolloomooloo and Whakapapa. Cricket took me through five continents, 28 countries and 134 different towns.

I had more addresses than Salman Rushdie. I stayed in $10m Caribbean hideaways with a private beach and $10 a-week Australian digs with a lice infestation. I played for 41 different teams, from slick, international-quality outfits in South Africa to a bunch of hippies in New Zealand. Sometimes I didn't like them, sometimes they didn't like me. So I kept moving on, bat and gloves clutched under my arm. I was a cross between Ernest Hemingway, Giovanni Casanova and Ian Botham. The trouble is, Botham wasn't much of a travel writer, Hemingway didn't have a lot of success with women and Casanova couldn't play cricket to save his life.

I was searching for somewhere mostly warm and sunny and English speaking and not infested by insects with jaws like Esther Rantzen. I wanted seasidey places and a fusion of races and real people, rather than automatons who babble 'You're welcome, have a nice day' every thirty seconds. I wanted passion and papaya, classic beaches and cool bars, exotic cuisine and topless sunbathing. And, as a professional fast bowler, I wanted the air to be frequently rent with the clatter of leather on stumps.

Very important.

SAD. That was my problem. Seasonal Affective Disorder. Sunshine Access Denial. With a pasty face goes a pasty life. Through endless English winters I'd tried cheering myself up with sun lamps or sitting by naked light bulbs or by decorating my college bedroom with aluminium foil. But when I looked in the mirror I just saw a pallid bloke with spots and no spirit. If a weak sun did occasionally peer through the low tin sky, it was about as invigorating as a lukewarm jacuzzi. The only way to warm up in December is to eat a chicken pharl, but then your eyes water and your rear end frazzles.

I hated English winters. They were boring, dark and frigid and the only greenery you saw were the nodules of snot caked on people's hankies. After nineteen cranky, cruddy, crumby winters I'd had enough. I wanted to escape the getting up in grey twilight, the fetid air of mildewed jumpers, the kickabouts on slimy-dog-turd parks, the peaky-faced girls, the men in the street saying 'mustn't grumble' in as grumbly a voice as possible, the great aunts slumped in front of *Bridge On the River Kwai* at Christmas saying, 'Them Japs were awful to your poor uncle Bertie.'

My winter of discontent was 1979, at the end of my first year as a professional cricketer. England were one of the best teams in the world, but my girlfriend wouldn't sleep with me. It came to a head one December night, at the end of a week working as a general dogsbody in a factory canteen. I was taking Amanda, just eighteen, to see a band in Covent Garden. It was cold and drizzling and interlocking my hand with a girl's wet glove didn't exactly set my pulse racing. A surly waitress plonked in front of us a weak lager-and-lime for me and a triple vodka for her, and an hour and a half after we'd ordered it, a cold, emaciated chicken in a basket. The conversation was strained. The band didn't come on till 11.30. The last tube was at 11.45. We had to leave after one song.

The graffitied train was full of people shouting and vomiting. We finally crept back to her parents' semi in Kenton for a bit of festive nookie on the sofa, but her father snapped the light on and ordered me out. So much for the season of goodwill. I got drenched cycling home, narrowly avoided being minced under a truck because the brakes didn't work, and trod in the cat-litter when I sneaked back in through the kitchen window.

I lay awake with a draught down my back thinking how fed up I was with winter. Silly things irritated me. Drying wet Levis on radiators and finding just when you want to wear them that the arse is still sodden. Record collections warping in a cupboard by the boiler. Green bananas. Val Doonican Christmas shows. *Definitely* Val Doonican Christmas shows. Football training in decrepit gyms, injuries from slipping on damp patches in indoor cricket sheds, some old bloke coughing bronchially during the Bolero scene in *Ten*. Dickie Davies's *World of Sport* which was just three hours of wrestling. I hated stupid pub opening times, headless beers full of sediment and *On the*

Buses films. Everything seemed murky, even my chances of making it with a prudish girl with a prickly father. There must be a better winter place than this.

And there was. The next morning in the Around the World section of the weather page of the *Daily Telegraph*:

		°F	°C
Auckland	sunny	75	24
Barbados	sunny	84	29
Calcutta	fair	86	30
Cape Town	sunny	77	25
Colombo	sunny	88	31
Johannesburg	fair	84	29
Melbourne	fair	75	24
New Delhi	sunny	90	32
Perth	sunny	88	31
Singapore	humid	91	33
Sydney	sunny	84	29

Someone once said that people were like their weather. Obviously a warm and sunny place was the place to be. And that's where I was going. My means of travel? Cricket. Like beach lifeguards or palm tree loppers, my job followed the sun. My trade was fast bowling, and between October and March English professional cricketers were free agents. Out of contract. Effectively on the rock and roll. Once the last county championship ball was bowled in September, the sponsored car had to be handed back, the P45 collected and your employers virtually washed their hands of you. Until the following April you were on your tod.

So, rather than spend torturous winter days wiping down ovens and cleaning out chip fryers to pay for a weekend on Broadway – *Ealing* Broadway that is – I sold my bowling skills abroad. Other countries did actually want English pros then, to play for and coach their club teams. I could see the world at the same time. It was obvious. Cricket would be my wings and wheels for an expedition – to find a hotter, happier world where the light was bright, the pitches had zig and zag and the girls were game.

A life of sun, seam and sex.

You could say I was shooting in the dark. When I made this decision aged nineteen I hadn't ever been on a plane or to bed with a girl. Experience: zilch. The best beach I knew was Broadstairs and the nearest I'd got to a leg over was when I'd bowled five consecutive balls down the leg side in a 2nd XI match. What I did have was an enquiring mind. I wanted to find out how other people really lived, what made them laugh and swear, whether they also always drank the dregs of the old milk in the fridge first, before opening the new. I didn't credit the accounts of cheap-skate backpackers who contributed to travel guides from flea-ridden doss houses, or the stories of older cricketing colleagues who'd never ventured beyond the confines of the Bombay Sheraton except if the BA hostesses were staying at the nearby Hilton. They'd barely dipped a toe in. I wanted complete immersion.

You met loads of foreign types in London and they just aroused my curiosity more. Sure, I was fascinated by the cricketers from these different places, intrigued to see great players like Viv Richards, Imran Khan and Richard Hadlee in their home environment. But there were all sorts of other unanswered questions, too. Like why are Australians so pleased with themselves when they live in a vast, useless desert full of spiders? Why are New Zealanders always stoned? How do West Indians manage to walk so slow and bowl so fast? Why do South Africans talk as if their jaw has been all wired up? Do Indians get ring sting?

I didn't know how long it would take to find the best people, the best places and the best cricket in the world. I did know it would involve quite a bit of legwork. Meantime, I would earn a bit of money, enhance my game and try to find my perfect match, then import her to England in March with my photos and trinkets and immediate intentions to buy a barbecue.

The first task was to work out some means of comparing places. I made up a formula to give towns/ countries a total performance:

$$(P + B + C) \times Ct = ?$$

You gave a mark out of ten for the local people (P), the beaches (B) and the standard of cricket (C), added them together and multiplied it by the number of female catches (Ct) you'd made there. My current London score was

People		Beaches		Cricket		Catches		Total
6	+	0	+	7	×	0	=	0

You can see why I wanted to get away.

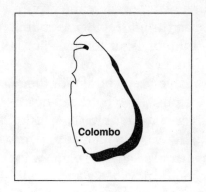

Colombo

2.
Sri Lanka

It Ain't 'Alf Hot and Cold Mum
I decided to get started straight away in my winter-off
before going up to university. On 1 January 1980 I
dumped the girlfriend, ditched the job and travelled to
Sri Lanka. I wasn't randomly venturing into the
unknown. My close friend and cricketing sidekick Dilip
came from Colombo. His family had offered to put me
up.

I flew there on Aeroflot. Well, someone had to. A
month cleaning chip fryers wouldn't buy anything air-
worthy. The return ticket cost £189. It was odd boarding
a plane for the tropics wearing a thick sweater, padded
donkey jacket, scarf, balaclava, my dad's spare
gardening gloves, hiking boots, long johns and two pairs
of Spurs socks. But the Aeroflot flight involved a change
in Moscow, where they were experiencing the coldest

winter for fifty years. The club I was due to play for in Sri Lanka might not have appreciated me turning up with frostbite. I soon wished I'd brought a gas mask too. The Russian plane smelt of a disinfected school toilet permeated with the lingering aroma of vomit. There was, I noticed, no sick bag in the seat pocket either, presumably because they'd all been used. Flying Aeroflot was not exactly what you'd think of as jet setting. More like cattle trucking.

The air-hostesses seemed to have been chosen for their bulbous noses and sour expressions. They betrayed not a flicker of emotion as they delivered us our braised gristle and carrots and Bulgarian wine in a paper cup. The springs in my seat had perished, and seeing the plane was only half empty, I asked if I could move. 'Nyet. You vil stay there,' they said, eyes locked on my forehead like lasers. The miniature scaffolding holding up their tight hair-buns must have also been clamping down their features.

I added them to my list of DWNs. This was a code for exceedingly ugly women devised by my Geordie friend Kevin and me. It was based on Kevin's habit of seeing a tasty girl in a pub and grunting, 'Wad yer? I definitely wad.' So we used it as a measure of fanciability:

The Fitness Monitor
DW (definitely wad) = Kevin's girlfriend Stella, anyone who looked like Debbie Harry or Jaclyn Smith or the blonde one in Abba.
PW (probably wad) = some minor flaw, e.g. big arse, too much blue eye shadow, bit stuck-up, could make half a lager and lime last all night.
DWN (definitely wadn't) = slags, swots, spotties, fatties, hairies, Greeks, Russian air-hostesses.

We landed in Moscow at 4 a.m. The outside temperature was minus 44 degrees centigrade. Stepping out into that was like descending into a giant packet of frozen peas. Naked. No wonder the people are so miserable. We were herded in a spluttering bus to a barn-like terminal building where they checked our passports. They glared at us as if we were criminals. I suppose anyone smiling was. Then we were herded into another bus and onto the connecting and equally repellent plane. The 8 hours, 40 minutes of tedium was interrupted only by the service of weak tea and dark bread that tasted of cod liver oil. To take away the taste I was forced to demolish a large proportion of the chocolates I'd brought for my Sri Lankan hosts. I nearly regurgitated them on the turbulent descent.

Three things hit me when I emerged from the plane at Colombo airport around midday. Relief, a wall of suffocating heat (making my arctic layers a shade superfluous) and amazement at the sight of a large proportion of Sri Lanka's sixteen million population. They clustered against the perimeter fences staring at the disembarking passengers and shouting 'What is your name?' when you got vaguely within earshot. One saw my cricket bat protruding from a holdall and yelled 'Iron Bottam! Sir! Autograph!'

The arrivals hall was besieged with relatives, rubberneckers, taxi drivers and baggage handlers, about twenty-seven of whom tried to relieve me of my luggage. Also various beggars with their limbs contorted into horrific positions as if they'd been reared in a shopping basket.

'They look as if they've been reared in a shopping basket,' I said to Dilip's cousin who was collecting me.

'They have,' he said, 'the parents think it makes them more effective beggars.'

They offset their diminutive size with a wiry determination to intercept you. Luckily, Dilip's cousin, an eminent Sri Lankan cricketer, had a well-fed physique and brushed them all aside. Most Sri Lankans have complicated surnames like Wikremasinghe or Wijegunawardene or Pushpakumara. His name was John Wilson. Meeting a Sri Lankan Christian is a bit like finding a Jamaican on Dartmoor.

Cling-ons

I didn't know a lot about Sri Lanka. Only that Ceylon tea was a posh version of PG Tips, and their curries made your eyes water. I had a vague idea that they were in the throes of civil war, but I was assured that in Colombo my chances of hearing loud explosions and seeing violence were nil.

This prediction was immediately disproved. A beaten-up car rammed a trishaw side-on almost as soon as we'd pulled out of the airport. Slightly dazed but otherwise unhurt, the trishaw man climbed out of his slewed three-seater, went over and lamped the offending driver. Then they both continued on their way. Admittedly, they couldn't exchange insurance details because neither vehicle had a license or a number plate. But if all minor accidents were sorted out as succinctly as this, it would help save the rain forests.

The ride to the city in John Wilson's reconditioned old Ambassador was like being in an episode of *Wacky Races*. We passed rattling trucks with their cargo precariously balanced, narrowly missed packed, badly dented buses, driven by crazed imbeciles lurching all over the pot-holed road, their passengers clinging doggedly to the side. We overtook large motorised tricycles bursting with bare-torsoed labourers brandishing picks and forks. Vehicles swerved round old men on knackered bicycles and aimless cows or mangy goats wandering across junctions; there were scooters weaving everywhere, their engines buzzing like baritone bluebottles. You half expected the Scary Coup or the Ant Hill Mob to materialise from a side road.

There was no such thing as braking. If you came across an obstacle you just weaved around it, blowing your horn permanently. In fact I came to the conclusion that there must be a design fault in Sri Lankan cars and they had connected up the brake pedal to the horn. It's hard to believe they had such things as driving tests, but apparently they did. I guess you passed it by managing to drive around for an hour without having a heart attack or killing anyone. The smart money was in panel beating. There was a repair shack on every corner. Or a tyre stall. I'd been promised my nostrils would be assaulted by powerful aromas the moment I arrived in Sri Lanka. Sure enough, I was overcome by exhaust fumes and the smell of burning rubber.

Somehow, John Wilson conveyed me unscathed to his father's house. This would be my home for much of the next four months. A square double-storey building in a quiet, tree-lined suburb, it was an oasis of calm after the bedlam of the main road. The house smelt of mothballs and Pledge. The walls were whitewashed and on some hung little wooden crosses or austere portraits of the Virgin Mary. The only sounds were the crickets outside and the highly-polished wooden floor tiles squelching under your feet.

The residents of the house greeted me on the doorstep. All eighteen of them. There was John's father, Dr John, his wife and several generations of their family; recently-married Sri Lankan couples sort out weekend parent-visiting disputes by living with them. Usually for about twenty-five years. My eye quickly alighted on Dr John's niece, Menaka, a dark, desirable eighteen-year-old creature with glossy hair and mischievous eyes who I immediately marked a DW (definitely wad).

After prayers and passion fruit cordial all round they showed me my room. It was large and spartan with a fan in the centre of the ceiling and a double bed. It was directly opposite Menaka's guardian-aunt's bedroom so there was little prospect of luring her in silently in the night. I might have been off my own parents' leash, but there were ten other adults and God Almighty checking my every move here. The walls had ears.

I didn't spend my first night abroad totally alone, though. My co-habitee was an enormous spider. Now, there are spiders and spiders. This one had hairy legs the width of pencils and a body the size of a golf ball. It was descended from an orang-utan. It clung to the outside of the wash basin as I went to clean my teeth. I was in a dilemma. It was too big and dangerous-looking to try the old glass and postcard trick. It would have probably eaten through the postcard in a flash. Yet I didn't want to seem pathetic and call out for help within hours of arriving. I fetched my cricket bat. One swipe did it, and the spider's body exploded like the squeezing of an enormous zit. Bat and sink survived intact. It was the best stroke I played all winter.

Fire Extinguishing
I got my spider-exterminator out again twenty-four hours after I'd arrived. I'd been invited to play in a friendly match for a Tamil XI at the best ground in Colombo. I was excited at the prospect of my first bowl against the local talent on their own patch. Then I discovered the oppo-

nents were Richmond CC, Surrey. I'd travelled 8000 miles to play not against dashing, Asian strokeplayers with flailing wrists and twinkletoes but a bunch of blotchy-faced, leaden-footed bankers from London commuterville.

Having not played for three months, I decided to have a bit of a knock up on the outfield. Some grubby-looking children were messing about with the fraying innards of a ball under the stand. I beckoned a few of them over to bowl at me on the outfield. They couldn't have been more than nine so I didn't bother to wear pads. I threw them a decent ball. The first whirled his arms around and sent down a vicious leg break, which easily beat my forward prod. I had to go and retrieve the ball thirty yards away.

Another flexed his fingers and tweaked an off break which I could hear fizzing as it came towards me. I played it OK. A third managed, from a rather spindly action, to propel a spinner which I swore was a leg break. On pitching it became a googly, darting the opposite way to rap me painfully on the shin. The children were sniggering. This humiliation went on for ten minutes or so, me alternately playing and missing (and having to go and get the ball), hurriedly blocking or inside-edging deliveries into my unprotected legs before they gradually got bored and, one by one, ran off, the last with my ball.

I didn't have to bat at all in the match, or bowl till well into the afternoon. It was quite a relief as for lunch I'd had two helpings of curry soup and a huge beef biryani, served a bit like fish and chips in greaseproof paper, and eaten on your lap in the dressing room, augmented by rotis. A boy came in with a wooden carrier holding twelve glasses of water. As this had been siphoned from a reeking toilet area which was more or less an open sewer, I decided the sticky-sweet fizzy drinks – passion fruit, blackcurrant or cream soda – were a safer option. By 3.30 p.m., having completed five overs in 34°C heat, I called for a drink and poured the liquid on me rather than in me. I took one wicket – an accountant who worked in Sheen – before retiring into the shade of a telegraph pole. And that's more or less where I stayed for the rest of the match. It wasn't an auspicious start.

At the Wilsons' house, the evening meal was a mini-banquet of aromatic fish, a variety of meat curries flavoured with coconut milk and coriander, which I'd never heard of, then steaming bowls of bright purple or orange vegetables and oodles of rice. The food was hot and fantastically tasty. I would have got horribly fat if I had managed to get much of it in my mouth.

But they ate everything with their hands, a skill I failed to master. Chicken legs were alright, but trying to scoop fistfuls of rice and oily aubergine into your mouth with any accuracy was like playing the piano with your feet. In gum boots. I just couldn't grasp the technique (or any food) and compounded my inadequacy by using both hands. This is regarded as both rude and unhygienic. The right hand is supposed to be for the mouth and the left for the waste-disposal unit. Well, how was I to know? It doesn't ask you that on customs forms. To: 'Have you in the last seven days been on a farm or in an abattoir?' they could add: 'Has your right hand recently made contact with your bottom?'

My burning mouth was cooled somewhat by a third course of 'hoppers' – a Sri Lankan delicacy – sort of soft, gossamer-thin popadums cooked in mini-woks. But fruit was the real saving grace. There were delicious fresh mangoes – not those awful tinned, paraffin-flavoured gobbets of slime you get in England – sweet little bananas, juicy pineapple (which they had a disgusting habit of sprinkling salt on), and papaya, which I know some people say tastes like cat's pee but I adore.

Dr Wilson, an eminent GP, sat at the head of the table in a clean white vest and a sarong. Somehow, with his combed, ashen hair and distinguished features, he looked quite respectable and not at all like the similarly-dressed old slobs you see buying their morning copies of the *Sun* in a Tenerife supermarket. Menaka-the-DW was seated near the other end of the table, next to one of her girl cousins to whom she was manacled like a Siamese twin. It was a hopeless pulling situation, and she quickly lost her *wadness*. She also belched at the table after every few mouthfuls. This may be perfectly acceptable etiquette in Sri Lanka, but I couldn't see it going down well with my friends at Crusts Wine bar in Ealing. The New Lad hadn't been invented then.

The Wilsons weren't especially rich but they had four servants permanently at their beck and call. Brought up in liberated sixties London I found this idea slightly repugnant at first, and tried to help by collecting up the plates and sweeping the floor. That seemed to genuinely upset them, so I soon stopped. Anyway I was too mesmerised by a vision that strayed more and more into my eye-line as the days wore on. Venita was the cook's nineteen-year-old daughter. Her face was flawless, she had lustrous hair and a delicious milk-chocolate body, accentuated every day by a thin slip dress that clung to her magnificent breasts and wafted round her sleek hips. When I could occasionally wrench my eyes away from her top half I noticed she also had long, slender legs, well-defined calves and delicate ankles. A sort of dusky, innocent-looking Julia Roberts. A DW, no question. She glided about the house barefoot helping with the chores. She barely spoke any English. Funny how that makes women seem sexier.

She was preoccupied most of the day and constantly under her mother's beady eye. In her occasional fifteen-minute break between jobs, I used that old ruse commonly tried by fathers on sexy young au pairs and helped her learn some English. Importantly, this means you can sit next to them at the table hip to hip, accidentally brush across their pert breasts when you're leaning over to correct a spelling mistake and give their creamy loins a good congratulatory squeeze when they get a word right. Learning something useful makes them so grateful and gives you such a strong, manly image. It's sort of public foreplay.

Over a couple of weeks these sessions developed quite promisingly, especially when most of the rest of the household (but unfortunately not Venita's younger sister) took their afternoon nap. Particularly effective was my human biology lesson when I pointed to all the different bits of her anatomy and then pronounced the name. I lingered over certain ones and made her repeat them several times. She hugged me briefly when I said she'd got them all right. It's incredible what you could get away with around the sub-continent then as an English cricketer. You'd be lucky to be allowed in anyone's house now.

I didn't get away with it for long, though. Venita tore her only dress on a nail a few days later and, despite not knowing one end of a needle from the other, I tried to help her sew it up. Unfortunately the younger sister saw me fiddling with the fabric, shouted something unintelligible like 'Aiiyooo' and within seconds uncles and aunts and servants were staring at me kneeling on the floor beneath her. Venita was sent back to the kitchen and polite arrangements were made for me to stay with a fat female relative who only employed male servants.

Once Bitten . . .

Apart from being attacked by marauding red ants at deep mid wicket one day, which made my leg itch for a week, the cricket was going well. The weather was ferociously hot but the pitches were quite lively. Spurred on by that and the opportunity to play every day, I found an extra gear in my bowling, and a jumpiness amongst frail-looking local batsmen.

It was a stimulating environment to play in. There were crowds of several thousand at most of the club matches, instead of the couple of moany old blokes on push bikes I was used to at English club games, and fresh pineapple vendors wandering about in easy reach of fielders on the boundary. Pineapple juice, I found, was a useful aid to polishing the ball.

There were some marvellous players, many completely unorthodox. Diminutive batsmen would charge down the wicket at you from the first ball of the day and try to clobber it back over your head. The concept of playing yourself in was totally alien to them. There were wonderful spin bowlers with weird, contorted actions who, if they'd been in England, would have been told to go away and get a proper MCC-approved action. The fast bowlers were gangly and slightly wild-eyed and had hysterical lbw appeals. They issued loud instructions to the captain in Singalese, which was quite disconcerting, especially when you only found out afterwards that *'bumpa ekak danna'* meant 'I'm going to stick it up his nose.'

There was a cunning wicketkeeper, Russell Hamer, who would privately tell his fast bowler (me) to sling the next ball way down the legside. As I ran in for this delivery he would be sneaking up to the wicket from his position twenty yards back. By the time I'd bowled it he was virtually in the batsman's pocket. He'd gather the errant ball one-handed down the legside and whip off the bails before the overbalancing batsman had had time to regain his ground. It was craftily conceived, brilliantly executed and exemplified the daring, virtuoso nature of their cricket. It's just as well the Pakistani umpire Shakoor Rana never saw him.

Being one of only two white players in the country – the other was the Leicestershire hothead Gordon Parsons – and the only one who got immersed in the local culture and didn't call people 'fackin' cheatin' cant' on the field, I became something of a minor celebrity. I was interviewed on local radio and in the *Ceylon Daily News* by a journalist whose teeth jutted out of his mouth like grounded shrapnel, was invited to parties and to coach at the major schools.

I could do little to improve the perfectly-groomed techniques of the schoolboys, and factually they knew far more about the game than me. They could recite laws or records off by heart ('Most Test vickets for England Bob Villis, sir.') Cricketing-intrigue was pulsating through their blood. It was as exciting and essential a part of school life in Sri Lanka as smoking behind the bike sheds was in England.

I came across one diminutive, bow-legged kid aged fourteen who looked about nine, and kept whipping across my best straight deliveries in practice, flicking them through mid wicket with a flourish. Then he was laying back and pulling virtual half-volleys. I told him if he didn't play straighter with more restraint he'd never get far. He smiled and did that funny wobble of the head that Asians do and blocked a couple of deliveries with great care. Then he carried on pinging the ball everywhere. His name was Aravinda de Silva. He went on to become Sri Lanka's most prolific player. By the end of the century he'd made eighteen Test centuries, all distinguished by that idiosyncratic whip off his legs and audacious pulling.

'Pulling' was not something you did at their evening socials. Sri Lankan sporty types loved their 'functions'. They could drum up a lavish welcome party for a visiting round-table's snail-racing team. Unfortunately, these tended to be rather staid affairs in someone's house where the men and the women plonked themselves down in separate groups on chairs pushed back against the wall, and remained there as if they were waiting for some sort of performance. They only opened their mouths periodically to spoon in a mouthful of curry. At least cutlery was provided at these dos.

One party was different. It was a bash thrown by a cricket-mad Maharajah round the pool of the Galle Face Hotel, a lovely old Raj-era building overlooking the sea with white shutters and wicker chairs and bare-foot waiters in embroidered tunics. Most of the Sri Lankan and touring West Indian players were there, plus wives and girlfriends or aspiring wives and girlfriends. A superb buffet was accompanied by a band playing awful cover versions of Boney M songs.

Midway through the evening, I was cornered by a smartly-dressed Sri Lankan who introduced himself as Rohan Pieris. He was tall and thin and in his thirties and he had a handshake like a withered tulip. He mingled about while I talked to various other players round the swimming pool. Many of them began drifting off by 11 p.m. as there was a one day international the next day. Rohan was still there and kindly offered me a lift home, which I gladly accepted.

But once in the car we set off in the wrong direction. After ten minutes he turned off the main road down a dark lane which led to a wide beach. The night was moonless. 'Come on, let's take the air,' he said. Slightly grudgingly, I obliged. He talked matter-of-factly about cricket as he walked. I meandered along the sand with him, listening to the waves and drinking in the balmy sea breeze.

Half way back to the car as he complimented me on one of my recent bowling spells, his hand entwined with mine and, not wanting to appear rude, I didn't withdraw it. Silently we got back in the car. The light of a departing ship glinted on the water. He beamed at me and put the key in the ignition. But instead of his other hand grasping the gear lever it wandered into my lap. He fumbled for my flies and temporarily had hold of my penis. Momentarily, I froze. I tried to shout but nothing came out except a sort of muted yelp, not dissimilar to Dominic Cork's strangled appeal for lbw. I shoved his hand away, opened the door and hurriedly got out. I stood there for a second, trying to understand what had happened. Then I legged it.

I ran for several miles on dusty tarmac, not a bad effort in leather, open-toed sandals after about ten bottles of beer and a bucket of curry. I hurtled through the container area of the harbour, slipping on metal crane tracks, through Colombo's old fort district, past hotels and train stations and government buildings. It was developing into quite an interesting un-guided tour, until I was all but flattened by an errant bus careering round a corner with no lights.

Eventually I reached my house, minus my sweat-sodden Polyester shirt, which had been rubbing my nipples red-raw (so that's why footballers wear vests under their shirts). It was only then, sitting on my bed with the fan on full blast, dripping with sweat and still panting slightly, that I began to shake. My whole body trembled, my stomach convulsed and I was violently sick. People say you are born homo or hetero. That night was confirmation that I'd definitely come out straight. Thank God. I didn't want a life consigned to listening to Barbra Streisand records.

Sri Lanka being a place of large, close-knit families spreading wild, exaggerated stories, the news of my escapade was soon out and embellished. The grapevine was so profuse that by early afternoon the following day at a well-supported club match, a small contingent clustered round me as I walked out to bat. 'How was Rohan's *Pieris*?' one of them said cheekily, deliberately emphasising the word 'Pieris'. 'Not my type,' I said, failing to look back, trying to hide my humiliation.

Now, one thing you learn about the sub-continent is that people say and do provocative things purely to get a reaction. They are world-leaders at inciting a riot over the tossing of a stray orange. Ignore them and they soon turn their attentions to someone else. Give them a response, even so much as a wink or a smile, and they'll never let up. I hadn't grasped that yet.

Before long, half the ground was chanting 'Rohan, Rohan, Pierrissss' and rather than calling my name, which they could only pronounce 'Oo-gez', shouting 'Come on Middle-sex!' which soon became 'Come On Sexy!' I must have been the first virgin in the world who'd been outed as gay. Well, on a cricket field, anyway.

On the Beaten Track
To escape daily references to Rohan whenever I was spotted round town on a brakeless, one-pedalled bike, I went up country for a while. I squashed in third class on a creaking train to the little resort of Negombo. Squeezed in with me were overburdened mothers and their happy, grubby children eating smelly food out of newspaper, ragged goats, and leaking sacks of rice. The twenty-mile

journey from Colombo took two hours because each time the train jolted into motion it ground to a halt again beside paddy fields or tumbledown huts just because a person had stuck their arm out. It was the first time I'd experienced train hailing.

In Negombo, a place famous for cinnamon, I ate a sumptuous four-course hotel lunch for £1.20, and then went for a walk on the beach. I chatted to some fishermen mending nets. As soon as I mentioned cricket they asked me about 'Iron Bottam' and offered me a trip at dusk in their primitive boat. This, a hewn-out tree-trunk smeared in coconut oil to make it waterproof, would have sat four comfortably. There were eight of us, which meant the boat itself was largely underwater. They didn't seem to be bothered much about that or about fishing. They spent most of the time staring in wonder at me. I only realised afterwards this was because I had a mosquito bite on my neck that had swelled up to the size of a Malteser.

Back on shore we sat in their shack under a naked light bulb and they laughed when I flapped at mosquitoes around my head. I had often wondered what mosquitoes were put on this earth for. They weren't a significant part of the food chain, and they didn't break down dung or clean up bacteria or pollinate orchids. I reckoned they were just one of God's sick jokes, soiling the beautiful parts of the world with a tiny pest armed with shark teeth and a whine louder than Germaine Greer. But then one of the fishermen showed me a great new sport. He allowed a mozzie to land on his arm, then pinched the skin around it trapping its sucker. It quickly swelled up into a red bubble the size of an olive, then the whole mass burst in an apocalyptic finale. It's a satisfying end to the little bleeders. If only you could do the same to human parasites like sports agents.

22

For a dash of culture, I boarded a coach to the historic city of Kandy, site of the famous Temple of the Tooth. As with any drive east of Athens, it took an eternity because of the state of the roads. It's not the enormously deep pot holes that slow you down, but the odd islands of existing tarmac between the potholes. I assumed this was the problem as a procession of cars and trucks snaked single-file up a hill ahead of us. Twenty minutes later we reached the front of the queues to see that the delay was being caused by a man practically on all fours occupying half the road, stoically pushing along a large urn of tea and ten cups on a small tray with wheels. He had a klaxon strapped to his leg. Our driver just shrugged and overtook him. It's against Buddhist doctrine to practise road rage. People just exchange automatic gunfire or bombs instead.

In the Temple, a gaudy pink building, you can't actually see the Buddha's tooth – allegedly smuggled into Ceylon in a fourth-century princess's hair. It's in a casket which is inside another casket which is in a box which is stationed in a display case. No one is quite sure whether there's a real tooth in there or not. It's a bit like going to look at the Ashes in the Lord's museum.

There was a plaque nearby advertising The Way to Nirvana:

1. All life is suffering.
2. This suffering comes from selfish desire.
3. When one forsakes selfish desire suffering will be extinguished.
4. The middle path is the way to eliminate desire.

Someone had written underneath. 'Ice creams 100 yards on the right.'

I took another bus to Nuwara Eliya in the verdant hill

country. Some of the mountain roads were so narrow and twisty the back of the bus virtually hung over the edge of a precipice as we went round a corner. I stayed amongst tea estates with a planter. He had a rambling old house with a sundeck that overlooked a valley of tea, speckled with the brightly coloured sarees of the (female) pickers. He ate fish curry and sambals for breakfast and, therefore, so did I. I soon broke the chain on the lavatory cistern through over-use.

Nuwara Eliya was a favourite hill station with the British. The departing colonials had left behind the very essence of an English village – red letter boxes, a bar with pictures of hunting, a golf course and a post office with a perpetual queue. Nearby is the Dimbula Cricket Club, where I had been invited to play a match, 7000 ft. up in the tea plantations. Saree-ed women – relieved picking duties for the day – rolled the pitch, marked out the creases and laid the boundary rope.

The patchy wicket played surprisingly well but thinking wrongly that I would find the cooler conditions to my liking, I tired quickly because of the altitude. The undergrowth was particularly thick beyond the boundary and I was told it was infested with snakes. There's never a better incentive not to let the ball past you, and I did some spectacular stops at long leg.

The centrepoint of this social match – tea, of course – was a disappointment. The cucumber sandwiches curled up at the edges and were practically bereft of filling and despite thousands of hectares of fresh tea out the back, we drank a liquid of tea-dust, powdered milk and sugar that tasted like toffee-flavoured Carnation milk. The best tea, I was told, was exported. It's like trying to get decent fish and chips in Grimsby or a strong cheese in Cheddar.

Paradise Spoiled

There are two types of beach in Sri Lanka. Ones you couldn't swim at and ones you definitely couldn't swim at. The undertow at Mount Lavinia, a southern suburb of Colombo, would test the seaworthiness of a cross-channel hydrofoil. I only ventured out ten yards from shore and yet it took me the best part of half an hour to thrash my way back as I was constantly sucked towards rocks by a vicious current. They don't tell you this in the brochures full of golden, palm-fringed beaches and silhouettes of happy couples lolling into rich purple sunsets. If you meet people back from a beach holiday in Sri Lanka who are either gaunt, have developed enormous shoulder muscles or are mourning a loss, you'll know why.

Thirty miles down the coast is the beach resort of Bentota. It should have been within easy reach of Colombo. It wasn't. It took about half a day to negotiate the decimated road and the trucks loading up with fish and rice sacks and the fallen coconuts and the wandering cows and dogs and the children playing pass the machete, the men pissing on what's left of the tarmac and the women beating their washing where the men have just been pissing.

Bentota, on first inspection, is paradise – azure sea, a wide, unspoilt beach, fine, silky sand that slips between your toes – and is not littered with fat Germans or other tourist detritus. When I arrived with three friends, including Dilip, out for a fortnight's holiday, it was practically deserted. Not for long, though. A stream of locals hawking precious stones buzzed around all morning. 'Vat is your nem?' they asked.

'Simon,' I said for about the ten thousandth time since arriving in Sri Lanka.

'Ah, S.i.m.o.n. Velly nice nem. Like some coral for your girlfriend?'

'I haven't got one.'

'Boyfriend? Ha ha ha ha ha.'

I didn't share the joke.

To escape any further sales spiel, I took a running jump into the sea. I was almost instantly dumped back on to the sand by a huge wave, which also deposited half the beach into my trunks. I tried again, with similar results. Swimming was a no no here.

I had just got rid of a fourth set of hawkers and was dozing off on the sand when there was a shriek. I cricked my neck and noticed two large branches lying about twelve inches away. Then one of them wriggled. They were two enormous snakes that had emerged from the undergrowth and were making for our picnic hamper. My friends had stopped playing beach badminton – just as hopeless a game in a tropical sea breeze, incidentally, as it is at Great Yarmouth – and were throwing handfuls of sand at the beasts, which only succeeded in shooing them more in my direction.

I had two choices. Bolt into the treacherous water or stay put and remember the first aid instructions if bitten – 'wrap wounded limb in bandage and immobilise with splint.' As there's never a handy splint around when you need one, I headed into the water. For once in Sri Lanka, it was a relief. I remained there being dumped by breakers while the snakes ate our picnic, before retreating back to the bushes. Slumbering blissfully on a beach has never been quite the same since.

A Man's World . . .

Back in Colombo there was the biggest celebration since independence: it was the hundredth cricket match between the island's two most prestigious boys' schools, Royal College and St. Thomas's. The Royal-Thomian was Sri Lanka's version of Eton v Harrow, except that in Sri Lanka the standard was high and everybody cared about it. There was a week-long carnival with stalls and rides, street parades with garlanded elephants, brightly coloured floats conveying fire eaters and snake charmers, and schoolchildren waving flags and blowing trumpets. Whereas Eton v Harrow is an annual opportunity for the masses to blow raspberries.

The game itself was ferociously competitive, attended by thousands and carried live on radio. And that was just the over fifties match. The actual contest between the schoolboys – preceded by a march-past of all former captains – lasted three days; each one was watched by a crowd of over 25,000. It got front page headlines for several days before during and after. It made English schools cricket look like kids scuffing about in a puddle.

For several successive evenings, old boys of the schools lounged around on padded sofas in club bars reminiscing about how they shouldn't have taken that risky single in the 1956 match, how much better the wicket and the players were in those days, and supping the local spirit, arrack. This, an evil toddy made out of coconut palm, tasted as if you'd swallowed a marine distress flare. Wisely, their rapidly-expanding wives sat in a separate room drinking cordial.

I supposed the girls Menaka and Venita would end up like that. For the moment, Venita had been sent to America to work as housekeeper for a rich Sri Lankan. Menaka had met a boy her age at the Methodist church. They were allowed to go unescorted to the Fountain Café once a week to eat ice cream sundaes. It closed at 9 p.m. That was not the kind of fun I was looking for.

After all the initial anticipation and promise of being away from home, I felt slightly let down. The two girls I'd met and fancied were unsuitable or out of reach, and the only liberated (i.e. European) girls I'd approached in what passed for Colombo's night club spoke barely a smattering of English and didn't shave under their arms. I certainly wasn't going to meet the love of my life amongst the arrack drinkers loitering around the cricket clubs. The nearest I'd come to making it with someone was with a thirty-five-year-old bloke. I'd completely failed to get off the mark in that department. In fact I hadn't even got to the wicket. Except the wrong one.

I loved the country, though. It was hot (constantly), sociable (masculinely) and always entertaining. Every day there was some cataclysmic incident on a nearby road that made the car crashes in Bond movies look pedestrian. I was inundated with offers of hospitality (and requests from local cricketers to find them an English club for the summer) and I loved the food. Once I'd been eating curry morning noon and night for two months, I managed to keep my daily bowel movements to single figures.

On my last day I gathered up my souvenirs – sachets of spices strung together, a book of curry recipes, a length of saree material (for my mum and my sister), and several bottles of passion fruit, pineapple and guava juice, which you couldn't get in England – and packed them in my suitcase. I hope they'd give my life a lingering essence of Sri Lanka, and they did. The bottles broke in transit, leaking sweet stickiness laced with chilli powder all over my clothes and the saree material. It was impossible to remove.

The Score
In the harsh twilight of an English April, I tried my place-

rating formula. The Sri Lankan people were welcoming and generous and the colonial legacy still ran through their veins so that wherever I went, they put themselves out whether they were a millionaire or a mopper-upper. Cricket certainly opened doors with everyone.

They seemed a bit unsophisticated, though. Either earnest and quiet and teetotal, or boorish alkies. It was probably a result of their material backwardness. There was no telly, the radio news sounded as if it was being broadcast from someone's bedroom and long-distance phone calls had to be booked. Often ten hours elapsed before the operator roused you from a deep sleep at 4.30 a.m. to say, 'Your call to England can be put through now, sir.' Then, when you spoke, all you could hear was yourself echoing back at you.

Their humour was as under-developed as their country. They'd laugh hysterically at some cricketer's nickname – Graham (Picca) Dilley or Allan (Legga) Lamb – and keep repeating it over and over. But when I told them a joke – like, what d'you call a Mexican girl with one tooth? Huanita – they stared at you blankly. Out of 10 I gave them 5. The beaches had been beautiful to look at, but the sea was a health hazard and so, to some extent, with the spectre of snakes and sun burn, was the sand. The beaches scored 6/10.

Sri Lanka's cricket had a vitality and individuality I hadn't experienced in England, their natural enthusiasm to give the ball a hearty clump wasn't inhibited by regimented coaches telling them to 'get your foot to the pitch and play straight.' In fact their batting was like their (car) driving: absolutely no guidelines whatsoever – so extremely dicey but compellingly exciting. 'Defend' and 'draw' were forbidden actions, like 'brake.'

Cricket gave them a spontaneity they lacked socially.

Their abandoned exuberance on the field was worth 7/10. Unfortunately their lack of 'sophistication' meant that the ICC still didn't think they were worth official inter-national recognition. Myopia in the extreme, particularly when you consider that in 1980, the Test match 'world' consisted of only six countries.

Now I came to the important bit – female catches. Despite some respectable efforts I was back where I'd started. At nought. The only positive thing was I'd dis-covered I wasn't gay. That was worth a point. Definitely.

People		Beaches		Cricket		Catches		Total
5	+	6	+	7	×	1	=	18

So in my book Sri Lanka had a popularity rating of eighteen. It doesn't sound much, but compared to the number of runs I made the following summer, in my first year of proper county cricket (0), it was certainly worth muted applause.

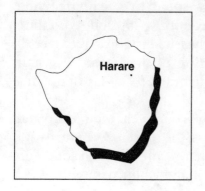

Harare

3.
Zimbabwe –
the Tour

Trolley-dollies

The strength and confidence I'd gained from the Sri Lankan experience made me a faster bowler, which helped in county cricket. It also tempted me to become a more uninhibited batsman, which hindered. Trying to emulate their daring stroke-play, I charged the fast bowling of Imran Khan at Hove, feeling the wind of the 88 m.p.h. delivery as it just grazed my right ear. I essayed a wild hook at his next ball, a bouncer, failed to connect but succeeded in completely flattening all three stumps as I overbalanced.

'It's terrible what they teach them at comprehensive school,' some old buffer in the crowd said within earshot of my father, who'd worked himself to the bone to give me a private education. He didn't speak to me for several days. I decided on a more circumspect approach until the following winter, when I'd be out of parental sight, in Zimbabwe.

Unless you're a hairy backpacker, an amateur zoologist or an adventure-sports freak, you've probably never given Zimbabwe much thought as a holiday place and probably never will. Why spend twelve hours flying to a warm but anonymous country with dodgy politics, no excitement and no beaches when you could get to the Costa del Sol in a fraction of the time? It's a fair question and I can't answer it, but you can't turn down a free trip.

Middlesex had just won the county championship and after a summer of high success, the players were ready for a month of high jinks. Anywhere with a bar and some sun would have done: Bangkok, Bali or Bournemouth. Well, maybe not Bournemouth. We were invited to Zimbabwe with the idea of fostering relations with a newly-independent country and emerging cricketing nation. The main idea in the players' heads was to soak up some rays and get laid. I was near the head of the queue. Well, what else was there to do in a sunny, landlocked country teeming with air-hostesses on four-day stopovers?

If the flight over was meant to douse the burning in your loins, it worked. The interior of the plane, operated by Zambian Airways, resembled the inside of a toilet roll with seats designed for pygmies, and the pilot was clearly practising for the Farnborough air show the amount he made the craft list and leap. Several players threw up (including me) and as there was no carpet, trickles of vomit shifted up and down the plane with each dive and climb. If there had been a nutritionist on board, it would have been a quick way of assessing the players' diet.

We finally landed with an alarming bump for a short food-and-Hoover-stop in Lusaka, Zambia. Judging by the spartan zone of scrub punctuated with grubby white shit-houses visible outside, that's all you'd want to do. A man got on wheeling a prehistoric upright vacuum cleaner with one of those elongated rubber balloons attached to the back. It wouldn't go under the seats so he finished up just smearing the mess around with newspaper and the handle end.

We lurched up into the air again for the brief hop to Harare, then clinging on to its old name, Salisbury. From the air this looked a much more prosperous and well-watered place, with lakes, blossoming trees and high-rise blocks. Tall, modern buildings were a surprise as my only visual experience of Africa was the jungle and straw huts in *Daktari*. Being in team uniform accompanied by a local liaison officer seemed to cut through the legendary layers of African red tape, and we were whisked to our hotel in two Rothman's *kombis*.

Compared to the battery-hen Post Houses professional cricketers were used to staying in, the Jameson Hotel was a palace. The mahogany swing doors, the dark polished floors across which brown-tuniced waiters glided, the rattan chairs and pot plants and brass clocks in the reception area telling you the time in London, Delhi and Sydney, all gave it a sort of colonial feel.

So often smart hotel foyers are just a prelude to cramped, stale rooms speckled with the remains of squashed insects. This establishment appeared to be the opposite. Amidst the hubbub of people checking in I was advised to take the lift to two-one-five and the porter would follow with the bags. The door to 215 was ajar and I pushed it open to reveal a decadent, sunfilled room with a completely circular bed, a matching mirror on the ceiling above it, an upholstered chaise-longue and, sunk into the floor, a white enamel bath with gold taps. The walls were black with gilt trim and the curtains were ruby red. It was an ensemble that said sex.

There wouldn't be any problem pulling with this boudoir. I thought my luck was changing. 'I think my luck is changing,' I said to the porter who was just behind me.

'It is, Boss,' he said. 'This is the honeymoon suite. You're in 219.' I followed him down the corridor to a cramped, twin-bedded room, which at least wasn't speckled with the remains of squashed insects. There was, however, a rodent in occupation. My room-mate Roddy the Rat, alias Rajesh Maru, the young Middlesex (later Hampshire) left-arm spinner and scavenger of vital information.

'There's no pool here,' he said, which was obviously a matter of utmost importance on a hot morning after a tense twelve-hour flight, 'but there is one at the Monomatapa International just down the road.' We made a beeline for it.

The British Airways hostesses were lying there in numbers and we soon got amongst them. Twenty years ago, a BA hostess was a symbol of sexiness. She was young, toned and tanned with glistening hair, a pillar box smile and perfect teeth. You definitely wad. Look at one now. She's haggard and jowelly, the face is leathery, the hair's lank and the smile's degenerated into a blank stare. She's a symbol of sullenness. I suppose you would be too if you'd spent two decades of trudging up and down aisles at 37,000 feet trying to make people buy bottles of Drambuie. It's about time British Airways had an oil change.

Compulsive Hookers
The air-hostesses were all perfectly good company but they were so well groomed and worldly. They were a bit

daunting for a pale, gab-less novice like me. I thought I had more chance with the local talent. Anyway, I didn't want to break my romantic duck in some far-off land against a crimson sunset beneath the canopy of a Baobab tree, and then discover my female opening partner lived in Staines.

That first evening the only women in the Monomatapa Hotel bar were black and buxom. Buoyed by the presence of several Middlesex players of Caribbean extraction, I beckoned two over to our table. I thought I was doing everyone a favour. One, Prudence, soon struck up a rapport with the batsman Wilf Slack. But instead of gazing adoringly at another black player, the other, Crystal, immediately plonked herself on my lap. As her lumpen backside lodged against my groin and her heaving breasts sought to extricate themselves from a tiny silver boob tube, she leant over and whispered a sweet nothing in my ear.

'I wanna fuck you,' she said.

I was rather taken aback. She didn't even know my name. I didn't fancy her either: she was in the DWN category. I didn't have a lot of choice though. She clamped my hands round her bulging midriff, as I slumped under her weight, gagging on her cheap scent. Every time she laughed, her whole mass juddered. It was like being pinned down by an enormous jelly.

After a few drinks and a serious build up of pain in my prostate area, someone suggested going back to our hotel. On the way out, Crystal linked arms with one of the black players, and I thought I was off the hook. But halfway along the road she grabbed me from behind and yanked me towards her.

'I wanna fuck you,' she said again, tripped on a kerb and her pendulous breasts spilled out of her minuscule top. She laughed and wrestled them back in. This happened twice more before we reached the Jameson hotel. It was a miracle she wasn't arrested (for possession of offensive weapons).

The hotel receptionist wouldn't allow the two women upstairs – 'no guests permitted in the bedrooms after ten o'clock under any circumstances,' he pronounced dictatorially. He wouldn't relent even after an offer of a sheet of paper autographed by the team. The offer of a sheet of paper autographed by Robert Mugabe (a twenty dollar bill) elicited a different response.

'OK, Boss,' he said beaming.

We trouped into Slack's room, six of us, and sat on the beds swigging Castle lager. Crystal sprawled all over me, tits everywhere. 'You gonna fuck my pussy now?' she grunted. I shrank away in fear and embarrassment. This wasn't how I'd envisaged my sexual initiation at all – performing with a rampant 200lb. mamma in front of her mate and half the team.

As coolly as I could manage, I said I had to go to the bathroom. Instead, I slipped out of the door, crept down the corridor to my room, and, despite The Rat's enthusiasm to go and peek through Slack's keyhole, I barred the door with a chair and table. It was a good decision. By morning we discovered our intrepid threesome were Z$200 the poorer and one had already paid a visit to the local clinic.

Losing the Plot

This was the prelude to our first match of the tour – a one day game at the Salisbury Sports Club, a pretty ground bedecked with stripy marquees and surrounded by blooming jacaranda trees. In it, a hungover John Emburey conjured a remarkable win by bowling six dot balls with

Zimbabwe requiring just two for victory from the final over. Attempting to show off my speed and variety to new opponents, I tried too hard and bowled like a drain.

After a bat-dominated three day match on the same ground, we headed east to Umtali (now Mutare) for a one day game. The parched, arid landscape of scrub and bush around Harare suddenly gave way to dramatic pine-clad mountains, many sugar-loaf shaped. It could have been Scotland or the Lake District. We came through Christmas Pass and saw the town down below, set in a hollow. It was surprisingly green and lush, and some of the mountains were blanketed in mist. It made you feel quite sentimental.

The featureless game, on a damp wicket under cloudy skies in front of a few diehards, was a less gratifying reminder of home. The chilly post-match barbecue was little more invigorating. One local player gave what he thought was an entertaining imitation of a day at a motor race, making odd sounds with a scrap of paper and a comb. Another tossed into his conversation a list of Zimbabwe achievements, including the world press-up record held by their captain's brother. The captain, Duncan Fletcher, a combative all-rounder and jovial consort, was nearby. At an opportune moment I asked him about his brother's press-up prowess. Fletcher's expression darkened and he said solemnly, 'My brother hasn't got any arms,' and stared at the ground. Just as I was about to splutter a profuse apology he burst into rolling laughter. I didn't see the funny side, which just made him laugh more. I suppose if you're a white losing your racial superiority in a hot, beach-less country riddled with tribal disharmony and corruption, you're bound to develop an unusual sense of humour. Almost two decades later Fletcher hadn't lost it, either. In late 1999, he accepted the job as the new England coach.

Another fanciful tale the local players were keen to tout around was the presence in their team of a prolific lad called Graeme Hick, the son of a tobacco farmer, who'd scored his first century aged nine-and-a-half months and was about to take world cricket by storm. He was going to be a run machine, they said. Yes, I replied, and I'm the Milky Bar kid.

They did have some talented players, though. The best Zimbabwe batsmen, Fletcher for instance, complemented elegant, classical styles with robust instincts. They were naturally strong and fit. The best Zimbabwe bowler was unnaturally stroppy and fat. Richie Kaschula his name was. He was pleasant on the field and bowled amiable left-arm spin but he turned nasty in the bar after a couple of drinks, often head-butting people if they disagreed with him.

Being head-butted, even lightly, by someone weighing twenty-two stone is not funny. There's a lot of momentum to deal with. This man didn't have a pot belly, he had an overflowing wheelie-bin. His waist was fifty inches. Obviously he'd been suckled on bloater paste. He made Mike Gatting look like a refugee. One day, when he was out on the field bowling, Gatting and Emburey each got into a leg of his shorts and waddled round the boundary like Siamese twins. There were some sore heads in the bar that night.

Kaschula wreaked his revenge in the next match, a day's drive south in Bulawayo. Quite apart from causing our bus to break down in the boiling desert because of excessive stress on the suspension, he took ten wickets in the game. The pitch was like dried Weetabix, perfect for his spin. Then, at a private barbecue after the second day's play, he tried to lob Emburey fully clothed into the swimming pool. Emburey clung tenaciously to a small rockery, saving himself but injuring his bowling hand. He was unable to grip the ball the next day. As our other spinner – The Rat – was incapacitated after being hit on the head at short leg, it was left to me to bowl spin. I'd done it before and I was never asked again. We lost by a mile.

On the journey back, Kaschula made amends, suggesting a detour to his family's private game park. This was Fatville twinned with Plumptown. All the inhabitants were the same size as him. Even the dung beetles looked overweight. Antelope mooched about, fat, rodenty things called dassies lumbered off the dirt road in front of us and a large community of vervets hung around in a sprawling acacia tree, the branches buckling under their collective weight. This was my first direct experience of free-roaming wildlife apart from a couple of trips to Stamford Bridge.

We were ushered into a small compound where various jeeps and other contraptions were parked. Each brandishing a plastic chair, we clambered on to a small trailer which was then attached to an old tractor. This was our 'safari sunseeker'. It listed dangerously when Kaschula got on, so most of us sat on the other side. After bumping across the savannah for some time seeing distant animals, which on closer inspection turned out to be either boulders or tree stumps, we came across a huge, lone ostrich egg. We were just about to jump down and take a look when the mother appeared from nowhere and charged us. We held up the plastic chairs as shields and, sheltered behind Kaschula, beat a hasty retreat.

When we were back at the family homestead, Kaschula pulled up his shirt to reveal how dangerous an ostrich could be. There was a deep, ugly scar across his enormous stomach. 'It looks as though he's had a Caesarean,' I whispered to Emburey.

'Yeah, and they weren't able to get the baby out,' Emburey sniggered, rather too loudly.

'EMBUREY!' Kaschula bellowed. He frogmarched him to a leopard pen, locked him in with three young cubs and threatened to let the annoyed mother loose from her cage unless he agreed to bowl badly in the third match of the series.

This was probably the first instance of attempted match-fixing in Africa. It would never have come off, because Emburey was incapable of playing with less than total commitment, even against his young daughters in the back garden. Perhaps realizing this, Kaschula made him sweat for a bit before letting him out.

Salisbury Seduction

We'd been on tour in Zimbabwe three weeks. While several players had prospered on the field and were virtually living with local girls off it, I hadn't taken a wicket, made a run or even had a slow dance with anyone. In short, I hadn't troubled the scorers. It didn't help that, as visiting cricketers go I was a complete nobody and I had only a quarter of the muscle definition of a local male, an eighth of their ego and none of their chauvinism. Instead of bragging about my steak-eating, tree-pulling prowess, I was polite to the local girls and they soon excused themselves. What they clearly wanted was a bit of rough. Preferably toned, tanned rough.

I was heading for my second goalless winter when I suddenly received a beautifully weighted through pass with only the keeper to beat. A decent-looking blonde in blue top and pedal pushers approached me in the beer tent after a day's play. She asked me if I was the guy in the sun hat who'd nearly done a brilliant diving catch on the boundary close to where she was sitting. That's me, I said, the nearly man, and stared at the floor as usual, thinking it was a wind up. It did occur to me, though, that she was at least a PW.

There were two spare chairs in the corner of the tent and we had a drink. I was quite nervous and didn't really know what to say. It was quite crowded and no one noticed us except a bloke from Castle Corner, near where I'd been fielding, who recognised me and said, 'There's the *puss* in boots' on his way to the bar. 'Puss' was local slang for wanker. It made the girl laugh and seemed to break the ice. I found out she was nineteen, a hairdresser and hoping to go to England to do a Bachelor of Education. This was handy information. At university, it was always assumed girls doing a B.Ed. were a pushover, which (apparently) they usually were.

After two beers, I began looking at her more intently. I noticed she had blue eyes, delicate, slightly freckly skin and a wavy fringe of blonde hair. She was actually quite pretty. She was half Dutch and I had a bit of trouble with her accent. Because of the general hubbub I thought at one stage she had said 'Shall we go fearsome fucker?' and I thought I was going to have to go through the Crystal situation all over again. I looked at her agape, and was even more worried when she said that Roots of Africa on Livingstone Avenue was the place. I was conjuring images of a sort of communal brothel, when to my relief she said the steaks there were great, and that it served plenty of other good 'tucker.' I heard it right that time.

We sat in a booth in the corner of the restaurant and talked animatedly. I told her about Crystal and she laughed and said women like that were notorious in the city and were an absolute harbour of diseases. She told me about her last boyfriend who had dumped her because she'd been out for a drink with a mate of his and worn her most expensive bra. He'd accused her of being a scheming whore. It sounded a typically juvenile male reaction.

So she was single and bought lingerie. Things were improving rapidly. She was swiftly moving from a PW to a DW, and it had dawned on me that I was wearing some ropy old underpants which I'd have to surreptitiously remove if there was to be any extra-curricular activity.

The meal was fantastic. The steaks lapped over the plates both ends and we had a side dish of gem squash which was the smoothest, sweetest vegetable I'd ever tasted. Our black waiter, Ruler, was incredibly attentive and memorized every request without writing anything down. The evening flew by, and after our second Don Pedros – a delicious velvety drink of vanilla ice-cream whipped up with whiskey – I was just wondering how to pop the question. Out of the blue she said she had to go because work started early the next morning, but maybe she'd see me at the match later.

I was too confused to protest. She'd chatted me up, asked me out, told me she was single and mentioned her racy underwear. Not only had she supplied the through pass, but apparently offered me an open goal. I had the ball at my feet and it was harder to miss than to score. Then suddenly the posts had closed together and the goal had vanished.

I lay in bed listening to The Rat chuntering in his sleep. I felt hopeless, a failure. Again. I dropped off to sleep and dreamed of playing in a Cup final at Lord's and being required to bowl the ball straight at a completely unguarded wicket to win the match. There was a woman umpire and I'd bowled a wide.

I woke up in a muck sweat. Women seemed to send me all in a tizz. I felt conflicting emotions. Hostility and desire, aggravation and titillation, appreciation and

complete bewilderment. One minute you were in harmony, the next in total discord. I went over the events of
the night and wondered whether I'd overstepped the
mark somewhere. I hadn't bored her with talk about leg
cutters and lbws, or given her my family's medical history
or pissed on my shoes when I went to the bathroom or
asked her if she'd inherited her bulky calves from her
mother. But something wasn't right and I knew the maybe-
see-you-at-the-match-tomorrow was just an escape route
and that there was no way she'd turn up. She admitted she
didn't even like cricket.

Still, I wore clean underpants to the ground for the
second day's play, and kept watch for her throughout. My
fixation was so all-consuming I kept straying out of
position on the boundary and the acting captain Mike
Gatting had trouble getting my attention to move me
back. I bowled moderately and was also slow reacting to
another high catch so that in the end I didn't lay a hand on
it. Later, when we batted, I roamed the boundary in a
tasteless pair of blue and red striped shorts hoping to
catch her eye. All they attracted was some good-natured
abuse and an invitation at the notorious Castle Corner to
take part in a shoe tossing contest during the tea interval.

Either she hadn't turned up, or had chosen to ignore
me. A couple of beers in the tent helped me overcome my
disappointment. We were just on the point of leaving for
a rendezvous at the hotel when I felt a nudge in the ribs. It
was her. My heart leapt. She looked absolutely ravishing
in a white slip dress that really enhanced her tan. I fancied
her like hell. She said she'd stay for a drink and give me a
lift back to meet up with the boys.

Two hours flashed by and when we eventually arrived
at the Jameson, the others were long gone and the hotel
bar was deserted. I lingered uneasily not knowing what to

do, but she suggested having a drink in my room. The goal seemed to be opening up again. There was a problem in the six yard box, though. I was sharing my room with The Rat. To my relief, he was out with the rest.

His cassette player, which he invariably carted around with him, sat on a low table. After ordering the beers, I put on the only tape I could find, Donna Summer's 'I Feel Love'. It created the right mood and before the drinks had even arrived we were kissing. Frantic, teeth-clashing, lipstick-smearing kissing. Suddenly she drew away and pulled her dress over her head.

'*I feel love, I feel love, I feel love* . . .' Donna Summer crooned.

Saying nothing, she lay down on the bed in her white underwear. I took the cue. Nervously, I jammed the table against the door tripping over my half undone trousers in the process. She'd removed her bra. You almost couldn't tell, as the area round her small, pointy breasts obviously never saw the light of day.

'I *feel luuuuuurrrrrrrrvvvvvvv* . . .'

'Take off your pants,' I said, suddenly assertive. She obliged, silently drew me towards her and we docked. Almost simultaneously the tape ended. I jumped up and turned it over. I actually stopped in the middle of my first ever shag *to turn the tape over*. I really understood how to please a woman.

Reclining on the bed one and half minutes later, I reflected on my consummation.

1. After the interminable build up it was an enormous anti climax.
2. How was I?
3. Did she know I was a virgin?
4. What now?

5. I could start by finding out her name.

There'd been such a din when we first met the night before I hadn't heard it. Things had moved on so quickly there hadn't been the opportunity to ask again. I mean, you can't just suddenly break the vacuum seal on your clamped mouths and say, 'Er sorry, who did you say you were?'

I rifled through her handbag when she'd gone to the bathroom. No help. Only the usual girly things – lipstick, sunglasses, purse, keys, ancient laundry receipt, dirty tissue, the lid of a mascara, a stupid expression on a crumpled passport picture, stray earring, several mint wrappers. No spare knickers, I noticed, so this wasn't a pre-planned exercise.

When she reemerged and stood there in the all-together I suddenly didn't find her attractive any more. I felt a strange distance and nonchalance, like a predator who had chewed off the best bits from the bone and wasn't interested in the scraps. I was conscious The Rat would be back soon. I thought she better go.

'I think you better go,' I said.

She shrugged, but didn't seem that disappointed. Presumably the answer to 2. was 'not much cop'. I pecked her goodbye on the cheek and said I'd see her tomorrow.

Reap and Pillage

The muggy overcast weather of the previous days in Salisbury had given way to a fresh, sunny morning. A stiffish breeze wafted the jacaranda blossom on to the pavements and sent cotton wool clouds spinnakering across the sky. Pulling on my whites for the last day's play, I was overwhelmed by a cleansed feeling. As if my whole body had been internally douched. The

interminable build up of sexual bewilderment and anticipation had been released. It was as if I'd been constantly
shinning up an unconquerable wall beyond which lay a
bevy of beauties. Now I'd made it to the top, the pleasure
was all mine. I felt elated and almost lightheaded as we
took the field. Instead of being slightly intimidated by the
task of bowling the pugnacious Zimbabweans out, I was
energized by it.

Their batsmen started confidently in pursuit of 416 for
victory, until I got in amongst them. One was caught in the
slips – my first wicket on the tour – another caught behind,
a third clanged on the head by a bouncer before he had
scored. Another took several blows in the chest. The ball
was whizzing through to wicketkeeper Downton at a fair
old lick, though it seemed effortless to me. My colleagues
were urging me on. The shoe-tossing, insult-lobbing louts
from Castle Corner remained silent.

It was a hot afternoon, but I bowled throughout it, and
after tea I took my fifth wicket in my twenty-ninth over. I
still didn't feel tired. The immense Kaschula came in no.11
and I ripped his middle stump out first ball, sending it
cartwheeling back several yards for a most satisfying end
to a 'satisfying' tour. Middlesex had won the match by
eighty-one runs.

At a small impromptu ceremony afterwards I was
presented with the match ball, a Kookaburra, scarred and
chewed as if it'd been prised from a dog's jaws. It was
more, of course, than just a memento of my career best. It
was as the tacky Old Spice ad said, 'The mark of a man.' I
caught sight of The Hairdresser during that final evening,
but through a combination of arrogance and embarrassment, I didn't go over to her. Somehow, she felt like a
stranger. Not knowing her name didn't help.

Actually, I was being paid far too much attention by

other girls to worry. There was Charlene (PW) and Melissa (DW) and Bev (PW). They seemed to be practically queuing up. From drought to flood in forty-eight hours. Bloody typical, the night before we were due to leave for England. It's incredible the instant confidence a decent sporting achievement bestows on you. It's like a natural form of Ecstasy. I suppose two-year-olds who win the Derby feel the same way, and that's why they're put out to stud.

Bev, a dark, tactile girl lingered longest and I went back to her flat in a nearby suburb. She cooked a delicious late supper, then we frolicked on her bed for a bit before I said goodnight. Our flight was departing at 9 a.m. and I hadn't packed. She was misty eyed as I kissed her goodbye, and she promised to write. She did too, sometimes proclaiming undying love. I didn't see her again for five years when she was introduced to me at Grace Road, Leicester, as Mrs Jonathan Agnew (mark I).

The Score

People		Beaches		Cricket		Catches		Total
5	+	0	+	5	×	2	=	20

I had mixed feelings about the Zimbabweans. The (white) men were mostly hospitable and matey when sober, racist and cruel when drunk. The (white) women were smiley and pretty and a bit stereotyped. They all had sleek jaws and crocodile skin handbags and wanted three kids and a two-car garage. The men were happy to oblige, provided they could play their sport and sup their beers and chew their T-bones. Their life was happy, yet limited. They lived in a tidy white theme park wedged in the middle of chaotic black Africa.

It served its purpose for me, though, and whetted my appetite for more exploration. Now it was time to get out and see the real world . . .

Pretoria

4.
South Africa
– Pretoria

Forced Isolation

I had to get my degree first, though. For three winters I traded sun, seam and socializing for digging my Renault 5 out of a Durham snowdrift to give lazy, impoverished students a lift to a geography lecture about plate tectonics. University was a riot, but it does give you work-itis and negative dress sense. How I ended up with a decent degree (2.2) or a steady girlfriend (Julia) is a complete mystery. I still dream of walking to a finals exam ragged and unshaven, frantically trying to memorise whether the Cretaceous geological era was in between the Triassic and the Jurassic, or later.

Between June and September my soft student under-belly had been significantly toughened with three solid summers in county cricket. Now, in my first winter out of university, a season playing provincial cricket in South

Africa beckoned. I felt I was ready for it. Unfortunately they weren't ready for me. Hired as Northern Transvaal's first official overseas player to give a sharper edge to their fast bowling, I was promised a flat, a car and sundry other perks.

Deceived by the posh pad with which Southampton had lured Kevin Keegan from Liverpool, I'd built up the impression of a luxurious apartment with chintzy furniture, electric curtains, a swimming pool and panoramic views, a swanky car and free membership of the best golf clubs and nightclubs in town. What it didn't say in the contract was that the 'other perks' amounted to the (generally inebriated) company of several boorish Yorkshire players, that the car was 1000 miles away and the flat was totally devoid of furniture or utensils. Obviously I hadn't read the small print.

After a fortnight of sharing Chris Old's motel room, I did finally move into 110 Jaspitt, 670 Schoeman Street, one room in a faceless sixties apartment block. It had prison cell windows and the kind of clangy metal outside stairs that enabled you to immediately estimate age, sex, height, lung capacity and blood-alcohol level of the user, which is not a major asset when you're just dozing off after an hour of mosquito-genocide. My REN (Ruptured Every Night) sleep patterns were not enhanced by a minuscule bed with only three legs, tissue-paper curtains, a thrumming fridge and plumbing that constantly groaned and grumbled as if it had consumed a dodgy prawn curry. On the third day, I listed the items the flat still lacked:

1. No bathroom light.
2. No carpet.
3. No table and chairs.
4. No cooking equipment manufactured after 1948.

5. No bath plug (I had to wedge my flannel in it).
6. No tin opener.
7. No plug on toaster or bed side lamp.
8. No screwdriver.
9. No saucepans.
10. No phone.

It was the absence of that last basic utility – the eau de cologne as it was called in English dressing rooms – that caused most consternation. My dad couldn't ring up to ask about the cricket, or my mum to check whether I was eating properly, or my girlfriend Julia to say she still cared. It made me feel totally alone and isolated and Pretoria was not the best place to be in that condition. Twin Basingstoke with Baghdad, infuse it with Afrikaaners and apartheid, chuck it on a dusty plateau prone to violent electrical storms and you've about got the gist of it.

Pretoria is a functional, administrative Legoland run by accountants and pen pushers, most of whom are anti-social and speak an inhospitable, guttural language that sounds as if they're choking. Cars stuttered around the city's one-way grid system, a labyrinth designed for maximum inconvenience. A simple straight journey is constantly intercepted by traffic lights that are totally out of sync. You never get a clear run of greens, like you do in Manhattan or along Marylebone Road (occasionally). If you want to turn left, say, the chosen street is always 'No Entry' and you have to go all the way round the block to get at it from the other end. Then you discover you're a block too far up the (one-way) street you wanted, so you have to go through the whole process again.

The street names are also invisible or written in unintelligible Dutch ('Kerk weg'), meaning the inside lane is cluttered with meandering drivers trying to establish where they are. Walk? Are you crazy? Afrikaaners are like West Virginians. They only walk on golf courses (if all the buggies are taken) or all over black gardeners who've left grass clippings on the gravel drive. A farmer, Mr van der Crook, whipped a 'kaffir' labourer to death for accidentally running over his dog. He got a three year suspended sentence.

Afrikaaners are called rock spiders. Pignoramuses would be more appropriate. They were privileged and the blacks were ostracised, but the lawmakers got it the wrong way round. It's the Afrikaaners who should have been consigned to the gutter of life. They were dense, arrogant, hostile and often obese. Otherwise delightful. Most took a daily ration of ugly pills, exacerbating the effect by wrapping thin strands of greasy hair across their bulbous, perspiring pates from ear lobe to ear lobe.

The Afrikaans traffic cop haranguing me after an innocent manoeuvre in a quiet back street, was a typical specimen.

'Don't you know the vuckeen rules?' he grunted, having flagged me down with irate gesticulations.

'What Vuckin rules?'

'Getting vuckeen cocky are you, you vuckeen yank?'

'Look, I'm English, and I don't know what I've done,' I said.

'Licence!' he snapped. I'd left it in the flat. My insurance too. 'No vuckeen papers either,' he ranted on. 'That's vuckeen sheet.'

He radioed to a colleague, his voice getting quite high pitched, though I couldn't understand what he was saying. Then he turned back to me. 'OK, you kom to the station, or you gif me eighty rand,' he said sternly. I gave him eighty rand. My crime: failing to come to a *complete* halt at a stop sign. Afrikaaners were the curse of Pretoria. And it's a day's drive to the nearest beach.

At least it was sunny most of the day. The heat builds up from scorching to stifling through a Pretorian afternoon and you yelp in pain when the backs of your thighs make contact with the black leather seats of the car you've neglected to park in the shade. Big anvil clouds balloon on the horizon until at 4.30 p.m. – so regular you can almost set you watch by it – there are the first rumbles of thunder, followed twenty minutes later by a tumultuous downpour of hailstones often so large and jagged the local A & E department is on red alert. I liked staring out of the window at these mini-apocalypses, watching the roads turn into a sea of white gravel, hearing the rattle on tin roofs, sniffing the doused-hot-tarmac air, the smell of cool water on baked dust.

After the storm, calm. In fact at night Pretoria was totally dead, and, as Afrikaaners never invited you into their homes or spoke to you in bars, it's lonely for the visitor, especially one with no telephone. In the hills of the Highveld beyond the city, there are snakes called boomslangs that are supposed to have a lethal bite. Believe me, after three weeks living in Pretoria, you go about trying to find one.

Predatory Tactics
The inter-provincial cricket was the saving grace. It got you away from that blighted city for a start. Throughout South Africa, there was an immense array of talent, magnificent manicured grounds and brilliant facilities. Playing against these muscular predators, you would either grow stronger or perish. I nearly perished a number of times, but the kindly dressing room attendants – mostly Ndebeles – nursed me back to life. There was even a boy

to whiten your boots. In my case these were one adidas and one Mitre, bound together with gaffer tape. I still hadn't entirely suppressed my student habits.

The players prepared for first class Currie Cup games with great thoroughness. You arrived at the venue around lunchtime the day before, and after a bucks fizz welcome at the smart hotel, wandered down to the ground for practice. The practice areas were excellently equipped, with immaculate playing surfaces and small armies of waiters to bring you drinks and new bats, and there were always newish balls to bowl with, not those ragged, roughed up English things that only Imran Khan knew what to do with. Then after a lengthy team chat, we'd be back to the hotel bar to get trashed on cane and Coke.

My first match for Northern Transvaal, two days after I arrived, was against Griqualand West. We flew over the arid plains and parched rivers of Orange Free State to Kimberley, and after practice, I visited the Big Hole – 1000ft. deep, hewed out by 30,000 diamond prospectors in the 1880s. It's the biggest manhole in the world. Gazing into the orifice with ghastly honky-tonk music emanating from a goldrush-themed bar nearby, I wondered if all the lucky female diamond-recipients knew the trouble these men had gone to. It must have been hell digging down there, on your hands and knees in relentless heat, yet there still seemed to be a few optimists poking about in the depths. When three of my first five deliveries were dispatched to the boundary in the opening over of our match, I wanted to go and join them.

We won that match, but during a protracted trawl around the country to play one day games in Port Elizabeth, Durban and Cape Town, we lost all the others. We flew everywhere. The skies were usually clear and looking down across the landscape was like a live geography lecture. My constant eccentric exclamations about inselbergs (desert outcrops) I'd seen from 33,000ft. earned me a new nickname – they called me Koppie. This was Afrikaans for 'small hill'. I later found out it also meant little head. It was coined by the wag of the team, Anton Ferreira, the ex-Warwickshire player, a hairy bear of a man known as Yogi. Though good natured, he spoke only in brief sentences invariably containing at least three derivatives of 'fuck'. As in: 'Fuck me this fucking pitch is fucked,' or 'Fuck's sake Koppie, get the fucking fucker in!" There'd be more bleeps than words if anyone recorded an interview with him. Not that anyone ever did.

The other provincial teams were far too strong for our motley band, and I was left with an indelible impression of South African willpower. The batsmen were tall and beefy and they punched the ball vigorously without much backlift. Their eyes narrowed when you tried to talk to them at the non-striker's end, like you did in England, and they didn't reply. They didn't want to be distracted from their task. The bowlers were fast and unrelenting and their deliveries rapped the bat harder and closer to your fingers than you were expecting.

If you got a lucky snick that fell safely, they glared at you in mid pitch and screamed 'FOOTSAAK!!' or 'YESUS!' and the fielders licked their lips, hungry for the next chance. There was also a madman quickie called James Carse who ran in with dilated pupils and nostrils flaring and flung down 90 m.p.h. hand grenades which either exploded off the pitch or flew straight at your head. He burst out laughing when batsmen got hit. He'd been in the army serving in Angola and you could tell.

I guessed they derived this total commitment from their macho society and their legacy as pioneers. There was still a feeling in bars and at *braais* that men should display their manhood by revving their V6 motors round the block or eating sizzling lamb's testicles or piling up the beer cans they'd guzzled in 10ft. pyramids while their womenfolk sat together in a corner looking on admiringly and trying each others' lipstick. There were only brawny fast bowlers and no slowies. Spin was for wimps.

It was all a sort of primitive show and just one aspect of the white South African make-up that suggested their instincts were quite basic. Sporting prowess was (and still is) a by-product. Provincial cricketers were paid by the match so they had to drive themselves hard to win the swanky cars and the trophy wives that came with national selection. It was part of the South African every-man-for-himself culture that stemmed from the whites' historical isolation, and their discovery of gems in the nineteenth century. Chest-beat, dig deep and the rewards will come. It seeps through in their cricket.

The floodlit games were the most enjoyable. After a decent lie in, you wandered into town to have an early steak lunch, and be at the ground in time for the 2.30 start. The stadium would be half full and atmospheric by then, and the harder white balls would ping off pitches, bats and hoardings to provide great entertainment. By 6 p.m. dusk would be falling, the lights were on and the *braaivleis* fired up. People would bring down their sirloins and curly *boerewors* sausages and chops and cook them on the boundary edge and the whole area would be cloaked in a meaty, smoky mist like vaporized Bovril that made the fielders instantly ravenous.

Luckily there was a supper interval at this point, which made the escape from being larrupped around by Graeme Pollock, Barry Richards and their other attack-shredding batsmen all the more attractive. Wolfing down a tranche of steak and a hunk of pecan pie and ice cream is a lot more sensible when your team's batting next rather than fielding. But brought up in county cricket, food is like junk bowling – if you don't help yourself to it, someone else will.

I made this mistake once at the Wanderers in Johannesburg. I staggered onto the field against Pollock's Transvaal nursing a badly distended stomach. The great man emerged through the Bovril mist just before 9 p.m. as if a god had suddenly descended through a cloud. He was in his dotage as a batsman but was still an icon to the spectators. He was much taller than I had expected, too, and he wore an alarmingly carefree expression.

His status was enhanced by an accessory to the scoreboard which ran a running tally of Pollock's current bonuses that season, based on fifty rand a run in all competitions. The figure that day stood at R77,100. Not the greatest morale booster if you were about to bowl to him. Nor was the knowledge that umpires worshipped him and rarely gave him out. I looked at the small, already knackered ball in my hand, and this colossus wielding a railway sleeper of a bat twenty-odd yards away and the umpire smiling sadistically at me, and I was conscious of the hubbub of expectation all around. I was the errant courtier about to be slain by a machete-wielding king in full view of his loyal subjects.

He didn't disappoint, swatting my second ball to the midwicket fence as if it were a pesky fly. He leant on his bat, chewing contentedly. The fourth was dextrously carved past point and rasped to the third man boundary. The bonus meter clicked up greedily like a London taxi fare. He made a masterful and rapid 78 not out and would have done so even if we'd had twice as many fielders. 'Jeeps', they called him, which might easily have been because he rode roughshod over bowlers (JCB would have been more apt). The real explanation was simpler: his initials were GP. Several things struck me about him, apart from a vicious pull straight on to my knee.

1. For such an exceptional batsman, his stance was extraordinarily rigid, legs akimbo, planted astride the crease, like guards at a gate in a thou-shalt-not-pass pose. He didn't stray from this position, whatever shot he chose, unless he had to run. In other words, never. Most of the junior population copied this idiosyncrasy and wouldn't be persuaded otherwise, making my attempts to coach them the 'MCC way' even more pointless than usual.
2. For such exceptional lankiness, he had enormous power. Balls fizzed from his bat as if they were TNT-assisted and sluiced through fielders' hands on the way to the fence. Two had to leave the field for first aid.
3. For such an exceptional sportsman, he drank remarkable amounts of liquor in the dressing room afterwards.

Animal Passions

In between provincial games there was the occasional chance to play a local club match. Soon after I'd arrived in South Africa I was subjected to a humiliating auction where I stood in a room and various Pretoria club chairmen bid for my services. I felt like a prize cow. Then I'd been paraded in the club bar by the winning official, the chairman of Adelaars CC, and forced to stand on a chair and down a pint in one.

Playing for the club was an equally dubious pleasure. Hardly any of the Afrikaans players – called Klopper or Oosthuysen or Roos – spoke anything other than pidgin

English and they had little idea about how to play the game. Field settings were hopeless and went from one extreme (hundreds of slips) to the other (everyone on the boundary).

Matches often began at the unearthly hour of 8.45 a.m. and the Adelaars ground was scrappy and unfenced so you couldn't really tell where it began and ended. A really powerful shot disappeared into a wasteland and took for ever to retrieve – particularly embarrassing if you were the unfortunate bowler. There were large ankle-wrenching holes in the outfield where rugby posts had been and the nets were more of a nature reserve than a practice area. Straddling the outfield were two electricity pylons and to one side a turd-coloured barn containing squash courts and a windowless steakhouse.

The bar was men only, as all Afrikaans club bars were. There was even a sign up saying 'no dogs, no women.' They needn't have bothered. Not even the mangiest pooch or ropiest slapper would have wanted to set foot in there. Beer dregs laced with cigarette butts and morsels of *biltong* swilled around on the concrete floor. The drinkers and darts players were augmented by a huddle to one side gawping at big-busted nudes spatchcocked across the centrefold of a porn mag. There was a coarse Afrikaans clamour, accompanied by lewd laughter. Or maybe they were just choking in the Rothmans-clogged air. Women, it seemed, were only marginally above blacks in the social strata (the word for daughter is 'dogster'.) I was not going to improve my cricket or meet the girl of my dreams amongst this lot.

I did meet one intriguing female. At Pretoria zoo, of all places, and she was human. I visited the place several times, partly because it harboured much more intelligent life than your average Afrikaans cricket club. Garbi was studying biology and worked in the reptile house part-time. She said it was the best bit of Pretoria, and I couldn't disagree. At least I could look at her there. She had mousy-coloured shortish hair, an attractive if slightly angular face with arched eyebrows and a fantastic body with strong, square shoulders, a trim torso and slender legs, which her masculine, zoo-issue shorts didn't do justice to. She was a PW verging on a DW. I feigned interest in snakes to talk to her (staring at a green mamba shedding its skin in mock fascination) and we arranged to meet for a drink at the Sticky Fingers café.

Over an odd combination of beer and strawberry yoghurt she told me about the purifying philosophy of her conservative Dutch-reformed family, the hopeless inter-tribal conflicts amongst the blacks (which I'd already witnessed when next door's cleaner, a Shona, attacked mine, an Ndebele, for trying to borrow an iron) and her thesis on genetics.

I thought nothing of this at the time, nor a few days later when she invited herself to dinner. I suddenly remembered the sausages I was going to cook were off, so had to trim the mould off them before grilling, but she ate them happily and drank a bottle and a half of wine. Then, without further ado, she started to unbutton her shirt.

I was slightly taken aback. Images of my girlfriend Julia flashed into my mind. Even though we had a fraught relationship and had split up twice, she wrote to me every week. I had gone away for six months, but I felt some loyalty towards her. We were still sort of an item. I'd feel awful cheating on her with a woman I hardly knew.

After we'd done it on my drainpipe bed, Garbi fetched her bag from the kitchen and fished about in it. She produced a swab and a small plastic container and transferred some of the fresh discharge on the sheet into it.

I watched dumbstruck. When she then asked if she could measure my testicles with a pair of callipers, I jumped up and put my trousers on. I'd just read *The Boys from Brazil* and knew all about Dr Mengele's 'cleansing' methods. I suddenly conjured up this notion that the 'purifying philosophy' Garbi had talked about in her family referred to people not organic food, and that I was just an extension of her wider scientific ambition. Before I knew it all my organs would be removed and pickled for public contempt. I subtly encouraged her to leave and never set foot in the zoo again.

White Power

I didn't have the requisite hot wheels, brawny appearance or star status to interest any other women. I drove a clunky, bile-coloured Golf, found most of the supplied cricket kit on the large side – so the sleeveless sweaters drooped limply beyond my shoulders and the trousers draped on the ground – and was constantly harassed by local sports reporters who thought I was overpaid, overrated and overawed. They were right about the latter.

I had not been prepared for the glaring unfriendliness of virtually everyone in Pretoria, nor for the great swathes of idle time to kill (there were only two first class games a month). I tried to learn a bit of the language. I got as far as:

drankwinkel – bottle store (with a separate window for blacks and whites)
twee castilles assablief – two beers please
speerwidgies – cheese portions
onderbroekies – underwear
het twee palkies gevat – I've got two wickets. I never had cause to find out how to say three.

The Afrikaans also said '*lekker*' (nice) a lot about their three basic staples – beer, meat and cars – but were extraordinarily offensive to the mild-mannered black barmen. The air turned blue with their offensive demands, 'You fuckin' kaffir, clean up this fuckin' mess, *doerce*.' I tried to help, but that just incensed them more.

I resorted to befriending the blacks whom I encountered digging the road, or walking about swinging battered tape-decks or lounging around under trees in parks, transistors clamped to their ears. Then P.W. Botha's government suddenly announced that all the city's parks would be closed to blacks. This was as facile as it was inhumane, since they were the only people using them, and there was little other shade around. The crippling injustice of apartheid really dawned on me after this superficially trivial episode. I think I'd been careering around a bit oblivious to it before. You were sort of sheltered from their hardships. Out of sight, out of mind. Now, seeing this barbaric system operating before my eyes, I understood the world's outrage. (It's incredible to think that in an essentially modern country, such an oppressive regime lasted almost fifty years.)

I tried to do my bit, paying Phinah, the lady who came to do my washing and ironing, twice as much in spite of her saying she was 'quite happy' and helping Franz, a gardener who worked nearby, whitewash his 'quarters', which were barely more than a hovel. I also honoured the pleas of another black man whose van had just run into the back of my car. 'Please don't report this,' he begged. 'I'm not insured.' I told my sponsors I'd accidentally reversed into a wall.

'So your drifing is as goot as your bowling,' they said (I'd so far taken only eight first class wickets). They made me cough up half the repairs. It was then that I finally flipped. I went straight to a travel agent and booked myself on a flight to Malaysia.

Asian Interlude

There was reason in my rashness. Not much, I admit. I'd gone to Pretoria with the aim of shaking up my cricket and shaking off my dependence on Julia. But it was all becoming counter-productive. My personality had won few admirers and my cricket had won none. In the last Northern Transvaal match before the Christmas break, I'd gone into bat no.11 wearing a sun hat instead of a helmet.

I was clonked between the eyes first ball by a bouncer from Neal Radford, a muscley fast bowler who was so vain he always took the field with a comb in his pocket. The ball virtually rebounded back to the bowler, but I felt nothing. Then two overs later, as everyone was still wondering why I wasn't on my way to Casualty, I collapsed to the ground for a laugh. The opposing players all got the joke when I stood up again, but I didn't. I'd ricked my ankle and couldn't bowl in the second innings.

I might have suffered brain damage too, but I could see straight. Pretoria was a dump, and if I needed any more confirmation it arrived at 11.30 p.m. on Christmas day. There was a loud rap on my door, and I opened it to be confronted by three drunk, purple-faced Afrikaaner oafs.

'Achhh you roiineck,' one of them slurred, veins bulging around his temples.

'You moo four fucking cow or veal fuck you.'

'Uh?' I was non-plussed.

'Moof your fucking cow . . .'

'What fucking cow?'

'That Golf. Isssit yours?'

'Yes.'

'Well fucking mooffit. We wanddogeddourcowout.'

63

And a Merry fucking Christmas to you, I mouthed through my windscreen when their leaning, lurching Datsun was a safe distance away. I wouldn't piss on you if you were on fire.

Sod it all, I thought, as, without telling any of the Northern Transvaal officials or players, I climbed aboard a British Airways flight from Johannesburg to Hong Kong via the Seychelles. Then a short hop from Hong Kong to Kuala Lumpur on Chinese Airlines. I hardly noticed the sixteen hour journey, I was that relieved to get away. I was so desperate that I'd flown 5000 miles to be reunited with the girl I'd been trying to make a clean break from. Julia was spending Christmas with her expatriate parents in Malaysia.

Two weeks of R&R in the tropics is not the approved method of rediscovering your lethal away swinger, but it certainly rebuilt my self-confidence. It was a lot better than M&M (Misery and Masturbation) in Pretoria, that's for sure. At Julia's parents', we slept in a huge double bed and ate delicious local food – for my money a Malaysian Chicken Rendang is the best dish that's ever been conceived. We hung out at the Lake Club, a luxurious leisure complex where you could perch on stools in the pool sipping Singapore Slings, and be fawned on by waiters serving you spicy, aromatic snacks.

We spent three days in a simple chalet-hotel at Port Dickson, windsurfing and swimming at a pretty sheltered beach with all the Bounty ad trimmings. It seemed the perfect setting until the second night we went skinny dipping, and discovered on emerging from the water, that someone had pinched our clothes. It reactivated our quarrelling, and I had to go to reception to get a replacement room key clad only in a large banana leaf.

I was invited to a cricket match and New Year's Eve

party at the fusty old Selangor Club. At the party, tables of legless Chinese-Malays sang Auld Lang Syne together and then chucked each other in the pool. The match, on a matting wicket, was poor and forgettable except for the sight of one insufferable Brit, who had driven from Singapore – a tortuous six-hour journey – in the pretentious expectation of scoring an easy century. He was out first ball. Watching someone else look a prat was wonderful restoration.

Natural Selection

'Had a good holiday?' asked Yogi Ferreira at the first provincial practice after I'd returned to South Africa from my sabbatical. I had explained my absence from a one day match in December by ringing the Northern Transvaal office on a crackly phone-line from Kuala Lumpur, lying that I'd caught deng fever in an up-country game park and couldn't travel. They'd obviously seen through it, but it was partly true. I had sort of been ill. The tough, unforgiving cricket, the austerity of Pretoria and its primeval women had sent me delirious.

Whether it was the steamy warmth or the red chillies or the emptying of my sacs, I don't know, but Malaysia cleansed me. I returned to Pretoria a different person. I turned up early to practice, sorted out a persistent no ball problem, didn't roll up to airports for away matches in board shorts, painted some murals on the walls of my flat, and booked some touristy trips – in the same country this time – that didn't compromise my availability. I even deserved my place in the team, though Trevor Chesterfield, the cricket writer on the *Pretoria Daily News* didn't seem to think so, implying he could have done a better job. This was a touch mortifying bearing in mind he was 5ft. 3in. with an artificial leg.

There were some scheduled days off here and there, and I used them well. I took my family, who paid a brief visit, on safari in the Kruger National Park, a controlled area of undulating bushland the size of Wales, bordering Mozambique. We saw everything from prowling lions to paroling elephants and were mesmerized by the sounds and smells and the parched, shimmering distance. This was Real Africa, Attenborough-land, the place of our zoological imagination. Despite our stay in 'Jock's Bungalows', a swim in the Mac Mac pools and a meander down Burns Drive, I couldn't think of anywhere less like Scotland.

Looming 2000ft. above the Kruger Park, amidst pine and gum forests, is God's Window, a peephole atop a precipice. Standing there looking down at the baked, rolling savannah was like looking at the innards of the world. If you really deluded yourself, you could perceive all those complex ecosystems and cycles of nature between the birds and the beasts and the plants and the trees that turn the cogs of the planet we live on. Here was pure nature, unhindered by man – except the odd Mozambique fugitive. Here in deepest Africa, these pro- cesses created us and will surely outlive us, without the aid of telecommunications or the Tetra Pak.

The predators weren't letting up in the human rat race either. Both my club and my province slid lower and lower down the league table, a process I was powerless to arrest. At least I enjoyed it a bit more, though. Northern Transvaal played a three day match in Durban, staying in a smart seafront hotel. The beach looked inviting, though when I went for a walk on it I was appalled to find signs up saying 'No black bathing.' They were allowed to paddle in up to their ankles (presumably so African nannies could accompany white children) but never to be seen in swimwear on a white beach. Can you believe someone actually passed that bylaw?

Durban was certainly less hostile than Pretoria. In fact, it seemed rather British Empirish, with men in tropical suits and wide-brimmed hats and cut-glass vowels. They didn't speak with the pinched, Dutch-spiced accents of the Transvaal. They batted with the same flair and crushing effectiveness, though. That was Natal in general (548-6 in a day and a half) and Barry Richards in particular.

Richards, a languid figure with a shock of blond hair, was close to retiring, and admitted as much to our wicketkeeper. After one extraordinary shot played from nowhere near the wicket or pitch of the ball, he said 'I can't wait till this season's over to hang up my boots.' He had such a benign presence reclining at the crease, like a cat that was barely awake. But as soon as the ball came down he was poised, ready to pounce, able to caress it in virtually any direction with a precise cuff of his paw. In between balls he returned to snooze mode. He made a majestic 123 and never broke sweat. If he'd grown up in England he'd have probably been told to 'Move your feet to the pitch, play straight and don't hit the ball in the air.' The cricket world would have been denied one of its greatest-ever talents.

Richards' sublimity was in direct contrast to the bustle and bristle of his famous team-mate Mike Proctor. Proctor was the bull terrier to Richards' lynx. Now only able to bowl spin following a knee injury and concussion after falling off a first floor balcony, Proctor still brought a fast bowler's fire and brimstone to this subtler art.

I stood at the non-striker's end as he rapped a batsman on the pad with an off break.

'HOWZAAAAT!' he yelled.

'That's not out,' said the umpire.

'Why not?' Proctor declared, wheeling round to glare at the official.

'. . . Er, well, I don't know really,' replied the agitated umpire.

'Well why don't you give it out then?' demanded Proctor. Which the beleaguered official duly did. In his next over exactly the same thing happened.

'HOWZAATONETHEN?!' cried Proctor again.

'That's not out.'

'Why not?'

'It was the same as the previous one.'

'But you gave the previous one out.'

'So I did. That's out.'

And they say star players don't influence umpires.

Binned

Northern Transvaal's last opportunity to haul themselves off the bottom of the Currie Cup table came in Cape Town. A stunning place to finish. Newlands must be the most beautiful ground in the world, in spite of an adjacent railway track and a brewery puffing away beside. Surrounded by oaks, the enclosures blend into the surroundings with Table Mountain standing majestically above, often with its thin layer of cloud – the tablecloth – blanketing the peak.

Our opponents Western Province were studded with stars – Graham Gooch, John Emburey, big Garth le Roux, Peter Kirsten, Kenny McEwen, Steven Jefferies – a whole team of umpire-controllers. The wooden spoon beckoned. I watched their explosive skills in the nets and absorbed their confident banter. I knew that

1. We were going to lose, and
2. A contest between Yogi Ferreira and John Emburey to see who could naturally pack more 'fucks' into a

conversation would definitely go to penalties. Emburey, you may remember, was the south London lad who, when asked once how his injured back was, unthinkingly replied, 'Well the fackin fackers fackin facked.'

Ferreira and Emburey had another thing in common. They were both, beneath a welter of expletives, eternally good-natured and long-suffering. Yogi demonstrated this consistently with his attitude to Northern Transvaal's other overseas fast bowler, Chris Old. 'Chilly' had an unrivalled reputation for pulling up the ladder with an unlikely ailment, which both Yorkshire and later Warwickshire had become well accustomed to. He used several in one game in South Africa. He turned up initially with handkerchief over his mouth saying he had a cold (it was about 90 degrees) and he'd sneezed and gone in the neck. He made it on to the field but then claimed his left little finger was hurting and he might have to go off for treatment. Finally he complained of double-vision, without seeing the irony of his reputation as one of the biggest drinkers England has produced since Oliver Reed, and dismissed himself.

Yogi must have been getting thoroughly cheesed off with Chilly, having to bowl most of his overs for both Warwickshire in the English summer and Northern Transvaal in the winter. He never complained. He just got on with the job. Weighing in at probably little under seventeen stone, he always arrived back in the dressing room bedraggled in sweat, a lone Saharan trekker staggering into an oasis.

He knew a thing or two about adversity having been a good amateur boxer who once fought the South African heavyweight champion Gerry Coetzer. The count, he was fond of informing us, lasted longer than the fight. Even before that encounter Yogi was no mental giant, but on the cricket field he ran in with the same gusto for the last ball of the day as he did for the first. He was the archetypal indomitable South African.

He ran gamely into the Western Province artillery but he didn't get much help. I did manage to trap Gooch with a fast yorker, but only after he'd made eighty-nine. We eventually bowled them out for 450 on a helpful pitch, and long before Northern's last wicket (me) was humbly sacrificed, the words of a recent Status Quo hit were ringing in my ears – '*Down, down, deeper and down . . .*'

We battled hard, and it could be said the umpires had again conspired against us (you have to make regular use of this excuse in a weak team.) What actually happened was the ball conspired against us. It flew off their bats and somehow avoided ours. We weren't good enough, lost the match and came last in the Currie Cup.

The winning runs were hit off me, and I trudged back to the pavilion, on the way dumping my ragged, taped-up, odd boots into a convenient litter bin. I didn't want any souvenir of what had been a largely fruitless winter. I wouldn't be coming back either. I was certain of that. Not to Pretoria. They wouldn't want me anyway. I sounded out a few people in Cape Town about playing there the following season. It had beautiful scenery, a sense of place and stunning beaches apparently littered with blonde bouncy-castles. Unfortunately we were back on the plane to Pretoria before there was time to conquer any. It summed up my trip.

The Score

My first winter in South Africa was effectively six months of self-obsession and soul searching. Searching for everything, in fact. Furniture, friends, fornication and five-wicket hauls. I hadn't had much luck with any of them, but like a six mile run which you don't look forward to or particularly enjoy, I felt it had done some good in the end. This was a tough, unforgiving, dog-eat-dog place, and you had to keep your wits about you to avoid being picked-off. South African provincial cricket flossed your body and soul, flushed away the gunk.

With the bits that remained, I resolved to be more ruthless and disciplined on the pitch, to get fitter off it and buy a decent pair of boots. I also vowed never to chat-up a biologist or set foot in Pretoria again. Well, a place with a rating of

People		Beaches		Cricket		Catches		Total
–2	+	0	+	5	×	1	=	3

you wadn't wad yer?

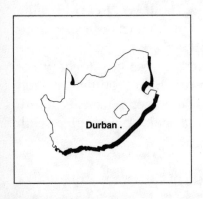

Durban.

5.
South Africa
– Durban

Call Me Bluff
A first taste of South Africa had taught me three basic things:

1. Wear matching (and reasonably new) footwear on the field.
2. Don't go on holiday in the middle of the season.
3. Get umpires on your side by, a/bribing them, b/congratulating them on their choice of tie/after-shave/original flourish when signalling a four.

No. 3 worked to some extent in county cricket. I got some sneaky wickets, including some lbws I knew were dodgy and Clive Rice given out caught behind when the 'snick' was actually his gold chain clanking on his visor (I wonder if Channel 4's snickometer would have detected that?). But the umpires took their compliance too far. When I was batting, they kept giving me the benefit of the doubt during fraught sparring contests with terrifying West Indian fast bowlers. 'No, no, that rapped his shoulder not his thumb, Sylvester,' they'd say to the marauding Clarke, a one-man assassination squad. 'You'll have to do better than that.' Several times I narrowly escaped being seriously maimed. Also, bribing the men-in-white-coats (with drinks, money, use of hotel room for shag) was quite expensive. I was out of pocket. I had to get another winter job. The Hampshire captain, Mark Nicholas, who I had a good record against, persuaded me to join him playing club cricket in Durban.

Durban, during the English winter, was actually Hampshire. It contained virtually the entire county cricket staff for a start, lured by Robin and Chris (Kippy) Smith and their father John, an engaging Brit who brought his sons up there. It was inhabited by people with plummy accents who lived in large white detached houses with gravelled drives and spent most of their time riding or playing golf, and a lot of very pretty, debonair young women in pearls and camisoles who cruised around in Mummy's two-door Beema. I'd have to admit that Portsmouth doesn't resonate to the cackle of cicadas, or offer a round-the-clock supply of voracious mosquitoes, and there aren't 18ft grey nurse sharks in the Solent. But the human similarities between Durban and Hampshire are evident.

I'd been hired along with two other English pros, Nicholas and his Hampshire team-mate Chris Goldie, to pull a struggling local club side, Grosvenor Fynnlands, out of the mire. I was welcomed properly, this time. I was immediately supplied with a red, souped-up Renault 5, a spacious one-bedroomed flat overlooking the beach and a handy salary.

Encouraged, I decided I was going to be more assertive this time, and initially, it worked. I made a few runs and took a hat-trick in the first match, two days after I'd arrived, which placed us temporarily at the top of the table. Punch drunk, I chatted up a DW girl for approximately six minutes at a party that night, before propositioning her.

'Want to come back to my place and make love?' I whispered enticingly.

'I'm afraid I don't make love on first dates,' she replied, reeling back slightly.

I wasn't going to be rebuffed that easily. 'Well . . . how about tomorrow?' I persisted, blithely ignoring her negative body language.

'No,' she said.

I'd hoped as I got into my mid-twenties, I'd understand women better, but they were more and more baffling. When they wanted you, they got you whether you liked it or not (I still hovered around Julia, usually on her terms). When you wanted them, you generally got nothing. I decided to hang back and leave it to the experts (the Smiths) for a while.

Within a week of settling in, the car had been broken into and the cassette player stolen, I'd wrenched my bowling elbow playing squash and discovered the 'Coastlands' flat was actually to be shared with another English player, Geoff Miller, who was excellent company but tended to slump into bed either at 8 p.m. or 8 a.m., neither of which quite fitted in with my schedule. And my burst on to the Durban cricket scene was doused by frequent and unseasonable storms meaning constantly ruined weekend matches. After six weeks in Durban I'd bowled twenty-five overs in anger.

My own image wasn't entirely enhanced by an article appearing in the South African *Cricketer* magazine which seriously questioned the value of English cricketers. Headlined 'Are English pros here just for the sun?' it was written by the sceptical, diminutive Pretoria correspondent Trevor Chesterfield and contained scathing criticism of various individuals. Among them Chris Old was cited as a waste of money and the page featured a picture of me beneath which was the caption: 'Simon Hughes: went on holiday.' So, our cover had been blown.

I did the decent thing and wrote a defensive reply in the *Durban Daily News,* arguing that English pros improved the local standard (it was true then) and disputing the claim that overseas players blocked local talent. There are eleven men in a team. If the locals are good enough they'll get in. I had to admit there were a lot of us. It was as if there'd been a ruling like the Bosman one in football and all the clubs had instantly jumped on the bandwagon and bought abroad. There was one major difference. We were lucky to get £200 a week, never mind £15,000.

I suppose the critical assessments of English pros were right in a way: we did live the life of Riley, whoever he was. We got up at 11 most mornings unless we were playing golf, had a leisurely poolside lunch of steak, salad and ice cream (usually prepared by a maid at someone's house), did an undemanding spot of schoolboy coaching between 2 and 4 p.m., and twice a week were obliged to stretch ourselves to attend evening practice at the club. There was only usually one day's play at the weekends, so Sundays we got up even later, went sunbathing or waterskiing or to a *braii*. It wasn't exactly slave labour.

The Grosvenor-Fynnlands ground was on a windswept bit of reclaimed land known as The Bluff, inhabited mainly by second-hand car dealership employees and owners, so the area was appropriately named. It had a wild, uncut outfield into which the ball kept disappearing from the ropy asphalt nets, so the practice nights were largely a waste of time. Players practised in an assortment of garb: from full whites and boots to people who didn't bother to change out of their blue office shirt, grey strides and hush puppies, and turned their arm over desultorily for half an hour before retiring to the bar to play pool. My cricket stagnated as my potting improved.

The coaching had its moments, though. I visited four different primary schools a week, for two hours in the afternoon. The kids were all desperate to get out of lessons, as kids always are, but while some were keen to play sport, others just used the opportunity to duff each other up. At one rougher school I had to keep confiscating knuckle dusters and stop a couple of eleven-year-olds sniffing glue.

Little boys invariably fidget, talk and don't listen when people are trying to tell them things. After I'd made them play eight-a-side roll-ball for half an hour in 95 degrees and 98 per cent humidity with the goals at least 100 yards apart, and forced anyone who didn't try or threw the ball instead of rolling it to do twenty-five press ups, they listened alright. One of them was a lad with a carrot top and freckles who was unfailingly polite and very talented. He seemed a bit cautious about expanding his repertoire, so in the nets I taught him some offside shots with the bat, and the inswinger with the ball. His father had been advising him to keep on swinging it away and improve his legside play, but I told him to ignore all that and be inventive. I was sick of parental meddling. Who was his father anyway?

I found out at a parents' afternoon a few weeks later.

'So you're the chap who's been telling Shaun to bowl

inners,' a tall, distinguished-looking man with hefty shoulders said politely. 'I must tell you, I had more success for South Africa with my outie.' It was Peter Pollock, the great Springbok fast bowler who took 116 Test wickets and later became South Africa's chairman of selectors. His son Shaun is now, at the turn of the century, rated as the no.1 bowler in the world. He gets most of his wickets with a wicked outswinger. *And* he scores all his runs through mid-wicket.

Off the Straight and Narrow

If you're a good golfer, Durban is very rewarding. There are hundreds of courses on many different terrains, each beautifully watered and manicured by more cutters and combers than you'll find at Paris fashion week. Caddies and buggies are plentiful and there's always a well-stocked halfway house with better fry-ups than the Savoy Grill.

If you're a bad golfer, Durban is very expensive. You lose all your wagers and wear out your shoes (or run the buggy out of gas), some of the courses are so junglefied you need an industrial strimmer to find your ball and you're regularly buying new ones from opportunist fairway-wanderers. I lost count of the number of times I shanked balls into lakes which were then dived for, retrieved and sold back to me at an inflated price by entrepreneurial little African boys.

At least I hadn't had to buy my own clubs. Raj, the friendly Indian doorman at my apartment block, loved cricket and cricketers and offered to lend me his.

'But don't you need them?' I asked.

'Sa'ab, it would be an honour to me and my family if you played with them,' he said – a sentiment he would definitely have withdrawn if he had actually seen me play. 'But you will have to come and collect them. I cannot carry them on the bus.'

I ventured into the townships one evening to pick them up. He, his mother, his wife and his four kids lived in Section 13 at B287, one in a huge battery of rabbit hutches – you couldn't call them houses – in a scrubby district about twenty miles outside Durban. It made Milton Keynes look like the Champs Elysée.

The accommodation was basic. There were two rooms plus a toilet. There was no furniture except one hard chair. The family squatted on the floor to eat in one room, and slept side-by-side on mats in the other. Each room had one barred window and a naked lightbulb in the middle of the ceiling. I've seen better equipped dog kennels.

Raj invited me in to share the family vegetarian curry, making a great commotion of introducing me to everyone and then turfing his ailing mother off the only chair to provide me with something to sit on. I protested, to no avail. Afterwards he presented me with the golf clubs, cleaned and polished, in a well-cared-for Slazenger bag. They were worth more than his home.

It's sad to relate, but this was the only time in a year in South Africa that I really saw how the 'other half' lived. Segregation was so effective that whites never needed to cross the racial divide and it never occurred to them to stray. Townships were deceitfully 'hidden' behind hills or in valleys off the beaten track and you were only conscious of this mass of incarcerated souls when you saw the over-laden buses, chassis scraping on the ground, heading out of the city at dusk.

Contrast this with the gilded surroundings of Durban Country Club, where we county cricketers spent many a pampered morning. The grounds were presided over by an elegant white club house with pillars and verandahs and contoured wicker chairs and polished marble floors. Black doormen in white tunics with gold-braiding and cream pith helmets saluted as you drove in. The golf course was luxurious. The fairways were like billiard tables, and there was so much sprawling natural undergrowth I kept expecting David Bellamy to suddenly appear out of it warbling about the delights of edible mangrove bark. Each hole was so different it seemed to be in a separate climatic zone. It was like that huge new glass-house at Kew Gardens where you go from the Arizona cacti room through a door into an Indonesian jungle.

The only hole I ever mastered was a piddly little par 3 with the green set 100 yards away from the tee on top of a little cone-shaped hillock. The banks of the green sloped sharply away from the putting surface on all sides. It was called the Prince of Wales hole and club selection was crucial, as HRH found out. He tried virtually every one in the bag and finished with an 18. A triple-quintuple bogey I suppose you'd say. Shit golf might be more succinct.

Learning golf is one of those experinces where you do tend to take one giant step forward and then lots of humiliating stumbles back into the crap. It's a beginners lambada class on grass. I was definitely the bloke with wild, flapping arms and two left feet, and Durban remains the only place in my sporting career where, for a whole (cricket) season, I averaged over 100.

Undeterred, I agreed to play in a pro-am one Saturday morning on a treacherous course at Umkemas, an hour south down the coast. Now there's one problem with 'celebrity' golf tournaments – you're supposed to be either well-known, or good at golf. Preferably both. I was neither. (Over the following years I became more and more humiliated at these events, turning up as the 'celebrity' to play with three blokes from Beazer Homes who had never heard of me and were even more appalled at my golf.) At Umkemas, I spent most of the round scuffing balls along the ground or shanking them out of bounds. My playing partners gave up waiting for me to catch up, and played amongst themselves. Then, at the seventeenth, a par-three hole where there was a prize for being closest-to-the-pin, I skimmed a grass-cutter to two feet and won a colour TV.

'Don't give it to him,' one of them muttered when I went up to collect it, 'he won't be able to lift it.'

Fish Slice

It sounds like golf was more important than cricket in Durban. It was. The cricket matches were usually rained off and when the sun came out again and the heat was really sweltering you couldn't go swimming at the beach for fear of finishing up in a shark's stomach. Shark nets are staggered protectively across some swimming areas. The ravenous beasts glide in, feel claustrophobic, and glide out again. That's the theory anyway. Out of boredom or perhaps morbid fascination, I thought I'd check out the reality by attending one of Durban's anti-shark board public 'dissections.'

This involves slicing open a fish that had recently snagged itself in the nets, to see what pond life or beach paraphernalia it might have swallowed. The 'catch' of the day was a 6ft grey nurse shark, a tiddler by Indian Ocean standards. What struck me, apart from the appalling smell when it was cut open, was the sight of two human feet in its stomach. The dissector shrugged. 'Ach, the tibia and the femur must av been too big for 'im,' he said.

I don't know what it is about that bit of the Indian Ocean – whether the prey is harder to catch or the passing cruise ships chuck out less edible garbage – but the sharks round there do seem to have a ravenous appetite for human flesh. There were often ugly sounding incidents of negligent people being attacked further up the coast. One batsman in the Grosvenor-Fynnlands team had actually had half his leg bitten off by a white pointer while surfing some years before. His name was Mike Manley but everyone called him 'Sharkbait'. He was allowed to have a runner in some games and was actually more successful than some of our fully-limbed players. He turned ones into twos and twos into threes. Unfortunately this was in the field. Chasing a ball to the boundary from slip, it was better if he failed to get there in time and the ball went over the line for four. Otherwise the batsman could run six.

Generally, it wasn't a very good team. The assortment of teachers, gauche car dealers and trainee accountants were a bit out of their league compared to the hardened veterans at other clubs. They regarded weekend cricket as a bit of a jaunt, to the extent that two players brought a tent with them to away games, and after getting totally bladdered in the bar, crashed out in it for a few hours kip on the outfield.

Their attitude was in keeping with their ground. The practice area was totally neglected and we pros couldn't do that much to rectify the situation. It's pretty hard getting bowlers to improve their accuracy when they're running up on rutted ground with a ropy ball shared between five, and landing on a piece of old, untethered lino to bowl at a batsman in blue jeans standing in front of a beer crate wicket. To improve a team's cricket there are three things you need. Facilities, facilities and facilities. It's why Derbyshire, Somerset and Sussex have won the county championship only once between them.

Smith Family Robin Son

What with the rain and the clamminess of the 12th floor flat, I'd been feeling rather cooped up. But midway through the season, a smart, rented house became fortuitously available which four of us moved into. Joining me were Hampshire's Paul Terry, Hampshire's Kevin Emery, and Bill Hunter, a club player born in Hampshire who was taking time out from his job back home. The house was large, white and detached with double garage and garden gnomes – very Hampshire – had four air-conditioned bedrooms, a verdant garden, a pool and maid's quarters.

The resident maid, Gladys, was an immense mother of four, never in danger of wearing herself out through hard work. She used the excuse of finding it difficult to squeeze through the narrow kitchen door not to do much work. The difficulty miraculously disappeared when we were out and she could snaffle our chocolate or pecan pie. We didn't begrudge her them, and at least she waddled into the bedrooms to change the sheets once a month. It was twice as often as we would have managed.

It was a gorgeous place to live only marred by a serious mosquito infestation. These were big ones, too, that could part curtains to get at you. They poured into the sitting room at dusk like fleets of Messerschmitts on night raids and the house cushions were soon covered in red shot-down squadrons of them. (I noticed they never seemed to bite Gladys though her body must have contained enough blood to start a transfusion service.)

Just up the road, twenty minutes north of the city centre in La Lucia was an even classier joint: the Smiths' house. Kippy (Hampshire) was home for a couple of months holiday while Robin (Hampshire) played for the Glenwood club. Their father John (Hampshire's no.1 supporter) egged them on to work at their game, which they did, every morning in their own back garden.

A net had been erected at the side of the house, an artificial wicket laid and a bowling machine positioned at the far end which Simalani, the garden boy, manned. Kippy always went in first at 5 a.m. – before it was too hot – and Robin an hour later. The neighbours didn't enjoy waking up to the incessant pherthump of the compound yellow balls pinging about, but John Smith was the master of placating people. Never can there have been such an energetic, eccentric man with such a plodding ordinary name.

By mid-morning the Smith-zone became a Hampshire free-for-all. Various of the county's other players staying nearby would arrive for half an hour against the bowling machine, a dip in the family pool, and a delicious lunch prepared by Florence the maid. I never got a go against the machine because when it was eventually free it had begun to overheat and Simalani needed to get on with his day job.

But it was instructive watching likely-opposition-batsmen's techniques while I lounged by the pool and was waited on hand and foot. If only all homework could be that cushy. Kippy, I noticed, flinched at the 90 m.p.h. bouncers (with a tennis ball) and took a number of stinging blows on the body, whereas Robin cuffed and swatted the same deliveries off his nose-end with aplomb. Kippy made up for his lack of sharp reflexes with exceptional concentration, triggered by habitual fidgeting with his abdominal protector, his helmet, his thigh pad etc. (You can always tell a meticulously prepared player by the amount they fiddle with their box. Atherton, Steward, Hussain, Dean Jones, Sachin Tendulkar. Everything is habitual and has to feel right, which makes them wonderful batsmen and presumably boring lovers.)

Kippy treated every practice as a match situation, talked to himself constantly, and set himself perpetual little targets. In a match he'd just look ahead either ten runs or ten minutes at a time, always focusing on small statistical milestones. Derek Randall used to do this too. At 3.20 p.m. during one England Test, he met his batting partner and captain Mike Brearley in mid-pitch and said ''Ere skip, in twenty minutes it will be twenty minutes to tea.'

Other than the Smith family's hospitality and facilities, they had another major asset. Close by was a public phone box with an invaluable design fault. If you dialled the code for England very slowly, you heard a clunk which you learned had convinced the contraption you were making a local call. Then by inserting a ten-cent coin, you could talk to your mum, girlfriend or girlfriend's sister-who-you-actually-fancied-more, as long as you wanted. Word got round quickly, and initially there was a mass exodus to the phone box until it became obvious that whoever got there first would hog it for hours. Luckily, others were then discovered with the same malfunction. You could always tell where they were by the sight of several cricketers' sponsored cars parked outside.

For most, it was an unexpected bonus. This was the era of the £2 a minute international call, so being able to talk to your family at length rather than the usual 'What's the weather like? . . . No it's been lousy here . . . Yes, I am eating properly, OK bye,' made you feel much closer to home. For me, it just meant conversations with Julia developed into prolonged arguments about commitment, which I now couldn't terminate with the usual 'Well, got to go . . . this is costing me a fortune . . .' In the end, she was the one who terminated the call, with a 'just piss off and leave me alone.'

Anyone for Tennis?
With the Smiths' orthodox good looks and muscley bodies and metallic-blue Porsches, they were permanently surrounded by tanned, tasty women. Generally cricketers were a better catch in South Africa than they are perceived to be in England. They were browner, and leaner and always got the VIP treatment at the local night spots.

Occasionally you got the Smiths' cast-offs. At one of their poolside Sunday barbecues, I lingered around their group feeling a little self-conscious that I didn't have a 44 inch chest or a Colgate smile or a coiffured hairdo. I ended up chatting to some floosy called Karen who, amidst a kaleidoscope of bright clothes and bottle-blonde tresses, was a little less ostentatious. She had a retriever in tow and was simply dressed in denim-shorts and a man's white shirt. But the longer we talked the more I saw in the hair and the pouty mouth her resemblance to Kelly McGillis out of *Top Gun*. She was a DW, no question.

Unfortunately I was no Tom Cruise and after a few minutes she was drawn, hardly kicking and screaming, into another conversation. I imagined she was totally out of my range, especially when I passed her waiting outside a toilet which I'd just left a rather nasty smell in. I nodded politely and she smiled and said, sort of conspiratorially, 'Hey, d'you play tennis?'

'Er, sometimes,' I blurted out, noticing a large rock on her wedding finger.

'Why?'

'Will you have a game with me?'

'Sure, when?' I said, warming to the idea and realising

that the longer I kept her talking the more the smell would dissipate. We arranged to meet at her tennis club in Glenwood the following night. Then she left. I admired her supple, Steffi Graf-legs as she went.

She wore too much make-up to play tennis – foundation, thick mascara and an oil slick of lip gloss. I didn't like girls who wore lots of make-up. It was as if they were trying too hard or had something to hide. She was a well coached player with a strong serve which I had trouble returning. It didn't help that her T-shirt rode up every time she threw the ball up, revealing a tanned, trim midriff. When I stabbed balls into the net she came up to it and beamed at me. Her stare was slightly unnerving, but we had a drink afterwards and she said we should do it again next week.

She intrigued me, which is another way of saying I wanted to have her over the back of a sofa, and my mind wasn't on the cricket that weekend. Perhaps that's why I took five wickets against the Old Collegians club in Pietermaritzberg. It never does for quick bowlers to think too much. Or any sportsmen come to that. I've often thought that people like Mark Ramprakash, Colin Montgomerie and Tim Henman tend to fall at the final critical hurdle because they've mentally over-complicated the situation.

After tennis the following Monday, Karen invited me back to her house. A man's jacket hung by the door and there were wedding pictures in the hall.

'It's OK my husband's left,' she said, 'he buggered off nine months ago.'

'Oh what a shame,' I said, in mock disappointment.

'No it's a relief,' she said. South Africans never did get sarcasm.

I was slightly mystified, but I drank the rosé she poured

me, relished the flash of inside thigh she offered me every time she crossed and uncrossed her legs, patted her slavish retriever when it slobbered on my knee. She guzzled three quarters of the bottle, took a couple of pills from a jar, and started getting quite intense.

'He used to slap me and tell me I was a starfish in bed,' she said. 'I miss him though.'

After a while, she beckoned me upstairs 'to see her rococo furnishings'. The dog followed. She led me into the decorative master bedroom and slipped into the ensuite pastel bathroom.

'I won't be a minute,' she said. I looked around at the hunting and riding pictures on the walls, and the enormous four-poster bed with a tasselled eiderdown precisely spread, and the nest of ornamental tables displaying wedding photos and silver knick-knacks, all arranged just so. A collection of men's shoes were aligned neatly under the bed – size twelve I guessed – and a pair of braces were slung over the arm of a chair. It looked like one of those rooms people leave untouched when there's been a death in the family.

She reappeared naked, displaying a flawless tan and a pubic mound trimmed into the shape of a heart, and draped herself across the bed.

'What are you doing?' I asked dumbly.

'Take me,' she crooned. 'Come on. I haven't had it since Andrew left.'

It's funny how a ravishing woman can suddenly become quite unappealing when you discover she is desperate. I was beginning to find the whole situation rather demeaning. Being seduced by someone else's wife who was begging for it, surrounded by wedding mementoes and the couple's personal effects. This is not what I'd been christened and put through expensive private education and endured the vows at friends' weddings umpteen times to do. No no no no NO.

Afterwards, I got dressed very quickly and let myself out despite her protestations. I couldn't linger in that embarrassing scene. She had thrashed about on the bed like a beached salmon, crying 'Oh My *God*' before I'd even got my pants off, and the more she pleaded for it, the more tense I became. It'd been the equivalent of being handed the new ball on a green flier against careless batsmen and taken one for plenty. Well, how would you perform if someone with heart-shaped pubes was virtually forcing you to have sex, beside pictures of her beefy-looking husband, with the constant spectre of him returning unexpectedly, while the couple's dog looked on accusingly or licked your feet? I was less apprehensive facing an over of Curtly Ambrose at Northampton having forgotten to wear a box.

She bombarded me with phone calls and we played tennis a couple more times (though I never dared go back to her house) and once she turned up to a cricket match in a dress that was little more than a napkin with straps. The players ogled her from afar. Once I'd told them that she had a violent estranged husband, and she was a cling-on who insisted on a menage à trois with her dog and thanked you for your 'gift' afterwards, they kept a respectful distance.

I added grateful, sex-starved South Africans to the Greeks and Russian air-hostesses on my list of DWNs.

In For a Shock

There was no club cricket for three weeks over the Christmas period, so two other young English pros and I decided to drive to Cape Town via the Garden Route. Equipped with shorts, T-shirts, a case of Castle lager and, negligently, only one working tape – the Commodores' greatest hits – we headed south. We drove through the Transkei, a self-contained 'independent homeland' you need a visa to enter. This is issued at a hick passport control where large Xhosas sit at tables with date stamps and ink pads, managing to look both bored and self-important.

We were warned about the dangers of car-jacking in the Transkei, but everywhere we looked, people moved about very slowly. They didn't look capable of winning a sack race never mind staging an ambush. When we stopped at a roadside stall and asked for a Coke, it took the girl an age to fetch it from a large fridge. It was warm.

'Can I have a cold one?' I asked.

'Machine done broke,' she replied flatly.

This, I imagined, was Normal Africa. No golf courses or swish houses or gleaming saloons on freeways, but red tape and run-down machinery and men loitering aimlessly by the dusty roadside, while their brightly dressed womenfolk plodded about dutifully carrying out their chores. Only 100 miles from Swanky-ville, it seemed untouched by modern civilization.

The 'rebel' West Indies cricket tours certainly hadn't impacted on the place. Any open ground was too rough for cricket and I saw no one playing in the road, either. In fact, the only game on view was a group of men playing dominoes in a dilapidated bus shelter. You looked at their fabulous physiques and wondered at the vast untapped cricketing resources here and elsewhere in Africa. If the continent does ever get its act together, England will be up a gum tree.

We bumped out of the Transkei, bypassed Port Elizabeth (sort of Basingstoke with docks) and drove on along the Garden Route, which is oddly named really, considering it's 200 miles of largely intraversible mountains. We'd heard Plettenberg Bay was something to write home about and it was. It's a beautiful beach defaced by a hideous multi-storey hotel protruding from a sand-bar, like a cruise ship that had run aground. It's an outrage. They'll stick a casino in the middle of the Serengeti next.

Having driven 2200 km through three days and two overnight stops, we finally reached Cape Town and collapsed on Clifton beach, just over the hill from the city centre. At last here was a stunning bay with glorious views everywhere you looked: the azure sky, the jagged rocks of the Twelve Apostles looming 1500 ft above the caster-sugar sand, the bronzed goddesses spreadeagled all over it. The sea twinkled and beckoned. There were no red flags up or warning notices, yet few people were swimming in it.

Running across the beach and plunging in headlong, I found out why. In Cape Town this is DIY shock treatment – a place to put a comatosed body to check if there's still any sign of life. The water is so ice-cold it's almost burning. Even a half-immersion in that Antarctic-fed sea is about as pleasurable as putting Ralgex on your knob. Worse, it makes your manhood shrivel to raisin size. You only go in that water if you've got a tube of sun-block to shove down your trunks afterwards.

Still, I was happy on the beach. I always am. I can't understand people who aren't. It's such a free, anything-goes environment. You don't have to dress-up or make conversation or sit up straight or worry about spilling your food. It's OK to nod off if people are boring the tits off you. And it's so egalitarian. Designer clothes and poncy cars and Rolexes are a western man's status symbol. They're worthless on the beach. The power there is with the dude who hires out the jet skis and no mega-bucked plutocrat can steal it from him.

By the sea the lifeguard is the alpha male. Actually, his life is similar to a county cricketer's. Idly sunning himself for most of the day noticed by no one, suddenly he springs into action, arousing a murmur of excitement amongst a sprinkling of observers, before everyone drifts back off to sleep. And there's another common denominator. Both often peer through binoculars looking professional. Batsmen on the pavilion balcony supposedly analysing an opposing bowler's grip, lifeguards scanning the horizon at 45°W for signs of trouble. It's all a mirage. Actually what they're all doing is scanning the beach / Bedser Stand for signs of 36DDs.

The difference is, of course, that lifeguards have rippling, sun-kissed physiques highly attractive to pneumatic blondes, but I can't see Pamela Anderson featuring with burnt bonces and V-neck tans in *Baywatch*. I considered joining the lifeguards' association immediately, until it dawned on me that they spend most of their time dragging fat Germans, who'd fallen asleep on lilos, out of freezing, shark-infested water, and thought better of it.

Under the Table

We spent New Year's Eve in Cape Town, at a party thrown by the Sussex and Western Province fast bowler Garth le Roux, a blond, hairy Goliath, not dissimilar in appearance to a tanned polar bear. He, in harness with Imran Khan, terrorized any batsman in the 1980s who had the temerity to stride to the middle at Hove. As an unsuspecting opponent walked to the wicket, the plaintive cry of the seagulls overhead would be drowned by some friendly advice from Imran at long leg: 'Gart, Gart, look

Gart, he hasn't got a fucking helmet on Gart. Remind him Gart.' Or, after Sussex's cockney sparrow Ian Gould had taught him some rhyming slang, 'Gart, Gart, hit him in the Gregory, Gart.' It was not a place for the faint hearted.

Neither was le Roux's party. South African breweries had supplied him with a shed-load of beer, literally. Cans and ice blocks were piled to the roof of a wooden shack and le Roux ordered that no one was allowed to leave until it had all been drunk. He was too big to argue with. By 4 a.m. several people had stumbled off the edge of the wharf and into the water and had had to be rescued, and as dawn broke, the area around the edge of the shack resembled a nuclear fallout zone. There were groaning bodies everywhere, a litter of cans and the air reeked of puke.

Beneath Cape Town's famous mountain, le Roux was still going, having seen off an impressive array of cricketers. It was an original take on drinking everyone under the Table. The people in his wake included England test players Graham Gooch, John Emburey, Chris Cowdrey and Paul Downton – all pro-ing in the area – as well as both teams from the unofficial Test match being played at nearby Newlands between South Africa and the rebel West Indies side. All the premier league drinkers like Sylvester Clarke, Collis King and Graeme Pollock were there, as well as Clive Rice, Lawrence Rowe, Alvin Kallicharran and many others. It was quite a multi-racial party.

It was probably all part of a cunning plan, too. The 1st of January was a rest day in the Test, but play resumed the day after. The West Indians were much the worse for wear and lost by ten wickets. Le Roux himself finished them off. In world cricket, his ability to destabilize the opposition both on *and off* the field was second only to Ian Botham. It was a priceless asset.

Still fairly bleary-eyed ourselves, we headed back to Durban through the undulating Karoo desert. There's nothing of notable interest in the 700 miles or so between Cape Town and Bloemfontein. There's even less of interest in Bloemfontein itself. Some places are cities without a plan (London, Los Angeles, Rio de Janeiro). Bloemfontein is a plan without a city. It's a grid of ugly modern tower blocks and tacky low-rise shopping complexes intermingled with some nineteenth-century colonial stuff. No wonder Allan Donald, who was born there, would rather live in Birmingham. After twenty years in Bloemfontein, the Bull Ring must seem like the Taj Mahal.

Back in Durban after a month off, we were positively gagging for some cricket, not a feeling I was used to during the relentlessness of a county season in England. Durban's fickle weather soon doused my enthusiasm though. It rained for what felt like months (it was actually only nine days) and successive weekend fixtures were cancelled. This is doubly disappointing for a cricketer abroad. You've been building up to it all week, talking about the opposition, checking out the pitch, cleaning off the golf-course muck from your cricket boots and suddenly it's a non-event. But what's worse is there's nothing else to do. At home you'd use the spare time to catch up with some old mates, or pop round to your parents with your washing, or replenish your record collection, or purge your wardrobe of some seriously naff items. In a foreign country, there are none of those options and while your club colleagues disappear off home to seed their neglected lawns (or wives) you're left with a bit of a void, which is inevitably filled by propping up some bar or other. Also, in Durban, rain just brings the mozzies out in legions.

We tried to use the time productively. Someone proposed football, but no one had a ball; golf was suggested, but Saturday was a members-only day and anyway most of the courses were waterlogged; squash – all courts booked up; badminton – hall shut at weekends; cricket net – indoor sports hall closed.

That's the irritating thing about sunny countries. There's no contingency plan for the times when it's not sunny.

The Durban season meandered to its end in late March by which time we English were all more than ready to leave. You can only take so much of golf in the morning, light coaching in the afternoon and heavy socializing in the evening. I was fed up with queuing for the faulty pay phones too. Grosvenor-Fynnlands were probably not sad to see the back of us as it happened, since Mark Nicholas and I had cost the club quite a lot of money in accommodation, coaching fees and pool bets and though individually we'd performed well, the side had still been relegated to the second division. It didn't please our benefactor (a nasty little textile tyrant who remorselessly exploited black seamstresses in pre-industrial conditions) and he withheld our bonus.

The standard of Natal cricket was quite disappointing. Mainly because most of the pitches were rolled meadows, the scores were low and the slip catches numerous. I took 50 wickets in 15 games without really doing anything special. I could see exactly why Mike Proctor, who learnt his cricket here, tore in with the ball and didn't hang about with the bat. Apart from Proctor and Richards, Natal has produced few really outstanding players. Like Hampshire. Perhaps in both places, life's just a bit too cushy, affluent and golf-orientated to knuckle down to a gritty team sport.

The club chairman invited me back with tempting offers of more money, less coaching and a better set of golf clubs, but I'd had enough of Natal. The cricket was too hit and miss, the weather was too oppressive, the beaches too dangerous and the women too slick or too scheming. Most of all, I'd had enough of being described as a 'mercenary' for working in this immoral, Black and White Minstrel society. I'd arrived home with a bag-full of dirty washing and £48.

The Score

People		Beaches		Cricket		Catches		Total
6	+	5	+	6	×	1	=	17

Auckland

6.
New Zealand

Who Left the Light On?
It's a common misconception that English professional sportsmen have exciting sex lives. Their physical fitness and the confidence they exude is compromised by zero dress sense, bouts of morose silence after a bad day and an obligation for the long-suffering girl to spend Saturday shrouded in jumpers and cardies, surrounded by manic young thugs (at football) or on damp, wooden benches surrounded by morose old blokes (at cricket). Team sports don't usually attract the cream of the female crop, I can tell you.

Occasionally in the provinces I encountered a PW, pretty in a bland sort of way, but they were out of bounds anyway because I was still plodding a fairly aimless course with Julia. She was my home peg, my ground sheet to rest on after exploring foreign fields. Like numerous county cricketers, I wasn't much of a partner. Having been frantically busy for the English summer, you suddenly develop serious lethargy at the end of it. In late September, while the girlfriend is out at work, you loiter around her flat all day eating toast and reusing the same mug twenty times to avoid having to wash anything up, and only stocking the fridge with beer and Dairylea.

It doesn't make for harmonious relationships and our on-off affair was full of complications and jagged edges. We'd made no progress in three years and now her clock was ticking, and my alarm bells were ringing. It was time to take the opt-out clause and go away again. I decided to go as far as possible. In early October, I booked a one-stop flight to Auckland.

I'd gained very little from Durban, apart from an awareness that I was never going to be able to hit two consecutive fairways with a three-wood. Going to New Zealand, would, I hoped, be a more valuable voyage of discovery, though I didn't know much about the place. I'd heard the usual New Zealand jokes reminding the last person out to switch the lights off, and that the air was so clear that from certain vantage points you could see back eighty years.

My background knowledge was sketchy to say the least. I knew Kiri Te Kanawa and Sir Edmund Hillary were New Zealanders, and that all self-respecting Kiwis were proud of their 'veggie garden.' So they could sing and climb mountains and plant courgettes. I'd also read somewhere that most New Zealand men could change a tractor engine with a fish knife and a piece of four-by-two, and so could their sisters. And that was about all. But Clive Radley, a Middlesex colleague, had told me the cricket was fun, and engineered me a contract to play for, and coach, Auckland University.

This sounded more my social scene. Mingling with intelligent students, hopefully some nubile ones, was just what I needed after two years of Julia trying to get her claws in, and five summers of the barrack-room slang in the Middlesex dressing room. ('Phorrr, you pen and ink. Did you have a Ruby last night or have you been sitting too near Gatt's arris?')

To my dismay, the University ground was out of town, miles away from the student halls of residence and any available talent. All the people at the club were men over thirty who arrived at matches already changed and stayed in the clubhouse afterwards only long enough to check their bowling figures or batting stats in the scorebook before bolting home to the missus. Like Glenn, the middle-order batsman, who had to get back to his wife 'Clear' because she was 'tin wicks prignunt.' Glenn rather undermined one description of New Zealand as 'a brighter Britain'. He told me, 'On 5 November here we have Guy Fawkes night. What do you do?' The only woman in the vicinity was June, a matronly figure who prepared the tea. This didn't overtax her already straining figure as it involved merely stuffing a dozen tea bags into an industrial sized pot and then slopping it into cups. If you wanted anything to eat you either had to bring it yourself or drive to the nearest deli for a meat pie.

This, I found, was very much the way in New Zealand club cricket. There were none of those hearty spreads you get at English clubs – the steak and kidney puddings and spotted dicks and spam sandwiches and chocolate eclairs. Not even a packet of nuts or a plate of bon-bons. Famished at lunchtime after a lengthy bowl, I'd traipse to the car in sweaty socks, and drive around till I came across a takeaway or a café. I felt silly standing in a MacDonalds queue in whites. Several times I got lost going back and was late on to the field or found I was running in to bowl with loose change jangling about in my pocket.

At least the club had a fastish wicket, but this advantage was offset by the fact that the senior player, Warren Stott, was a bowler and he always wanted to bowl with the wind, which meant I had to run into it. As this wafted straight off a sewage plant, I often felt nauseous during spells (especially straight after a Big Mac) and needed a regular supply of Rennies. We couldn't swap round because Stott – who played one day internationals for his country – bowled his medium pace so slowly it wouldn't have reached the other end into the wind. He was the original 'dribbly' bowler, which had nothing to do with excess saliva but described an indigenous type of seam bowler.

Dribblies were everywhere in New Zealand. They loped up to the wicket and dobbed the ball slowly but persistently on a full length, with a hint of swing. The keeper stood up to the stumps so the batsmen daren't stray out of their ground. At national level they played an important part, descended in a consistent line from Bev Congdon in the seventies through Jeremy Coney in the eighties (and Chris Harris in the nineties). In club cricket you weren't a team unless you had one.

They looked innocuous, but on the cabbage patches of Auckland (the original 'veggie gardens') they were unplayable. They coaxed the ball to misbehave, making it pop or grub almost at will. Regular shouts from the boundary of STD! (Smack That Dribbly!) only increased the batsman's anxiety, already intensified by the sight of what appeared to be about thirty-eight fielders. In Auckland several club matches are played on one not-very-large paddock, with the boundaries overlapping each other. From the air the ground must look like a giant Venn diagram. You know that the man standing with his back to you at short mid wicket is actually cover point in an adjacent game but it doesn't make run-scoring any easier, especially when, just as you're concentrating on the bowler running in, a ball from the next door match suddenly shoots across your pitch hotly pursued by a fielder. You would have thought in a country with a population density of 12.4 people per sq. km (1/20 of the UK), there ought to be enough space for everyone to play their own self-contained game, but this is how the Kiwis do it, and it does mean if your match is boring there's another one to watch nearby.

Consequently, the standard of club cricket was fairly ordinary. They played two day games, usually on consecutive Saturdays. With Auckland's fickle weather this meant you could be daubed in factor 15 playing on a bone dry strip one weekend and battling a howling wind and a sticky dog wearing two sweaters the next. The umpires – both men and women – were awful. None had the first clue about the game, and seemed to have been recruited from the local tax office. They could count, but that was about all. The grounds were usually roughish, without sightscreens or proper scoreboards, and changing rooms were communal and chaotic, in some cases shared by about six different teams. It cut down the incidence of sledging. You couldn't exactly call a bloke a sheepshagger on the field and then, finding after play you were changing next to him, ask to borrow his shampoo.

A Family Affair
My Auckland accommodation was a constant headache. Literally. I was initially billeted with the Kennellys, a kind middle-aged couple who had six kids. Five of them still clattered about the house, making quite a racket as teenagers do. This wouldn't have been so bad if it hadn't

been for the barge-like house with its mint-thin dividing walls. My sleeping area was in the middle of a discordant din of The Clash from one room, Van Halen from another and Tina Turner from a third.

The family were staunch, law-abiding Catholics who regularly went to Mass and said Grace before dinner, quickly followed by one of the kids telling another that he was a little shit or a selfish prick, which made the mother wince with disapproval. A normal sort of family, really. It was quite reassuring having them around, but there was no peace or privacy to offer my prospective conquests.

I'd tried to find alternative accommodation, but it wasn't easy. The options I investigated were either louse-infested slums, or room-shares with ten-year-old boys or bohemian houses inhabited by drowsy, red-eyed, bra-less girls who asked through a fog of smoke and incense what I was 'into.' Not them, anyway. So I remained with the family, which had two distinct advantages: dinner in the oven whatever time I came home, and endless packets of frozen peas to ice my sore knee, which had had a severe collision with a boundary board. I was laid up for a while and didn't get out much. The club social life was non-existent and the other English pros I knew playing in Auckland – Bill Athey, Ian Gould, Dipak Patel and Jack Russell – were more interested in golf than girls.

I was rather put off exploring the city night life on my own by stories of machete-wielding gangs from Auckland's large Polynesian community squabbling there. There were, I noticed, a lot of people of all races round town with sticking plaster on their face. When I gleaned this was actually due to the high incidence of skin cancer in New Zealand caused by a large hole in the ozone layer, I ventured out more. In fact, the Samoans and Fijians did most of their beheading in the southern suburbs.

In some city dive, I managed to charm a DW, a foxy blonde called Tania McCall, a 21-year-old travel courier. She took me for a ride, in every sense. During our second date, I sensed she might be on for it, but she lived with her parents, and so did I, kind of. The only private option was my sponsored car, which had the added lustre of 'Simon Hughes: English pro sponsored by Pakuranga Motors' daubed on the side. She eagerly accepted my suggestion to cruise to the Auckland Domain, a city park which stayed open all night. I thought my luck was in.

When I'd parked at a suitably private spot, she got out of the car, I assumed to loosen her clothes and clamber abandonly into the back seat. Instead she came straight round to my side, opened my door and asked if she could have a drive. Her driving test was in a couple of months, she said, and she needed the practice. For the next two hours we stalled and lurched our way round the empty roads, bumping over several kerbs and scraping a low wall slightly. This, I said, gave her excellent credentials to pass the test, bearing in mind the normal levels of driving in Auckland. She pulled a stern face and asked politely to be driven home.

I was too tired to protest. Keen to please – some might say desperate – I endured this routine three more times, visualizing I might get what I wanted eventually. Each time I got nothing more than a routine peck on the cheek. She didn't even offer to pay for the petrol. When, after two weeks of no contact, she rang to ask if I wanted to go out for a drink I said 'I hope you fail' and put the phone down.

Bach Interlude
By late November I'd got rather depressed. I hadn't adjusted to the puddingey wickets, my knee was still sore, I was too busy and exhausted from coaching endless

groups of inept ten-year-olds to sightsee, and the only girls I seemed to meet were lank-haired dollops who needed to read *The Hip and Thigh Diet*.

I was hankering after Julia again. Why? The image of her superb body that improved every week I was away from it, and her slightly disturbed mind which I found alternately frustrating and stimulating. I began spending half my salary pestering her with late-night phone calls. These snatched conversations were played out in the living room in front of the entire TV-gazing Kennelly family, not the most comfortable place to be apologizing for your failings and trying to rebuild a relationship. Also, it was 9.30 a.m. in England, and she was at work.

There were no faulty phone boxes in Auckland like the ones in Durban. I know, I looked. Then I thought up a crafty ruse. As University club coach, I had a key to the pavilion, and there was a pay-phone near the dressing rooms. I arranged to be standing beside it at 10 a.m. each Monday when Julia would reverse the charges from a London phone box. Pretending I was in an office, I accepted them, assuming the bill would go to the University.

We actually had decent conversations. I knew it was crooked but it lifted my spirits and I started bowling better and earning my keep. The ploy was so effective, other English pros in New Zealand began using it to speak to their other halves, and some Sunday mornings there were enough there for a casual net while people waited for their calls. It never occurred to me that the only reason I was at the nets was because of a girl, and that if I'd spent half as much time and money improving my cricket as I had chasing and placating skirt, I'd have played twenty Tests.

As usual in the southern hemisphere, club cricket had a three-week break over Christmas, which puts single blokes staying with large families in a bit of a spot. They kindly invite you to spend it with them, hoping you won't. You say you won't ever get a better offer than that, praying you will. Fortunately I did. Bernie Maher, a Derbyshire player and honorary Kiwi, had borrowed someone's *bach*, 100 miles up the coast.

This is the definitive New Zealand experience. You sleep in a ramshackle wooden cabin perched on stilts, on a fern-enveloped beach yards from the water's edge. You slob around in a singlet and board shorts all day playing frisbee or beach tennis, and loll around the barbecue all night. Occasionally you extend yourself to fetch water from a pump or dig for 'pippies' at low tide and boil them up for supper in a big pot. You don't spend any money or wash or have any contact with modern appliances, and there's no sound except the soothing lap of the waves, and the sizzle of sausages over charcoal. Basically you're in a bit of a trance, a favourite state of the common-garden Kiwi. It had much to recommend it.

After three days Bernie and I had become so comatose we shouldn't have been in charge of a toy ship never mind a life-size catamaran. Sailing it in the bay, we managed to impale it on a rocky outcrop and had a hell of a job extricating it. Giving it one last heave into the water, I felt a searing pain in my already-damaged knee and when we had got back to shore, it had swelled up like a pomegranate.

Sportsmen can be joyless individuals at the best of times; when injured they're unbearable, alternating between self-pity and outrage, blaming everyone but themselves. I was not good company after that, cursing the *bach's* lumpy beds and draughty windows and the billy's interminable boiling time and the salty, sandy, burnt food, and the incessant lap of the bloody waves.

Damage Limitation

I was put on to Graham, the physio of the New Zealand team, as soon as I was back in Auckland. He diagnosed *condra malaysia patella*, the degeneration of the underside of the kneecap from wear and tear. He treated the joint with ultrasound. He should probably have applied it to my brain as well. As he, a single, thickening forty-two-year-old, plugged me into the machine, he also told me there was a spare room in his house. I moved in the next day.

I was not the only one. Bridget, an older brunette, checked in to stay with Graham, the following weekend, and then Lynn, a blonde slightly past her sell-by-date, the weekend after that. There were others. I kept hoping I might get one of his rejects, but after hearing some of the humphing and howling emanating from the next room at odd hours, I thought better of it. In any case, the only role Graham had in mind for me was as some kind of lacky to wash the dishes and mow the lawn.

He did help my knee to recover and took me along to the New Zealand nets to give the batsmen practice before a Test against Pakistan. The coach Bob Cunis, rescued from anonymity by John Arlott's famous comment on TMS: 'Odd name Cunis, neither one thing nor the other,' told me to give it a full go. Keen to impress, I made the ball fly around, hitting the opener John Wright on the shoulder and the star batsman Martin Crowe on the hand, jeopardizing their chances of playing in the match. This infuriated no one more than Graham who had to work overtime to get them fit, forcing him to cancel a date with another willing divorcee.

I was invited into the Eden Park dressing room for one day of the Test match and before play talked to Richard Hadlee whom I knew well from county cricket. He didn't answer back. In fact he didn't even seem to register that I'd spoken at all. He was staring into space with a slightly manic expression on his face and no one attempted to disturb him. He was in a trance, too. But he put it to good use. This was how he prepared for big matches – total focus, no distractions from his projected goals, which he carried around in a briefcase. A few of his colleagues raised their eyes skywards when they saw his impenetrable gaze, but they couldn't really complain. They rode on his back. Graham Gooch once described facing New Zealand's attack as, 'Hadlee at one end and Ilford 2nd XI the other.' Hadlee carried the team, illustrated by this Pakistan Test when he took a stack of wickets, bruised and cut a number of opposing batsmen and New Zealand won by an innings. Naturally, he was worshipped like a deity and constantly on TV, advertising anything from cars to paint to garden strimmers. If he'd been seen wearing a sarong, ship loads would have had to be imported from India.

Physical Quirks

The hot mid-summer sun and the volcanic soil made vegetation grow like wild fire, including cricket pitches. Suddenly they were lively and fun to bowl on, but the Kiwis were dogged and hard to dislodge. I suppose they got it from their feathered namesake – I mean you have to hand it to an ugly overweight bird that can't fly or see but still continues to survive in a hostile environment. The Kiwi shell is hard to crack. Except in rugby, they thrive on being underdogs. They're gritty, determined and opportunist. They're practical and uncomplicated, there are no pretensions. They are not coached regimentally. Quirky it may be, but they find their own way and stick to it.

Glenn Turner had a big influence. He came to England

in the 1970s appearing to be just a boring blocker, albeit quite a prolific one. As soon as he'd been introduced to one day cricket, he began pinging the ball everywhere, to some of the most unlikely places. He pioneered the chip shot – over the infield but short of the boundary – and, with an enormous bat that looked too big for his spindly arms, was frequently devastating. He was an early innovator and he set the ball rolling for the New Zealand approach in the eighties and nineties, picked up afterwards by Martin Crowe and then Stephen Fleming. You underestimate Kiwis at your peril.

Listen carefully to them too, otherwise you're lost. 'Right you jokers,' said the University captain at the critical stage of a game, 'no wogging of the drubblies, be a blob not a cocky, spicially against the currymuncher. It's a flat dick, just wait for the bad nut.' I felt like I needed to rifle through a dictionary of anthropology. I knew 'currymuncher' meant Asian person and that 'wogging' was slogging, but I was still a touch confused when I went out to bat. Second ball I pulled the bat out of the way of a nasty lifter only to be given out caught off chin-via-shoulder. I sat in the dressing room feeling thoroughly disconsolate. I couldn't get a run or many wickets or understand anyone.

Kurti, a team-mate came over and tried to console me. 'Don't pack a sad, mate, you fair sucked the kumera there. That umpire's out in the wopwops.'

'Look just fuck *off*,' I shouted.

He looked a bit put out. Then he said, 'Aw go puss yerself thin' and walked off.

You couldn't blame me for finding New Zealand speech rather confusing. Fit and fat both sounded like 'fet', 'deck' was dick and sex was pronounced 'six'. I suppose it's the Scottish influence that makes their accents so pinched. When a nosy Kiwi quizzes you about last night's date, saying 'Ewes hid six thin, dud ewes, ay?' you're not quite sure whether they're on about fornication or farming, or both.

The answer to the above enquiry was a resounding 'no'. It was four months since I'd seen Julia, she was getting terser and terser on the phone, and I thought I was justified in having a local dart. I took a nurse out twice, but each time well before I'd got within range of a double-top and bullseye finish, her bleeper went, and she was called in to work. I didn't know whether this was fate, or a friend baling her out. I didn't get on the oche with anyone else.

On the field I was at last contributing something with the ball, and slowly growing in confidence. Taking on extra responsibility abroad, and constantly having to prove yourself to new team-mates wards off complacency and keeps you sharp. It should be compulsory for every young English pro. It would definitely harden them up a bit. Added to that, playing on windy, ill-equipped grounds watched by more livestock than people is, of course, excellent preparation for county cricket.

Jack Russell, who was playing for another Auckland club, took these afternoon games as seriously as any Test match. He was out there hours early warming up, ate his customary Weetabix-soaked-in-milk-for-exactly-half-an-hour before play, was in full PE-teacher-voice behind the stumps and spent any breaks studiously sticking more little bits of padding on his dilapidated gloves or pieces of heavy material on his fraying sunhat to stop it blowing off. I played on Russell's side in a needle match between the English pros and a select Auckland XI (which we won easily). I was amazed to find in the dressing room he also marks out a no-go area round his chaotic kit with yellow tape. It looked like one of those zones cordoned off by forensics after a homicide. If cricket was a little more technologically advanced, Russell would probably be using laser beams by now. Obviously he's not the bloke to ask if you want to borrow a box.

Slimline Tonics
New Zealand couldn't really consider itself a cultural mecca in the eighties; their art and literature was of negligible interest, their film industry non-existent and their only band of note, Split Enz, split up. They later reformed as Crowded House and were claimed by Australia. It was a place where you were meant to be outside, windsurfing, snorkelling and sailing around to nearby islands, rather than fiddling about with a guitar indoors.

Auckland was growing on me. I liked the steep hills and undulating streets and glistening harbour and cliff-lined bays. It's a sort of mini San Francisco. The neat weather-boarded houses with their rattly tin roofs gave it an unpretentious air, and if someone didn't like where they lived, it was quite common for them to stick the whole house on the back of a large truck and plonk it down somewhere better.

I could see why so many British handymen had settled there. It wasn't dissimilar to home but the weather was slightly better, the golf courses were snob-free – you could play in a T-shirt and shorts without being turfed off by some snooty official telling you to wear tailored trousers – and there was a stack of outdoor work for painters and builders. I could immediately tell how long Brits had been there by the extent their voice went up at the end of a sentence. If they said 'I'm off down the Oaks for a few Stein-e es,' they'd arrived at least five years ago.

The 'Oaks' was an important bar because it had satellite

TV and every weekend showed Test matches from Australia on a big screen. The West Indies consistently blazed a trail Down Under. Holding, Marshall, Garner and Walsh regularly dynamited the Australian batting, much to the undisguised joy of the Kiwis jam-packed in the bar. If ever you had doubts about the bitter rivalry between Australia and New Zealand, Friday night in the Oaks would have dispelled them.

The February weather was roasting and I scoured Auckland's sprawl for the perfect beach. But on the east side they're mostly either too shingly or too small and in the west, bleak and assaulted by mountainous waves. I persisted and one day descended a flight of stone steps hidden behind a school which led down to a small cove, St Leonard's beach. After five years of looking, this was the spot – sandy, secluded, unspoilt, shaded by eucalyptus trees, with a couple of yachts bobbing on the horizon. The water was clear, calm and warmish and harboured nothing more dangerous than the innocent flounder. And it was deserted. So I thought.

When I looked beyond a large boulder, I saw the corpulent figures of about a dozen middle-aged men. Some were stretched out on the sand, one or two were perched on rocks. All were bollock naked. Not that I could see their bollocks (or wanted to) beneath their large expanses of juddering flesh. None were attempting to suck their stomachs in, knowing that if they did they'd risk crushing their lungs. If there's anything that can tarnish a beautiful beach more than the sight of wobbling, leathery female cellulite, it's the display of wrinkled, distended male torsos with their emasculated tackle nestling below a beer gut which is barely supported by a pair of wizened chicken legs. This spectacle brings on the same slightly sick feeling you get when you're lazing in a ski-resort sauna imagining unharness-ing the hotel barmaid's magnificent breasts, when a fat, hairy German wanders in and removes his towel. Men over forty-five should never be allowed to remove their clothes except in the privacy of their bedroom. With the lights out.

No one had been in my bedroom for months. There was no inclination to change the sheets, and the place was in a right state. Meeting Grant, a cricketer, badminton player and asylum-provider, changed all that. Grant was the antithesis of the fat lumps on the beach. He was so thin he had won a Mr Puniverse contest literally by removing his shirt (he'd auditioned to play a refugee in the movie *Merry Christmas, Mr Lawrence* and had been rejected on the grounds that he looked too emaciated). He was surrounded by slim, attractive women either keen to feed him or borrow his jeans. One who couldn't quite squeeze into them (she was a size ten) took a shine to me.

Apart from being practically a nymphomaniac, Chloe had two other advantages. She had a flat overlooking the beach, and she worked in marketing for a brewery. There was nothing in her fridge except ice cream, beer and durex. She was also very fit and liked tennis which kept her vertical for a while and gave me a bit of respite. She was frisky and intelligent and a bit unpredictable and I totally fell for her. It was a vigorous fling. We went running on the beach together and climbed hills and watched the sun sink into the sea and laughed and argued and hung out in cafés and played with Daville's Rum 'n' Raisin.

I was happier with a girl than I'd ever been. We had the advantages of a student-type relationship – no ties, no responsibility – without the disadvantages – no money, single beds. But it couldn't last. My knee injury had flared up again and I was booked to fly home in late March to have it properly checked out. A month after meeting Chloe I was saying goodbye. Perhaps that's why we enjoyed it so much, because it was finite, had a time scale. And it was just like all those holiday romances when you say 'I'll see you soon,' and promise to stay in touch, but never really do. At least we had a excuse. I mean, we couldn't just suddenly nip down to Brighton to a quickie, could we?

That, I suppose, is the major problem with New Zealand. It's so far from anywhere else. Despite Auckland's presence, there's no tangible escape from miles of wild, woolly countryside and sheep pastures and rocky bays. You can't just hop on a train and go and see the new Chagall exhibition or Vladimir Ashkenazy conducting the Berlin Phil, or get tickets for the Eurythmics tour. Urban types can only have so much fresh air, clean-water streams and pristine sand.

Still, I was sorry to leave New Zealand. The weather is about right – not too hot, never cold – the people are casual with a dry sense of humour, the beaches are tranquil and restoring and so, largely, is the cricket. It's quite an unthrusting, low key sort of place. The joke 'How do you set a New Zealander up in a small business? – Give 'em a big business and wait' sort of rings true, which makes the country endearing in a quaint sort of way.

I suppose it was a pastoral place.

You still got milk in bottles with a creamy bit on top and greengrocers twisted the corners of brown paper bags properly. New Zealand was the ideal antidote to the hurly-burly of an English season. I was keen to come back and the University were keen to have me. Until they were handed a bill from New Zealand Telecom totalling $1620 detailing thirty-six reverse-charge calls from the UK . . .

The Score

People		Beaches		Cricket		Catches		Total
8	+	8	+	4	×	2	=	40

7.
Australia –
Perth

Helping with the Enquiries

Immediately I got home I was in hot water. Auckland University demanded money for the phone, Julia demanded an explanation for not hearing from me for two months, and Middlesex demanded a fitness test. I satisfied the first, avoided the second and failed the third. I had to have a minor knee operation and was sidelined for a while. I decided to take stock.

1. I was a twenty-seven-year-old graduate who didn't have a secure job or own a house, a car, or a decent pair of shoes. With my £2320.87 savings (plus a £100 premium bond my dad gave me on my eighteenth birthday) I couldn't buy a caravan never mind a des-res.

2. I was in trouble with an employer at home and an

employer abroad and the local London borough's careers adviser had been made redundant.

3. My knees were giving me gip and my hair was falling out.
4. I was a compulsive liar and a habitual flirt and an incessant nomad.
5. I was unable to concentrate on anything for long.
6. I'm bored with this list now.

Middlesex won the championship that summer, but I played only a minor role with the ball, taking 24 wickets. I didn't really feel part of it. My knee didn't fully recover till July and in one match I suffered the ultimate fast bowler's indignity of the wicketkeeper (Paul Downton) standing up to the stumps for several overs after Allan Lamb had sidled up the wicket and casually smote my best effort over the sightscreen. I had lost pace without gaining accuracy and my career was idling, in tune with my relationships. Julia and I had come to a T-junction. I was stuck in neutral neither playing the field nor getting serious.

Conquering the art of bowling and pursuing women have some parallels. Both are complex and unpredictable and all the more addictive for that. Just when you think you've grasped how a ball will behave, it develops PMT and everything goes haywire. Also, they say size is not important in either, but it is really. You're always seeking perfection but it's never attainable.

I listed the ingredients I was looking for in my ideal woman against the components contained in my ideal cricket match, to see if I could draw any conclusions:

At a cricket match I want:	From a woman I want:
1. A firm pitch	1. A firm body
2. A big crowd	2. An extrovert
3. Tough opposition	3. Other men fancying her
4. Daring captaincy	4. Strip Poker
5. Surprising twists	5. Julie Christie twinned with Kim Wilde
6. Wickets	6. Sex
7. Applause	7. 'You're the best.'
8. Several days off afterwards	8. No obligation to 'clock in' every night

The middle order (i.e. 6 and 7) was not delivering the goods on either side. Prompt, possibly painful action was required.

If you're an English footballer the place to go and sharpen up would be Italy, for rugby players either France or New Zealand, for golfers and tennis players definitely America. In cricket, Australia has always been associated with an abrasive approach both physically and verbally – the place to find out if you were a man or a mouse. It was the oven of the game, where the soft dough of talent was baked to a hard crust of achievement.

The winter offers weren't exactly pouring in – they never have from Australia ever since we dumped about 200,000 convicts on them in the 1850s. I had to pay my own way. A good mate in Perth, Cookie – himself a former Middlesex player – said he'd find me a club and somewhere to live. That was the easy part. Getting into the country was like penetrating the Kremlin. There was an enormous queue at their London tourist office just to get an application form, then endless questions assessing your health and finances and moral codes ('Have you ever attended a meeting of, read a book relating to or told a joke about the Klu Klux Klan?' 'How many showers do you have a day?', that sort of thing). Then another enormous queue to hand it in. After a further six hour wait, which felt like six days, you were finally called up to the window to answer more personal questions and get your visa.

The inquisition continues when you arrive in Australia. The mass of travellers in the Perth arrivals area suggests a fleet of jumbos have landed all at once, but it's just the immigration officers quizzing everyone. Is this, I wondered, what Australians meant by 'the big ask'? They wanted to know precisely where and with whom you stayed in the last ten years and what your mother's aunt Flora's maiden name was, and the customs people poked about in your bags and shoes and lockets and asked you when you last cut your toenails. 'Got a criminal record?' they demand, to which it is tempting to reply, 'Didn't know you still needed one.' Finally they stare at you gravely and stamp your passport, saying 'Three months then, and not a minute longer' as if you're borrowing the family silver. Reminding them that Great Britons blazed the first trails here, and therefore we commanded a bit of respect, cuts no ice. They think Captain Cook is a make of gas barbecue. They don't appreciate history, think heritage is a load of old tosh. 'Recall' is just a button on the telephone.

Real Men Don't Walk
Perth is a brash, glitzy city built in a desert. There's a lot of money there and a lot of sand. It's 4000 miles from Auckland and even further away in attitude. Yet though the personalities of the two cities are markedly different, the people's accents are quite similar. Tell you what though, neither race likes being mistaken for the other.

There's a simple test you can conduct to avoid embarrassment if you're not sure whether someone's a Kiwi or an Aussie. Ask the bloke if he ever made love to a fourteen-year-old. If he's a New Zealander he'll say, 'Of course not, I wouldn't dream of it. That's a disgusting idea.'

If he's an Australian he'll say, 'A fourteen-year-old what?'

Whether it's because of their remoteness (2200 miles from Sydney) or their emptiness (Western Australia is ten times the size of Britain with 1/20 the population) there is a definite hard insularity about Perth people. They're narcissistic, defensive, narrow-minded xenophobes. There are a lot of Yorkshire people there. They obviously felt at home. Western Australians refer to other Australians as 'crow-eaters' or 'banana benders' and there was a sort of smug isolationism about them. After the great success of Alan Bond's yacht, this was reflected in every car licence plate declaring 'WA – Home of the Americas Cup.' Western Australians are desperate to make their mark. It doesn't make them great lifelong companions, but it does make them good at instant things like sport.

Their character comes out strongly in their cricket. Twice a week practice is an exercise in one-upmanship. Who can show up who. Everything's a macho competition from the biggest hit to the flattest throw to who can get into the nineteen-year-old barmaid's knickers first. Don't turn your back for long either, because there'll be knives in it, metaphorically speaking.

In matches they are overtly egotistical and more interested in trying to squeeze, and ultimately crush, the opposition by not budging an inch, than in having a 'good game'. The two day games (Saturday-Saturday) were

118

largely an endurance test. There were 90 overs in a day. You weren't allowed to bat for more than those 90 overs in the first innings. The wickets were always batsmen-friendly, so the bowling team went defensive very early on and the batting team did the same, determined to use up all the time. It became a kind of virtual stalemate for 70 overs and then an almighty thrash for the last 20. The lunch interval didn't break the tedium either. All they gave you was a jug of water and a synthetic meat pie.

At the end of the second Saturday whoever led on first innings got the points. That was fair enough, but if the side batting second had overtaken their opponent's score with time to spare, they were allowed to carry on piling up runs – kind of having a net. It was utterly pointless and just an excuse for the batsmen to fill their boots and the victors to further humiliate the vanquished. It made me so mad that on one occasion after we'd lost but were still detained in the field, I asked to bowl, sent down a succession of bumpers and split a batsman's chin.

Still, you can see where the Aussies get their focus and discipline from. To them cricket isn't supposed to be fun, it's a ruthless, dog-eat-dog route to self-satisfaction. There is absolutely no compromise and zero honesty. Bowling at one typically resilient batsman, I moved one away and induced an edge to the keeper. There was a big appeal, but he stood there defiantly and the umpire was unmoved.

Accustomed to the majority of English batsmen tucking the bat under their arm and obediently striding off, I was incensed. The next ball was faster and took a bigger edge, which this time the umpire heard. As the batsman wandered off to the pavilion, I said, 'You hit the first one as well didn't you?'

'Yep,' he replied, 'but we only walk when the fucken' car's broken down.'

119

The losers don't stay afterwards, either, to, as we say in England, 'drink the fixture back.' No, no that would be much too compliant. They're powering away in their V8 penis-substitutes almost before the umpires have removed the bails, just to show that however lightweight they might have looked on the field, they've got a monster under the bonnet.

Sometimes they took it to extremes. During one club match, a player who'd been humiliated by a mouthy opponent left a dead mullet in the guy's car where it rotted malodorously. The victim retorted the next weekend by filling the first player's dog full of laxatives while he was on the field, then locking it in its owner's changing room. Cricket, to Australians, is not 'just a game.'

I played for Fremantle, a 'city' in its own right, thirty minutes outside the centre of Perth. Being next to a very active port, the club members were mainly older men with tattoos and gold chains who'd worked all their lives in shipping or farming. Old Australia, if you like. They had a raffle in the bar twice a week for a huge hamper of steaks or a whole lamb.

The players (average age twenty-four) were offspring from the multi-cultural society that had migrated to Fremantle – Italians, Yugoslavs, Croats – as well as some from older stock. New Australia. There were no blacks or Asians or Aborigines remotely connected with the club, or any other in Perth for that matter. There was a low level apartheid going on in Australian society. It was more blatant than latent in WA. They often referred to the kangaroo-proof bars on the front of their four-wheel drives as 'Boongs.' Why? I asked. 'Because that's the sound an Abo makes when he bounces off it,' a club official said, narfing.

The facilities were superb. The pitch was the fastest in town – quicker even than Perth's test ground, the notorious WACA – and it had a wide, well-tended outfield, beyond which was a block of six nets each of which you could have played a Test match on. The bland, modern pavilion sat atop a high bank, offering a great view on match days but a lousy obstacle at practice when you were expected to sprint up it twenty times before going in for a shower.

If you didn't turn up every Tuesday and Thursday evening for training you weren't picked on Saturday. At these sessions, there were two hours of serious nets – batsmen in head-to-toe protection fending off bowlers charging in from their full run ups – then fielding practice under lights followed by some fitness work which often featured a mini triathlon on the beach. I was considered quite fit for an English player, but I lagged behind there. The training was a good deal harder than anything I'd experienced in county cricket.

It needed to be. Quite apart from the heat, the standard was fantastically high, with legions of fast bowlers supported by fluid fielding, and remorseless, narrow-eyed batsmen intent not to give it away. And the following Saturday's opponents could well include a couple of current or retired Test players – Kim Hughes and Terry Alderman at one, Dennis Lillee and Rod Marsh at another.

The give-'em-nothing ethic was drilled into you at the end of the training session, when we were given a pep talk either by the head coach Mike Hirsch, a barrel of a man whose imposing twenty-stone appearance and resounding bellow belied a kind heart, or the club psychologist. In the bar, the team selections were read out and greeted with the same triumph or dismay you'd equate with opposite ends of Anfield when a goal is scored. This was serious, earth-moving stuff.

Verbal Diarrhoea
The art of sledging is rooted in these intensive prepara-tions. The players were instilled with large amounts of pent-up energy, often too much for a lil' ol' cricket match, so they got rid of some of it verbally. I was astounded by the extent and vulgarity of the comments, but if ever I was on the receiving end it just hardened my resolve. It didn't shut them up, though. Some players have a loose wire between their mouth and their brain, and sledging has become an Australian compulsion.

The Aussies are particularly good at it because you can't always tell who's talking. In general conversation their jaws hardly move – the usual greeting 'Giddaymay-owyagoan?' is grunted in one, long syllable, and some of the severest sledgers such as Merv Hughes or David Boon, had huge walrus moustaches making any slight move-ment of their lips imperceptible. (Boon usually had the short-leg helmet on as further camouflage.) The current Australian captain Steve Waugh has refined the art to such a degree, he could easily make a living as a ventriloquist if he retired from playing.

I sat down with a couple of Poms and listed some of the more common sledges we'd come across or heard about:

1. 'G' on avagoyermug.'
   'Rattle your dags, chief.'
   'We're not playing for sheep stations, mate.' (all said by bowler to annoying, blocking batsman)
2. 'How's the wife and my kids?' (wicketkeeper to new batsman). Alternatively, 'Your missus is a dud root, mate.'

3. 'Oi blue, you've got shit on the end of your bat,' (batsman looks at bottom of his bat) 'No, mate, the other end, prick.'

4. 'Better ease off a bit Macca, this one's still on the tit.' (captain to fast bowler as green-looking batsman takes guard)

5. 'There's two pieces of shit together.' (bowler, loudly, as the two batsmen meet for mid-wicket conference)

6. 'Back to the nets, idiot.' (Ian Healy to any young batsman out quickly)

7. 'What's the difference between a Pom and a bucket of shit? The bucket, dickhead.' (bowler to any English batsman)

8. 'Right Deano, we've got him four floors up, now take him to the sixth.' (bouncer threat)

9. 'Skip, let's put a chocolate eclair down, see if he comes out for that.' (spin bowler trying to lure stolid, fat batsman out of his crease)

10. 'Arsewipe!'

Occasionally, a sledge backfires:

11. 'It's four years since I last saw you, and you still haven't improved.' (Merv Hughes to Robin Smith, after a couple of iffy strokes) 'Neither have you.' (Smith to Hughes after he'd just twatted him for four)

12 'I've been waiting for two years to have another bowl at you.' (Shane Warne to the spin-vulnerable South African Daryll Cullinan) 'Looks like you spent most of it eating.' (Cullinan's reply)

Happy Hours

Because I'd travelled to Perth very much under my own steam, little was provided for me. I had no job (no Aussie school would let a Pom loose in there) and no guarantee of a place in Fremantle's first grade team. At least Rex, the club treasurer, lent me his battered 1972 Falcon, basically two sofas on wheels with a gas-guzzling 4-litre engine and rather loose steering.

I had to organize my own accommodation, as usual. The club coach, Mike Hirsch, said he'd put me up in his little townhouse for a while. Also living there were Hirsch's brother Clayton, who I had to share a room with, and the (then) Sussex all-rounder Dermot Reeve. It was hard to decide who was worse. Clayton drove a taxi till 4a.m. every night, then, exhausted, either accidentally tumbled into my bed – not pleasant considering he was a twenty-two-stone fast-food bin – or, having slumped into his own, snored so loudly it woke next door's dog.

If you did manage to get a bit of shut-eye, it was then frequently disturbed by the screams and gasps of whichever current girlfriend Dermot had enticed back. There was a wobbly headboard too, and like all good wobbly headboards, you could tell from its heightened rhythm when the session was reaching closure.

Next day Dermot would surface at around noon and proceed to give a full recount of last night's events, which we hardly needed, while creating an almighty mess frying eggs, bacon and tomatoes. Then he'd return to the action in the bedroom, leaving me to clear up. One afternoon a cute local girl he'd been seeing fairly regularly emerged from the bedroom in tears. I asked her what was the matter.

'Dermot won't tell me he loves me,' she cried.

'How can he?' I retorted. 'He only loves himself.'

I think I was just jealous.

Maybe she was expecting more, because Dermot was from English stock. There was no subtlety or sensitivity about the Australian chasing game. Pursuit was done with your ears-pinned-back and the accelerator on-the-floor. Even the cars were driven as if they wanted to mate violently. To the West Australian sportsman, shagging was just a Saturday night extension of their all-out efforts on the field in the day. The women seemed happy to wait until the drinking games had ended and the general abuse had died down and then play along with it.

Without really intending to, you get sucked into this malarkey. There we were enjoying our happy hour (6–11.30p.m.) at the aptly named Brewery Tavern – a cavernous cattle market – while the chicken we'd left in the oven at home cremated itself. We drank pints of XXXX with snakebite chasers – about ten of each – leered and threw drink at various partly-exposed boobs and butts and told crude jokes, to the accompaniment of thumping rock music. It was Western Australian nirvana.

Near closing time the staff began rescuing the bar stools from the puddles of beer everywhere. Out of the blue, I was accosted by a DW, a tall, slim brunette, who was quite touchy-feely despite my drunken state and drenched clothes. I have no idea what I said to her or how we got back to my house. (I've always doubted the credibility of people who say they don't remember anything about last night, but Castlemaine and Strongbow have definitely erased the early part of this encounter from my brain.)

I do recall stumbling through the front door to be enveloped by chook-smoke belching from the oven, then being pushed into the front bedroom, relieved of my soaking 'Save water. Drink beer' T-shirt and frenziedly snogged.

I drew away sharply. Firstly I wasn't used to this level of forwardness and secondly I had an uncontrollable retching in my stomach. I rushed onto the porch, clothed

125

a small bush with projectile vomit, then motored back inside for re-docking. She didn't blanch at this behaviour, nor at Clayton's unappetizing mass bursting in at an embarrassing moment, muttering 'Jeez, wouldn't mind catching it off her,' before crashing onto his bed in the altogether.

'Shit, he's got an awning over his toy factory,' she said. 'Glad you haven't,' and clawed my trousers down.

She had a vivid name to match her fearless methods – Kristina Schmack – and as a girl who owned two Dobermans, she was used to getting her own way. She was a psychology student and I sometimes felt I was just part of her thesis. She'd invite me round, deliberately arrive home late leaving me stewing on the step, but then behave so erotically once inside the door, it was difficult to complain.

She was an odd mixture – a control-freak who suddenly became totally abandoned – and I was hooked. We had a two month fling, staged largely in her gothic-inspired flat which had wrought-iron candelabra everywhere. Occasionally we escaped this permanent twilight to cool off in the surf at Cottesloe beach or refuel at the Ocean Beach Hotel, a big, popular bar with a terrible band playing Whitesnake, Meat Loaf and Creedence Clearwater Revival cover versions.

By mid-December I'd got more accustomed to hot wax dripping on to my exposed shoulder blades and the dozing dogs leaping up and barking every time she exhaled with pleasure. But supplying SOD (Sex on Demand) was becoming tedious. It was OK at 9a.m. and 11.30p.m. but not necessarily at several junctures in between, especially just after she'd indicated total indifference. I tried looking even more dishevelled than usual, hoping to ration the sessions a bit. That seemed to make her come on stronger.

Completely unexpectedly, Julia, who I *still* exchanged emotional letters with, phoned to say she was coming out to stay on Christmas Eve. It was in five days' time. Even though our doomed relationship was now largely platonic, my heart missed a beat when she told me. I tried to sound calm.

'Are you sure?' I said, in an isn't-that-a-bit-rash? sort of voice.

'Yes. Why, don't you want me to come?'

'No, no of course I do. Marvellous,' I lied.

I realized I had to get out of this Kristina thing or sacrifice my London bolt hole for ever. It's at a time like this you wish you could summon some impersonator to hold the fort for a while. I decided on a compromise. I'd temporarily slip out of Kristina's life (tell her I'd been summoned to Sydney for a while) which was risky considering my house was two streets from hers. It seemed worth it because Julia would probably only stay a month, by which time I'd be craving SOD, and could slip back round the corner.

It's incredible what you delude yourself you can get away with. Julia arrived as planned, but soon developed a dislike for the Perth lifestyle, my flatmates and particularly me, and went off travelling on her own. Worse, Kristina's friends had reported several sightings of me and Julia walking about, despite my various precautions such as always hunching and wearing a pulled-down cap while out. When Kristina heard my voice on the phone a month later she silently replaced the receiver.

I wanted a chance to explain things. But the flowers didn't break her resolve, and the phoney invitation, delivered in a reputable Aussie accent, asking her to do a radio interview about her psychology thesis, was greeted with an irate 'If you call me once more you little Pommie jerk, I'll have your nuts off.' I could hear the dogs barking in the background and I guessed she might be serious. Well, she had no tits anyway.

Too Many Blowies

For Poms, Christmases in Australia do feel weird. It seems wrong, almost slightly immoral, to be body-surfing at the beach on Christmas morning, daubed in factor 15, then lazing on the sand drinking sparkling wine and eating lamb kebabs, when you would normally be overduely wrapping-up your grandma's pot pourri. Instead of the Festival of Nine Lessons and Carols on the BBC, there's just the usual jangly pop on the radio, although bizarrely 'I'm Dreaming of a White Christmas' does get quite a bit of airplay. Rather than repeats of Morecambe and Wise and an old Bond movie, the TV is largely American sitcoms and self-satisfied Oz sporting highlights interspersed with ads for fitness gadgets or home-improvement products.

In fact, in keeping with the general tone of Aussie life, they were generally pretty blunt and calculating about Christmas. It wasn't a time for giving, just an opportunity for taking more than ever. An evening of blue TV comedy featuring Rodney Rude and Kevin 'Bloody' Wilson, dwelt on this. Rude told of the Melbourne bloke who hailed a cab after his office Christmas party.

' "Oi mate, got room for a case of beer and two pizzas?" he slurred.

"OK," said the driver.

The bloke opened the door and went "Blaaaaaaaaa-euugsh!" '

Wilson made up a seasonal song, including this observation from a ten-year-old boy:

'I've looked through all my presents, there's
  nothing here I like.
Santa Claus you cunt, where's my fuckin bike?'

When you're abroad the only presents you get from home
are calendars of damp, bleak, rural England (which
reminds you why you left), socks (useful, in Oz as dish
cloths) or books. My godmother sent me *Dangerous
Australians* which wasn't a catalogue of savage criminals
or vicious fast bowlers. It was an awesome list of the most
harmful creatures known to man, all to be found in the
area. The red back spider – keen on lurking under toilet
seats – the saltwater crocodile, the tiger snake, the
common scorpion, the blue-ringed octopus, ticks, stone-
fish, stingrays, sharks, and, worst of all, box jellyfish –
known as 'sea wasps' – capable of fatal stings.

If you found this book before setting foot in Australia,
you'd never want to land. It instantly cultivates a phobia
about every little nook and cranny. Harmless creepy-
crawlies assume deadly qualities and you feverishly
tourniquet the area around innocuous itches and smother
it in lotions. It's unnecessary alarmism, of course. I spent
one and a half years living in Australia and the only one of
those 'dangerous' animals I saw – a scorpion two inches
long – I flattened with a shoe.

What's never mentioned in the literature is how to deal
with Australia's no. 1 annoyance, the blow fly. Have you
noticed how those intense, alluring pictures of stunning
Australian beaches in glossy brochures never feature a
single fly, or an apoplectic sunbather flapping madly
about his head? As dupes go, those images are in the same
bracket as the breakfast cereal ads featuring the happy
smiling children sitting obediently round the kitchen
table. Nothing – late trains, burnt toast, dropped catches,

jock rash, or women who spend ages applying make up so it looks like they're not wearing any – has ever irritated me as much as the simple, six-legged blowie. They're every-where in Perth. On your ear, in your eye, up your nose, buzzing round your ankles, alighting on your arm, salivating on your steak. They're impossible to swat and if you spray yourself with Aeroguard, you pong so much you repel all the humans as well as the flies.

They make playing golf a fraught experience. Just when you're ready to drive, one settles on your hand or face. You swipe it off, and line up again for the shot; on the backswing, it lands on your eyelid. Another's on the ball. You flick at it and accidentally snick the ball sideways. 'One,' says your unsympathetic partner. You're sweating and they're congregating. This process goes on all after-noon. One hole takes an eternity. No wonder the Japanese love the Australian courses. It's the only place in the world where their six-hour rounds are regarded as brisk.

You can try the bush hat with dangling corks, or the Genuine Aussie Fly Net (made in South Korea) – a sort of mesh bag you put over your head. They do work but they aren't ideal for golf. You can't see properly out of them. The only thing that cures the fly problem in Perth is the famous Fremantle Doctor, the stiff afternoon sea breeze, regular as clockwork. But when that gets up, your four-irons are blown into territory it's wiser not to explore.

Actually, the best programme on Aussie TV is the weather forecast. There's this huge land mass filling the screen with not a cloud or an occluded front on it, and a madcap presenter who's definitely never studied meteorology or 'O' level English. He just stands there in a loud shirt saying 'Aw it's a *beaut* in Brisbane today' and slapping the word *BEAUT* over Brisbane 'and it'll be a *bonza* in Adelaide' and *BONZA* is plastered across

Adelaide 'and it's a real *bottler* in Alice Springs' and he sticks *BOTTLER* on Alice Springs. And they're all interchangeable, and he's dazzling and relentless, just like the Australian sun.

Runs in the Swamp

In January it was 40°C for nine days in a row, but, perhaps because I'd begun my overseas odyssey in the stifling heat of Colombo, I wasn't too bothered by the Perth climate. I liked bowling in a thin, sleeveless shirt rather than five layers, and on firm ground with no groin-twanging damp bits. It was better breathing in hot, clean air from the continental interior rather than cold, moist carbon dioxide from the Marylebone Road. The pitches were bouncy and true and edges carried easily to slip and the bowlers got a good grip from footholds which didn't disintegrate into a pile of soot after five overs. You could use the same 22-yard strip week after week.

The facilities – the pitches, the weather, the preparations – allowed talent to thrive, in spite of the infrequency of innings – one knock a fortnight on average. This wasn't such a problem for bowlers, as you got plenty of rest. If your team fielded the first Saturday, they probably batted for most of the second. I did quite well, while visiting English batters like Alec Stewart and Robin Smith found it a bit more of a struggle. Being used to at least five hits a week at home, they found the lengthy gaps extremely frustrating.

This is the key to an Australian's thirst for runs, and their conveyer-belt supply of prolific, no frills batsmen. You have to be disciplined and make *every* innings count. At Fremantle, we had the classic prototype – Geoff Marsh. Universally referred to as 'Swampy', he was an unassuming, quiet sort who'd erected a net at his family farm in Wandering in the Western Australian interior. There he developed a simple, secure technique through hours of facing a bowling machine fed by his wife.

The year I was there he didn't play for the club much because he was often wanted by the Western Australian state team. The Fremantle officials began to get worried that he might get picked for Australia and they'd never see him again. I reassured them that his game of cuts and nudges was too limited for Test cricket. He wasn't dynamic enough. Marsh made his Test debut a month later and retired in 1993, after playing 49 more and appearing in 117 one day internationals. Then for three years he was a very successful national coach.

Australia were at their lowest ebb when Swampy came on the scene. They had just lost a series at home to Richard Hadlee (OK, that should read New Zealand, but Hadlee took thirty-three wickets in the three Tests) and, having drawn three home Tests with India, they then flew to New Zealand and got beaten again. That was in addition to being regularly poleaxed by the West Indies. Well, everyone suffered that.

But the seeds of rejuvenation were being sown. The nucleus of a new team was forming, based round Border, Boon and the young Craig McDermott and now there was Marsh and another promising fellow called Waugh. Boon and Marsh formed a productive opening pair, matching each other for commitment and determination. There was one objective, and one objective only. To make Australia great again. They went to some lengths. Once, when they were rooming together, Boon woke up early on the first morning of a Test. 'It was about six,' he said, 'and I had this sort of sixth sense about something. I opened an eye and there was Swampy, in his helmet and gloves, with his bat, in the bollocky, and he's practising his forward defence in front of the mirror.'

I can't ever attest to such measures, and neither, I should imagine, can any other English player. Jack Russell did take his sunhat and keeping gloves to bed, but that was just in case they got nicked. We just don't *do* such total commitment. There's an in-built resistance in England to try too hard – in daily appearance, in business, in sport. Intrinsically we feel superior, in a been-there-done-that sort of way. Homage to self-enhancement is a New World thing. They've grabbed the pioneering baton. That's why we dislike the Americans, and they think we're a bit dotty.

Discovery Bay

It was all very well sitting around philosophising, working out what English sport/cricket needed to regain its slipping crown. What I needed was good hard cash. In three months in Perth I'd only earned $200, $40 for a man of the match award (five wickets up the coast against Wanneroo) and the rest from three days' humping wool sacks in a warehouse. I was sick of living on meat pies and pizza.

An acquaintance got me a job with the *West Australian*, a fat daily newspaper with ninety pages, only about three of which were worth reading. They needed casuals to contribute stuff to the other eighty-seven, and my first 'reporting' assignment was a seminar for local architects on catering for the disabled. I was planted in a wheelchair to experience the difficulties of negotiating kerbs and swing doors, and wore various masks to understand tunnel vision, partial blindness etc. For a joke, the story had been pinned up at the club, next to the 1st XI averages.

'Looking at your batting stats mate, you don't need a mask to experience blindness,' a player glancing at it said. I had made only eighteen runs in six innings.

I also had to process mind-numbingly boring bulletins from the Kalgoorlie gold fields ('Mr Henry Jarvo, deputy district commissioner for Kalgoorlie tourism, announced there would be a full review of long-distance bus arrival times after the Hannan mine-head café became over-crowded last week . . . '). And there would also be half a page of world news items to select from the wires for the *Evening Argus* in Geraldton, a piddly place even more myopic than Perth.

Still, it was a job in a smart office paying $95 a day and, best of all, I knocked off at 12.30 and headed straight for the ocean. Swanborne was a nudist beach, but mainly young, taut and uninhibited where St Leonard's, Auck-land was old, saggy and should-have-been-prohibited. Now definitely single, I could at least continue to admire the Aussie female form at Swanborne as one shapely secretary after another stripped off for their lunch-time top-ups. To nullify arousal you didn't have to recite 'Nora Batty, Nora Batty' to yourself, either. A quick glance behind the dunes at the wobbling women playing nude volleyball and the lapsed body-builders lying prostrate, their knob-tips glistening in freshly-applied factor 30, did that easy.

The newspaper arrangement was good while it lasted, but after six weeks of anticipating Alan Bond or Robert Holmes à Court financial scandals, and actually receiving stories about regional grant cuts and fishing disputes and broken-down suburban trains, I was laid off. The perma-nent staff were back from their Christmas break.

It gave me more time for practice and exploration. A few of the English players, including occasionally Robin Smith, met on Mondays and Fridays for an early evening net and then we'd retire to sit on Port beach and drink tinnies and watch the sun sink behind the vast sheep-ferries – looking like holiday apartment blocks anchored off shore. It was still 30°C at 10p.m.

I was determined to have a proper look at Western Australia. Perth, after all, was eminently forgettable – much of it was like Hull in a hot climate – and I thought I'd be bound to find some amazing beaches along the state's 13,000k.m. of coastline. I didn't. A three-day drive down south revealed only inaccessible coves or unsheltered sand spits. The most memorable sight, in fact, was an emu darting out from some copse and running at full tilt alongside my car for 100 metres, before vanishing into the undergrowth. It triggered a realization. I'd flown 12,000 miles and lived in Australia for four months and I hadn't spotted a single live kangaroo.

They're depicted on every signpost, billboard, stamp, T-shirt, drinks coaster, Esky and stubby-holder going, and I felt slightly cheated that I hadn't spotted a real one. I went some way north into the outback, but found none. Just wandering sheep, aerial-police speed checks, triple-trailered road trains, and miles of bush. The landscape was quite hypnotic, but every so often there was a huge warning sign proclaiming 'Drowsy Drivers Die.' Much more catchy and persuasive than the English 'Tiredness Can Kill: Take A Break.'

Western Australia, it seemed, was just a mass of nothing. No decent beaches, no kangaroos, hardly any people. Then I discovered, belatedly, the best direction to go from Perth was west. Not back to England, but the little matter of 20k.m. out to sea. There, lying like a little jewel in a bucket of cement, is Rottnest Island. It's only small (about the size of Guernsey) and you can easily cycle round it, but there's a beach for everyone, some wide and bracing, others tiny and secluded and you camp where you like. There's no traffic and *no flies*. You sleep and swim and drink and barbecue, in any order or quantity that you desire. There's a liberty and a laxity you associate with University summer term, post-exams. It's an outdoor free-for-all, and if the sun is shining, which it usually is, it's a fresh-air ecstasy tablet.

Playing beach cricket on the first day there I met Kate, a vigorous, well-endowed, 26-year-old blonde physio with a luminous personality and the ability to bowl a useful leg break. (Her leg rub wasn't bad either, as I soon discovered, though it was a bit of a struggle in her solo tent.) She wouldn't have qualified as a DW when I first embarked on my worldwide adventure (not Barbie-doll-head-turning enough) – but she was now, regardless of the fact that almost anything would have done at that point. We really hit it off.

She enjoyed direct, sporty types and I loved her bravura and energy and smutty humour. We talked for hours about travel and aspirations and how shit men were. We became inseparable, and by the third day we had explored most of the island's beaches and several levels of massage and I had decided Mary Cove – a quiet little bay beneath a low cliff with egg-timer sand, translucent sea and intimate hiding places behind large boulders – was the place for a honeymoon.

Those seventy-two hours were close to perfection. The weather, the setting, the situation. We'd stripped each other bare, mentally and physically, and were happy with what it'd revealed. We were cycling blissfully back to catch the ferry when some strange animals scuttled by. They looked like large rats, but were in fact Quokkas – small wallabies unique to the island. They were ugly and fat but it was the closest I ever came to seeing a kangaroo. To me it was a sign. My mission was over. Rottnest Island had come up with the goods. After a seven year, worldwide search I'd found the beach and the bird I wanted in the space of forty-eight hours on a tiny eight by two piece of land. I was ecstatic, particularly about the bird. I was already thinking about the future, planning where we could live and how to get a regular journalistic job in Perth and the deal I could do with Fremantle for next season. I wondered how quickly I could become eligible to play for Western Australia. It was very exciting.

Sitting side by side on the boat, she told me. She was engaged to Damian, a cardiologist, and had been for some time. They were due to get married in April and she'd had her doubts. Her mind was in a whirl and she had taken time out to think about it. I'd been the gust of wind that had cleared the air. Now she could see Damian's qualities – his stability, his sensitivity, his restraint – in a truer light. She thanked me for showing her that and for my excellent demonstration of the googly.

I nodded dumbly and contemplated the one she'd just bowled me. I thought about trying to step out and attack it, but there was no time. The hydrofoil was back in Perth and there was the sickening, smirking 'Damian' at the wharf to embrace her. I was stranded out of my ground and he had smugly whipped off the bails. I felt lame, an idiot, and wandered off, the defeated batsman, deciding that the only people in Perth shittier than the men were the women.

Fair Dinkum

I played a club match the following Saturday and bowled innocuously. To cheer myself up the day after I went to the WACA (which could be Aussie lingo for a big hitter but actually stands for Western Australian Cricket Association) to watch a one day international between

Australia and New Zealand. I caught up with Richard Hadlee – for a break from Australians, as much as anything – who became positively fulsome on the subject of gripping the ball in different ways and gave me some useful tips on swing.

It's flattering when stars like this take time to pass on their skills and I felt much better. I sat in the crowd and watched Allan Border carve the ball about. It was stinking hot. Two very slim girls in bright bikinis wandered in front of the open-air enclosure carrying drinks. Amidst the predictable leering and wheyheying, one oaf shouted out 'Oi, git some food in ya!' His mate added, 'I'll give ya a protein injection!'

There was predictable guffawing, and the girls laughed too. It annoyed me. Recent events had given me a humour bypass. I just hadn't been able to fathom the rules of the Aussie mating game and I felt a failure, as if the last five months had been a waste of time.

They hadn't, though. The cricket had been good, the most abrasive I had ever played. Hard but fair. The conditions and facilities were ideal and the players were extremely fit, well-drilled and determined. They had plenty of incentive. Doing well on the field raised their profile amongst family and friends in the neighbourhood. It was worth the effort and a more credible way of getting attention in the street than simply cranking up your V8 Dodge on ridiculous suspension or building a poncy conservatory. And, for almost everyone there was always the glimmer of being chosen in the state side. Then anything could happen. Geoff Marsh had jumped from club to country in the space of weeks on the back of two successive hundreds for WA. The system was as dynamic as England's was decrepit.

Looking at Perth's three Ws – weather, wickets and

women – I'd definitely profited from two and lost heavily on the third. The lifestyle was so healthy – lots of exercise, sun on your back, open space everywhere, larking about on the beach – that you couldn't fail to enhance yourself physically and I felt my bowling had regained some pace and discovered some accuracy. I'd been fast and penetrative and helped the largely fledgling Fremantle team to third place in the league.

Mentally, I'd regressed. I'd scored several own goals on the women's pitch, and hadn't made any genuine male friends either. I wasn't as confident socially anymore. I found Western Australians upfront and gregarious but pretty superficial. If the conversation wasn't about sport, it revolved around telling jokes and they didn't laugh at mine. They had a very limited sense of humour, restricted to crude one liners about sheep or Sheilas. (E.g.: 'What d'you do if a bird craps on your windscreen? You don't take her out again.' Or 'How d'you make a sheep go woof? Soak it in petrol and throw a match on it.') In fact, it would be fair to say they didn't really have a sense of humour at all.

Their lives were relatively uncluttered by conventions or moral dilemmas and they were oblivious of anything happening a hundred miles yonder. They lacked complexity. This, I reckoned, was the secret of their sporting prowess. Vim and vigour. A direct approach with no distractions. In every communal thing they do, they're at you – verbally and physically – rather than with you.

Everyone knew where I'd been when I got home. My speech had a nasally strine, and I kept using words like 'bludger', 'ripper' and 'dunny' and saying 'streuwth!' a lot. I also liked 'Fair suck of the sav, cobber', which attracted a few baffled expressions when I used it to accept someone else's point of view. My favourite Australian phrase, however, was 'Been home feeding the chooks again mate?' I'll leave the meaning to your imagination, but I can tell you, after my female flops of the winter, I was doing a lot of it.

The Score

People		Beaches		Cricket		Catches		Total
2	+	7	+	8	×	2	=	34

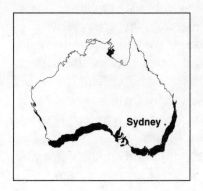

8.
Australia –
Sydney

Mucky Waters

In one way the Perth experience worked. The following summer I enjoyed my best season in county cricket, taking 63 wickets. I was 34th in the national bowling averages. It doesn't sound much, but when you have been at the depths of 134th, you feel a new man. I was tipped as an outsider for England's winter tour, but then who hasn't been at some stage in their career? Middlesex were obviously pleased, anyway. It was the last year of my contract and they immediately offered me a three year extension, plus a £1700 pay rise. After six years in the job, I had made it into the stratosphere of a five-figure pay packet. I was on £11,000 a year.

To celebrate, I took a taxi to Barclays. The cashpoint machine was out of action, so I had to join a lengthy queue inside to withdraw money to pay the driver, who'd kept his meter running. A ninety-second journey cost me £12.80. Then I went and bought a house, a three-up three-down terraced job in the London Borough of Hounslow. To help pay the mortgage, I filled it with friends, mostly Kiwis who'd come to Europe for their obligatory eighteen-month rite of passage in a VW Combi. At weekends it was like a doss house. Bodies in sleeping bags everywhere.

A successful summer of county cricket does have its downside. You're away a lot, and your social life suffers. You can't say yes you'll meet the gang down The Antelope, Friday about nineish, because you're on the way to play Derby at Chesterfield. Offer the girlfriend a toiletry-sachet-weekend in the Cardiff Post House while you're out chasing leather ten hours each day, and, if she's got any nous, she'll say wild horses wouldn't drag her there.

Your relationships lurch and stumble along, and gradually peter out because you're not around, or if you are, you're about as animated as a dead dog. Julia was long gone, and soon so was Sarah, the life-and-soul-of-the-party physio I was seeing (occasionally). She transferred her attentions to someone less absent and more interesting and better looking. Herself. She'd had enough of gauche, immature, insensitive, selfish, untidy 28-year-olds.

Winter set in and, unattached, I was getting cold feet again, partly due to my resistance to putting on the central heating. I was in constant denial about the end of summer, refusing to switch the lights on until it was pitch dark, going out in board shorts and a T-shirt to scrape the frost off the windscreen. Australia was where it was all going on – the Ashes, the Americas Cup, the gay and lesbian Mardi Gras. I couldn't hack Perth again, but I knew Sydney was a happening place. An acquaintance was captain of the University side and I set up a deal to play half a season for them. They pledged me half the airfare and help finding a job. I arrived at midday on 1 January 1987.

It was a bonza day, so I suggested to the University captain who'd collected me, that we spend the first afternoon of the new year on Bondi Beach. Big mistake. The area around it was jammed and we had to dump the car and walk miles. When we reached the beach we couldn't see it for bodies, mostly tubs of reddening lard emitting odd nasal sounds:

'Oiee, gizzanoderbeya'

'Goddanymorcheebs?'

''eard de Villascore, maate?'

Bondi was besieged by Brummies.

It was the defining moment in English cricket in the last twenty years. England, under Mike Gatting, had just clinched the Ashes in Australia and here, on probably the most famous beach in the southern hemisphere, the seeds of the Barmy Army were being sown. They've hardly ever had anything to shout about since. That just makes them shout more.

And on the beach, Brummies had become the new Germans.

The sand was extra crowded because no one was in the water. A major sewage pipe had ruptured up the coast, and more or less raw effluent had been floating in on the surf for several days. There was a big clean-up campaign going on to reverse the process and send the sewage back out to sea. It was called Turn Back the Tide. Unofficially, it had been renamed Turn Back the Turds.

Spiked

I was bounced around various players' spare beds for several days while my arrangements were sorted out. It didn't matter where I slept. I passed out at precisely 8.45 every night, irrespective of whether I was in a bar, a car, or ordering an Americano with extra pepperoni in a noisy pizza joint. Jet lag does this to you, I find. Leaves you alone all day and then jumps up and bites you just when you thought you'd conquered it.

Before I'd managed to get my bearings, the Sydney University team were off on the 'Country Tour.' This involved five days of driving round the baking interior of New South Wales with my new team-mates Greedy, Hondo, Jacko, Micko and Flapa (Face Like a Pizza). We played tough, needle matches in hick towns and crashed out five-to-a-room in pub annexes after mammoth tucker-less nights on the piss. I only survived by nipping outside around 10ish for a TC (Tactical Chunder). A member of the oppo saw me one night. 'All two-pot screamers, you Poms,' he said derisively.

Travelling south west from Sydney, the sheep-farming town of Goulburn had been our first stop. This is Bradman country. The Don played his early cricket all round the area. At Bowral, a short distance north, where he was brought up, there's a cricket ground and museum dedicated to Australia's favourite Pommie-basher. You can see sepia pictures of the nine-year-old Bradman practising solo. Behind his house he used to throw a ball against a water tank and hit it as it rebounded.

At the same age I used to play a similar game in my back garden. There was only one difference. I was hitting a sluggish tennis ball with a bat, Bradman was hitting a wickedly jagging golf ball with a stump. That is obviously why he scored 28,067 first class runs, average 95.14, and I had made 1208, average 10.67. It's my uncle Tony's fault. He's the one who gave me the bat for my eighth birthday.

After Goulburn we drove further inland to Yass. It got

hotter, less populated by humans and more by insects with large mandibles. The match, played on a surprisingly green field surrounded by wattle trees, was extremely combative, featuring the uncomplicated hitting of a beefy left hander with an orange beard who they referred to as Bushfire, and the nifty running and calling of his pocket-sized partner, a red faced man called Blood Clot. Stumpy, the wicketkeeper, had a nice line in acid comments when you came into bat: 'Mate, you're as welcome as a fuckin' turd in a swimming pool.'

Hostilities over, we quaffed several cases of amber nectar perched on the back of a ute, and headed for our lodgings, the Letom, which might sound like a good name for a brothel but is actually 'motel' backwards. It did in fact have an unusual line in home-made porn videos which ten of us crammed into the largest room to watch. To the accompaniment of thin, toneless music, a lank-haired wimp with elephantine tackle kept beckoning apparently vulnerable damsels into his apartment with a 'Come orn angel, you know what you want, let's go inside and get it orn.' The bedroom looked suspiciously like the one we were sprawled in, and I'm sure one of the girls was the pub barmaid before she'd filled out.

Wimp-man then proceeded to give them what he wanted them to want. Presumably. We could only judge from the sound as, once the girls had meekly submitted, the camera panned sideways and filmed just the couple's legs from the knees down. We saw the touchline occasionally but never once got a view of the goal mouth. There was much entwining of limbs and tensing of toes and sometimes extra legs slid into view, accompanied by deeper moans, as if the cameraman himself had decided to get on down with his microphone. He certainly wasn't looking through the lens. It should have been an excellent cure for insomnia, but it was so awful we were riveted. In a perverse way it was more titillating than the mechanical sex you see in the likes of *The Enchanted Pussy* or *Teenage Mutant Nymphos*.

The next place was Cootamundra, even further inland, and Bradman's actual birthplace. It's a raw town with lots of rambling weatherboarded houses, scrubby fields and nobbly bushes. The sun here bakes the skin the texture of tree bark. Someone could make a fortune selling anti-wrinkle cream. The cricket ground is in the middle of a dusty greyhound track, with a big lean-to at one side as a sort of primitive grandstand. The outfield is red, ant-ridden dirt and the wicket is hard and shiny.

A big farmer with dark muscles like polished hardwood comes pounding in to bowl, sending down a succession of chest-high deliveries at Jacko, a short fourth-grade batsman with a paunch. He's still woozy after a gallon of alcohol and hot, fitful sleep. Some prankster had switched his electric blanket on in the night and he hadn't realized. Bleary eyed or not, there's no gimmees granted or expected, and he takes several blows on the arms and shoulder. His team-mates laugh and slap the bruised flesh jovially when he comes off after gutsing-out a painful dozen. The concept of friendly, social sport doesn't exist in Australia. Cricket in the outback is as rough and spiky as the bush itself.

Country teams often give international touring sides a good game. They have no regard for who you are or what you've done. Test your tackle here, cobber. It's now that counts, not then. History is a burrow. You've got to come out, mate. The interior of New South Wales is the spawning ground of strapping, chirpy, chisel-jawed youths who aspire to one thing and one thing only. Playing for Australia. It's always been the same.

One of NSW's interior's first products was the colossal George Bonner, an explosive hitter often referred to as 'the Australian Hercules.' He was supposed, in the 1880 Test at the Oval, to have hit a ball so high the batsmen were turning for the third before Fred Grace caught it. He was proud of his roots and was described in his obituary as 'a man without guile.' The tale of his invitation to a dinner at the Johnson Club in Fleet Street, illustrates why. He admitted at the table that he had never heard of Dr Samuel Johnson. The resultant mocking laughter in the room caused him to rise to his full 6ft. 6in., take a deep breath and pronounce: 'What is more I come from a place where you can ride a horse sixty miles a day for three months and never meet a soul who has heard of Dr Johnson either.' Reputations to Australians are nothing. This is the source of their dynamism, and the reason they're so bloody pleased with themselves.

Heads and Tayls
On the way back from the Country Tour, I was dropped off outside the Sydney Cricket Ground. It was the first day of the final Ashes Test. England had already won the series. Standing in the shadow of an SCG floodlight tower, I realised I didn't have a ticket, or any money, and I didn't know where I was supposed to be staying that night, or even the actual name of the bloke I was staying with. Everyone just called him Logs.

I blagged my way into the ground as an England player, despite a soiled T-shirt and a pair of shorts covered in red dirt. 'Where d'you Poms keep your money, under the soap?' the gateman said, gaily waving me through. Having made contact with my Middlesex colleague, Wilf Slack, England's 13th man, I spent the day on the England balcony, and the night on a put-you-up in his hotel room.

The match was mainly memorable for the Test debut of the sandy-haired Australian off-spinner Peter Taylor, a virtual unknown dubbed 'Peter Who' by the newspapers because he'd only played one game for his state that season. There was so much confusion in fact, that it was initially assumed the selectors had called up Mark Taylor, the young NSW opening bat, until he'd gone on radio to say it wasn't him.

Peter Taylor's success in the Test – he took 8 wickets, scored 42 and was named man of the match – confirmed the wisdom, luck or desperation of the selectors and the enormous strength of Sydney club cricket, where Taylor spent 99 per cent of his time. Only in Australia or, perhaps, the West Indies, would you be likely to find a player who'd taken more Test wickets than he'd made first class appearances. Like the previous example of Geoff Marsh, it brought into stark contrast the freedom of movement across Australia's cricketing infrastructure, compared with the insular cul-de-sac that was English county cricket.

It was a kind of turning point. 'Taylor's Test' was Australia's first victory for fifteen matches. The domestic Sheffield Shield had been at a low ebb, and some wag said the definition of blind optimism was an Australian batsman coming to the middle with zinc sun block on his nose. But their sporting infrastructure wasn't burdened by bureaucracy, and developments like the Australian Academy were already underway. Within a year Australia had won the World Cup, and quickly became a fearsome Test opponent. England, on the other hand, didn't win another major Test series for twelve years.

As it happened, my first club game in Sydney was against Northern Districts, the club both Taylors played for. Mark opened the batting and looked an OK player, despite escaping an apparently plumb lbw on 15. Perhaps the umpire was a Taylor, too. He made a stodgy 40 and I chatted to him in the bar afterwards and heard about his background in Wagga Wagga and the surveying exams he'd just finished. I said I felt sorry for him, consigned to a life poring over maps and looking through theodolites, and he shrugged and said 'Aw no worries mate. She'll be right.'

Little did I or anyone else imagine that he would go on to play 104 Tests. Or captain Australia – with unprecedented success – in half of them. Or score runs and snaffle catches even more relentlessly than he chewed gum. He certainly kept Wrigleys in business and the turf where he'd been fielding had to be constantly relaid because of it. Whatever he munched, though, it energized his brain and electrified his baton. He had the knack of getting the necessary extra out of people, an alchemy similar to Mike Brearley's. Both seemed able to rub the lamp and conjure up something. They did, it is true, have one or two genies at their disposal.

Perhaps Taylor's most distinguished characteristic, however, was his humanity. He was always honest and approachable as captain, prepared to give frank answers to frank questions. He never shirked an issue, even when, some years later, a man from the *Daily Mirror* tried to present him with a 3ft. wide 'Duck' bat after a run of low scores. He was asked if his refusal to pose with it showed he had lost his sense of humour. 'No, I can still laugh at myself, but I don't think I have to stand next to a three-foot bat to prove that I'm a humorous chap,' he said.

He remembers my map-and-theodolite prognostications and laughs about them every time I see him. Having been given the freedom of Sydney, he's got no worries now, either. Perhaps that's why he's the first person on earth who *happily* answers to the name of 'Tubby'. And he might be interested to know that Hermès now do a leather chewing-gum holder, price just £120. (Amazing isn't it? We've flown to the moon, cloned sheep and created babies in a test-tube but no one has discovered a better gum disposal place than the underside of a desk.)

Home Alone

I was holed up in a bachelor flat in the Sydney suburb of Hurstville for a while. Sometimes, I dreamt I was back home in Hounslow as I watched the rain drip onto tasteless sixties apartment blocks or heard 747s thundering overhead on their final descent to the airport, or failed to find anything to eat except Kebabs and Chinkies.

I also had a loo that didn't flush, no kettle and only one saucepan. Having heated up the baked beans, I had to rinse out the pan to boil the water for a cup of tea. By which time the beans were cold. It made the ill-appointed 'studio' I had in Pretoria seem like the Ritz. You might wonder why, with a history of accommodation headaches, I was still attracted to these overseas trips. Well, have you shared a poky, fusty house in real Hounslow with various itinerant New Zealanders who fart all day because they exist on lentil soup and whose mates from home keep ringing your phone-by-the-bed at four in the morning because they've miscalculated the time difference?

I didn't have a car for a while, or any money, because the club officials weren't convinced I was worth anything. I was just a valueless commodity. I roamed about on the Sydney subway following up daytime job leads. The city's double-decker trains were fast and safe. The roads were slow and lethal. They were clogged during the day because no one walked anywhere, and at night they were ruled by pissed kids hooning about dangerously in five-litre Chevs. There were numerous hold ups while bits of man and machine were scraped off the roadside. Australia's road death toll is the equivalent of Italy's. Not entirely coincidentally, large groups of Italian panel-beaters now reside in all major Australian cities.

The Australians might be supreme on track and field but they display a clear inability to master the simple art of steering. This has forced the installation of traffic signals at virtually every mini junction: Aussie drivers can't be trusted with roundabouts or giveaway signs, even in supermarket car parks. This just slows everything down more. For a time I was lent a four-litre Torana by my friend, the club-captain (Greedy). I failed to discover how fast it went. I never got out of second gear.

Obviously I'd heard about the scenic pleasures of Sydney – the harbour, the opera house, the fish restaurants, the luscious totty perfecting their tans on Tamarama (nicknamed Glamarama) Beach. After a month I hadn't seen any of them. I had little money and my existence revolved around the flat, various cricket grounds and fruitless journeys to employment agencies. I knew every destination from every platform at Central Station and every back way to the University campus in Newton. (The sports club bar there was always full of svelte students and though I was only twenty-eight, I felt like a sad old voyeur.) I was Mr Frustrated standing at the Pearly Gates, somehow unable to climb over them.

And then everything changed. A youngish married couple I'd met, Chris and Carol, invited me to share their double-storey house in Stanmore, rent-free. After a useful five wicket spell on a dodgy pitch, the club gave me a lump sum of $2000. And, having had an article relating my impressions of bush cricket published by the *Sydney Morning Herald*, I was offered a sportswriting job by *The Australian*. Instead of being some home-sick bludger, I now felt I belonged. Summer, which had sullenly remained behind leaden skies for most of the time, had suddenly blazed into town.

I worked at *The Australian* three days a week which was ideal, split between sub-editing and reporting. The paper battled against the country's regional insularity, trying to be genuinely nationwide and reflect wider issues. (The sports desk was run by a Liverpudlian and a Californian.) It sold only 150,000 copies a day, which just underlines the reality that, hey, us blokes in the Barossa Valley don't want to know about you banana-benders in Queensland, thanks, all the same.

Because of the huge distances between the cities, I suppose you can understand it. I mean, you'd probably rather read about the woman with a singing pet iguana round the corner than the trend for domesticating wallabies 1500 miles away. Even the winter sport is regionalized. Aussie Rules is focussed on Melbourne and Perth, rugby union on Brisbane and Adelaide and rugby league in Sydney. Basically there are only three types of national news in Australia. Cricket, bushfires and dingoes. (What does a dingo call a baby in a pram? Meals on wheels.)

It was useful journalistic experience for me at least, despite *The Australian* remaining in the hot-metal age, and I earned some spending money. On days off I had a proper look around, soon quoshing the idea aired by some numbskull, that the Sydney harbour bridge and opera house were just 'an old coathanger and a few Pecan shells'. The harbour bridge looms up above you like an enormous roller-coaster uniting the north and south halves of the city. The rivet heads are the size of hub caps. Close up after dark, the imposing grey span and the web of metal suspending it, rumbling and clanking as a train runs across, resembles some large and ravenous monster. I found it quite frightening.

The opera house is one of those carefully-crafted constructions, like the Chrysler Building or Concorde or Liz Hurley, that you can't take your eyes off. It's a stunning vision of man-made beauty, with sleek lines and glimmering materials and gravity-defying components. The opera house has a fabulous exterior but is rather disappointing inside, (another link with Hurley). It's also much larger than it looks in photographs, which Paul Hogan discovered when, before *Crocodile Dundee* was even a glint in his bank balance, he had a job painting it.

There's no denying that the harbour and its contents make Sydney one of the most stunning cities in the world, and the inhabitants derive a lot of their self-assurance from it. But if Sydneysiders start getting excessively smug, just remind them that the opera house was an Anglo-Danish construction and the harbour bridge was built by a firm in Middlesbrough.

The Transparent Wife

An equally intriguing sight suddenly hove into my view. I was dozing in my bed at Chris and Carol's house about a week after moving in. Chris, an intelligent but meek chemical engineer, had already gone to work. I heard my bedroom door being pushed ajar and assumed it was Carol, a slightly bossy, self-conscious redhead, thirtyish, bringing in my morning tea. I was right. But she was wearing a knee-length, semi-transparent negligée with fluffy trim, and nothing underneath. My eyes pinged open.

'Morning,' she said in a slushy tone of voice I'd never heard her use with her husband, and she laid a red-taloned hand on my shoulder. 'Mind if I slip in?' She tossed her mop of curly hair back in sort of mock abandon.

More married female angst. No one's got any scruples these days, I thought. I should glare at her and say, 'What would your husband think?' Various questions flashed through my mind as I shuffled sideways obediently, allowing her to slide silently under the sheet.

Did I fancy her?

Did it matter?

Was this 'payment' for the room and if so was I a rent boy?

If I resisted her advances, would I be out the door?

Had I had a shower last night?

Though my mind was in a complete whirl, my body was able to make a clear response. It was active to the incitement yet numb to the consequences. It's the main cause of adultery, I suppose. And she did have creamy thighs. We jiggled around for a few minutes. She emitted several loud gasps which was unwise considering the front window was wide open and only four feet from the pavement. If it had been Somerset or Devon, the social services would have been called.

But instead of finding the event seductive and exciting, and the realisation of a classic male fantasy, it seemed forced and mechanical and a bit dispiriting. It certainly didn't seem much of a recommendation for holy wedlock. I wondered if I was just an unwitting target for her marriage frustrations – Chris's dithering, his constant vocal hunt for his wallet, his premature balding, the incessant picking of his toes. Maybe she was just bored.

Afterwards I felt a combination of embarrassment and

shame both of which intensified as the day wore on. I couldn't look Chris in the eye as we sat round the table for dinner that night. When she went round and massaged his shoulders between courses, I found her deceit faintly repulsive. She placed her hand on my arm once when he'd gone to answer the phone and I shrank away reproachfully.

It didn't stop me playing the game a couple of other times. Your moral judgement seems to go all haywire when you're woken by a buffed-up hussy at 8.15 in the morning. I suppose guilt and self-gratification are close bed-fellows. But I was getting more and more confused, and began to dislike myself. I couldn't eat breakfast or concentrate at work, and I stayed out at night until Chris and Carol were in bed. That just seemed to rev her up more for the morning.

I started waking in the night thinking I could hear the bedroom door opening, and having graphic dreams about Amazing Grace, the Madame Cyn of county cricket, whose personal services I'd resisted as a youngster. I contemplated moving out, but there was nowhere obvious to go. Instead, I went for the avoidance option. I got up at 7a.m. when Chris did, and got the train into the city with him. I lied that I had to be in work early, although walking out in beach-shorts and carrying a towel was a bit of a giveaway. Carol wasn't just cold towards me after that. She was positively glacial. The way she disembowelled a chicken with one of her comprehensive collection of Sabbatier knives gave me the creeps. I reckon she was the original bunny boiler. She had created a new category in my fanciability table: DWN ISP – Definitely Wadn't If Sense Prevailed. The trouble was, in this particular field, I didn't have any.

The Cold Swede

I had a good look around Sydney's harbour and beaches. The water seems to soothe the Aussie craving to be noticed. They stage twilight sailing races round a few buoys, spending most of the time on board quaffing sauvignon blanc rather than raising spinnakers, and looking for the most part, as if they shouldn't be in charge of a rubber duck never mind a 40ft. sloop. The lifeguards on Sydney's ocean beaches are unpretentious (the prospect of filming *Baywatch* on Bondi was hostilely rejected) and the people flexing chemically-enhanced triceps are in a minority.

Once they'd cured the turd problem, all the beaches were worth the trip. Bondi's rough and ready cosmopolitanism, accommodated by a strange melange of pebble dash and neon, contrasted with Tamarama's elite hedonism. Next door there's Bronte. A bit further down, the incomparable Richie Benaud lives with his English wife Daphne on an upper floor of a plain apartment block overlooking Coogee Beach. The view across the sand and out into the Pacific is spectacular, the sea glimmers invitingly.

'I bet you pop down for a dip every morning,' I said to him enviously as we chatted in the SCG commentary box.

'What a marvellous thought that is,' he replied. 'Actually, I don't.'

'Oh, too busy I s'pose?' I suggested in an admiring tone.

'No, I can't swim,' he said.

None of Sydney's southern beaches satisfied my 'perfect' requirements, though. Either they were too built up, too crowded or you spent too much time in the water narrowly avoiding decapitation by people's errant boogie boards. Take a bus an hour north and it's a different story. Especially if you have a Swedish blonde in tow.

Tina from Stockholm had landed on my doorstep, without warning. A mutual friend had directed her to my address when she arrived in Australia, and now here she was. She was fresh-looking and lively even if she didn't quite fit the Swedish stereotype; blonde yes, but petite and without the legs up to her armpits or an I-just-want-to-get-naked-with-you expression. Maybe it was just me. But this, after labouring through umpteen mainly fruitless overs being slapped everywhere, was a certain wicket. Well you know what they say about Swedish blondes.

I suggested a bus trip to Palm Beach, which I'd been told was the business. I paid for her ticket. The Sydney big wigs have their weekend homes here. On a thin finger of land jutting out parallel to the coast with water on either side, it's expensive and exclusive. The beach is curved and shaded by large palms, through which you get the odd glimpse of futuristic metal and glass buildings and grand older style houses. No beach huts, ramshackle *bachs* or fast food joints anywhere, and the whitewashed changing room contains lockers inscribed with Lord This and Sir Desmond That. It's the Australian 'Hamptons.' I visualized owning a retreat here when I'd made my money in cricket and journalism. The clatter of a resident's chopper overhead roused me from my delusions.

Tina and I had a fantastic day, jogging on the beach, swimming, reading, drinking the white wine I'd brought, eating the tuna salad I'd made, talking about relationships, and rehearsing essential Swedish phrases such as *'Var ar vilha ha bonke?'* – loosely translated as 'Your place or mine?'

The combination of hot sun and alcohol had a promising effect on Tina, but, lying there with her head on my arm contemplating how I was going to sneak her into the house without the depraved Carol noticing, I nodded off. So did she. I came round with a dead arm and a horrible realization that we'd just missed the last bus back to Sydney. There was no public phone to ring for a cab, no pubs or little hotels to stay in, and every house in the area was inaccessible behind large, imposing security gates and electric 'inclinators' to convey visitors up precipitous paths.

There were worse situations to be marooned in. It was still warm and I had visions of a night of beach canoodling. She had visions of a night of beach castration. She had gone absolutely nuts, ranting that all blokes were either crap organizers or scheming bastards and I was both and just a typical English cheapskate. She was yelling unintelligible curses between hysterical sobs. It was one of those instances when that old chestnut 'So, a blow job's out of the question, then?' could have incited a homicide. Swedes are not renowned for their sense of irony.

We spent the night in an old wooden boat house as far apart as possible. She had the padded bench in one corner, I had a deckchair in another. The nylon material scratching against my burnt legs and the prospect of funnel web spiders with a bite like a viper lurking within, ensured I hardly slept a wink. It was the worst night of my life. I must have dozed off eventually though, because when I woke up it was light, and she had gone along with my imitation Ray bans. No wonder Sweden has the highest divorce rate in Europe.

Lamb Tales

Later in the summer Down Under, I happened to be at the Sydney Cricket Ground for one of the most memorable one day internationals of the decade. Australia were rebuilding after the humiliation of losing the Ashes and were giving thrusting youngsters like Dean Jones and

Steve Waugh an extended run. I got there early to lob down a few at Gatting and the lads on the practice ground. I also managed to pass off three Kiwi backpacker-friends – Grant (Mr Puniverse), Mark (concave chest, Coke bottle glasses, hippy sandals) and Ian (pin stripe suit, beer gut, huge cut across forehead) – into the ground as England net bowlers. 'Net bowlers? They look like your opening attack,' said the waggish gateman.

The Aussies had already given England a good hiding in the first one dayer, and looked about to do so again. As they built up a healthy first innings score I sat on what remained of the Sydney hill and listened to the cocky, bare-chested locals airing their vocal chords.

'He's fat, he's round, he bounces on the ground, Mike Gatt-ing' and, after the youthful Philip DeFreitas had naively failed to back up, 'Oi Daffy, does your mum know you're out?'

I was quite relieved that the old practice here of downing a tinny, then peeing ostentatiously into the empty can before gaily spraying the contents on the people below, had been outlawed.

Looking up at the vast SCG scoreboard displaying all the players' names with their scores and analyses against them, I wondered why back home we had never copied the Australian prototype. The English equivalent is a mathematician's blackboard, a jumble of different sized numbers, some relating to individual scores, others to players, forcing bemused spectators to pore over minute scorecards with a magnifying glass to try and fathom out the information on the board itself. Reading logarithms is easier. (During the 1999 World Cup we even had absurd announcements saying that no. 2 on the board related to no. 8 on the scorecard, etc. etc.).

In this match, England eventually needed eighteen to

win off the last over, with three wickets left. It was 10p.m., the floodlights were on and the crowd were already in the throes of celebration. OK, they were just plastered. Allan Lamb, who'd so far failed to middle anything in a patchy 50, was facing the metronomically accurate Bruce Reid. He mishit the first ball through the covers and scampered two, diving in to just beat Jones's rifle-like throw. ''E couldn't 'it a boundary in a billabong,' they shouted. Sixteen to win, five balls to go.

The second was an attempted yorker which Lamb somehow inside-edged to the boundary past square leg. 'Oi Lamby, git out afore someone sees ya,' they yelled, and greedily slurped their beers. They weren't quite so vociferous after the third ball, on a good length, which Lamb swung at and deposited sweetly into the stands. 'Come on Reido, finish 'im off,' they beckoned, less than convincingly. Six needed off three.

The fourth ball was driven straight, the fleet-footed DeFreitas making it into a well-run two. The fifth was clubbed triumphantly to the midwicket boundary for the winning hit. Lamb and DeFreitas were running and jumping off in pure elation, while on the 'hill', men chucked down their plastic beakers and kicked them at each other and grunted that the oppo were that desperate they needed two foreigners to win it for them. The kind of reaction you regularly get behind the goal when Spurs lose to Arsenal at home.

We interested observers look at the incessant amount of English football and Australian one day international cricket and wonder how the supporters tolerate all the repetition, never mind get in a tizz about individual games. We shouldn't rationalise it too much. I mean, do we ever wonder why a dog never fails to slaver over a bone?

It doesn't matter that there are more one day internationals in an Australian summer than boogie boards on Bondi, a home victory is still anticipated with the same gusto as the Next Big Dumper. One day international cricket (and English football) is like surf. It's relentless, even though each wave/match is slightly different, and it sucks the brain out of you. Just the 'over-the-moon' and 'sick-as-a-parrot' lobes remain in the supporters'/surfers' heads, leaving a dead morass in between. If you doubt me, ask their wives.

Dinosaurs

England went on to win both one day tournaments in Australia that summer. They'd made a clean sweep, and the hosts were left licking their wounds. The amateur game wasn't totally sound in Sydney, either. The pitches were generally awful, since they often had rugby league played over them in winter and the halfway line created a ridge right through the middle of the wicket. In the western suburbs, the council groundsman at Petersham CC tried to get round this by cutting the pitch diagonally across the square. It sounded quite smart until someone discovered that he was actually a Vietnamese gardener who didn't know any better. He had also marked out a pitch a yard too long on a previous occasion.

Sydney, like London, was such a multifarious place and the younger brigade were more interested in surfing and socializing than cricket. There didn't seem to be that much emerging talent, except for the Waugh family and one virtuoso left hander who was a brilliant young player but a few snags short of a barbecue, even for an Aussie. He had a lot to say for himself when at the crease, little of it intelligent. Calling him 'Dinosaur' – big mouth, little brain – usually brought about his downfall. (It worked with a few other players, too.) He went the way of so much young blood at the time, to a life of girls and air guitar. How influential the success, or in his case non-success, of your national team can be.

I could see the flaws in other club teams. Some were too dependent on a couple of macho pacemen, others relied mainly on predatory fielding. Before I left I spurred mine, Sydney University, to a major effort that would nudge them several places up the table. 'After hitting a four, look for a single,' I said in a stirring team talk, thinking it was time I spelt out the canny, professional approach. 'And whatever you do,' I added, 'don't get out playing extravagant shots. There's all day to bat remember.' Everyone nodded sagely.

Ninety minutes later I walked in at 60–6, sliced my first ball streakily to the boundary, hooked ambitiously at my second and skied an easy catch to long leg. We were all out for 84, and the match was over by 3 o'clock. I tried a bit of sledging when we bowled, sending down a high bouncer after I'd been driven for four, accompanying it with a venomous 'Drive That Then!' The batsman looked at me sadly, muttered 'Why don't you sit down and give yer mouth a chance?' and larupped the next one over mid-wicket.

Due to the early finish, we retired to a Sydney pub festooned with car licence plates to watch the final stages of the Americas Cup in the waters off Perth. Dennis Conner wrested the Cup back without much of a fight from the Australians. In fact his *Stars and Stripes* made *Kookaburra II* look like an old whaler.

The atmosphere at the bar became extremely downcast as the *Kookaburra* limped back to port. Then someone noticed a recent Western Australian number plate by the pub door, with its little slogan 'WA – home of the Americas Cup' at the bottom. He defaced it by changing the dash after WA into an 'S'. They all guffawed at the lettering which now read 'WAS home of the Americas Cup' and out poured a torrent of anti-Western Australia jokes:

'Why do WA blokes have clear-top lunch boxes?' 'So they can tell if they're going to work or coming home.'

'Why do Western Australians wear shorts?' 'To keep their brains cool.'

On and on they went, through the yokel Tasmanians and the unsophisticated Queenslanders:

'What's a Queenslander's idea of foreplay?' 'Brace yourself Sheila.'

Maybe I was having sense-of-humour failure, but I listened to this fairly puerile performance feeling somewhat detached, and waded in with a more general quip.

'What's the difference between Australian men and government bonds?' I asked. They shook their heads. 'Bonds mature.'

They stared at me as if I had three heads. Then one said, 'What d'you call the useless piece of skin on the end of a Pommie's dick?'

'Dunno.'

'A cricketer!'

There was a lot about Sydney I liked. The layout is stunning, the weather fair dinkum, if occasionally too hot, and the light stimulated the endorphins. I could have certainly traded a terraced house looking on to the back of a Gateway supermarket in Brentford for a balcony view across Sydney harbour. A friend who was used to a stifling, three-train journey from Putney to her London office every day, could windsurf across the harbour to work here in eight minutes. It was probably a smoother ride than you get on the tube, too.

The place confounded the old joke that the difference between Australia and a carton of yoghurt was that the yoghurt had a live culture. Sydney's music scene thrummed, the Aboriginal art was intriguing, there was a mouth-watering selection of restaurants, including Thai, Vietnamese and Indonesian, long before London had them on every street. They were nearly all 'Bring Your Own', great because you weren't charged for bringing in a case of your favourite beer (the downside being that you drank six cans, then only remembered two days later you left the other eighteen in the establishment's fridge). Sydney was an open-minded, open-all-hours city, offering endless possibilities. Its attitude was symbolised by a sign outside the NSW art gallery: *Do* Walk On The Grass. Now how many times have you seen *that* by a manicured lawn in England?

I loved their words: 'yakka' – an Aboriginal term for work – 'tucker', 'slygrogging' (sneaking a drink); and phrases: 'don't come the raw prawn' (don't wind me up). I liked the fact that with subtle intonations 'mate' could mean so many different things: 'Mate!' (cheery), 'Maaayte' (cautionary), 'Mate?' (quizzically), 'Mahayte . . .' (sympathetic), and the fact that Durex was a make of sellotape. (Might confuse a few chemists in England if an Aussie walked in: 'Givvus a roll of Durex.' 'A *roll*? I say, sir.')

Sydney's overriding problem, though, is unavoidable. Australians. They are upfront and personable, they do have energy and drive and an engaging, if basic wit, and they are muscularly good at sport. But there's no depth, it's only skin deep. No frills or fancies or intrigue. You probe for something more, but you don't find it. They are the facade of a gorgeous house, but inside it's just a shell full of flies.

The Score

People		Beaches		Cricket		Catches		Total
5	+	9	+	6	×	2*	=	40

*This place rating formula was proving to be flawed. Female catches should have been recorded as 1, but then the total would have been 20, and Sydney was certainly a more attractive city than Perth (34). I'd lived in Sydney half as long as Perth, so I doubled 'catches' to 2 to balance the figures.

9.
New Zealand Retraced

Liquor-ice Allsorts

By the age of 30, Ian Botham had scored 13 Test hundreds and taken 343 Test wickets, Mickey Rooney had already been married four times and D.H. Lawrence had written 12 novels. I was approaching that stage of my life, and the most distinguished thing I could claim was my bowling had been pasted across every square inch of hallowed grass at Lord's. The only century I'd run-up was 3–115 against Worcestershire, after which I was 'fined' by the Middlesex lads for hiding the little slip of paper the scorer hands to the captain with the bowling figures on it. I wasn't experiencing consistent success in county cricket, or for that matter, in life generally. Here's a list of things I'd hoped (and largely failed) to have achieved by now:

Things you should do before you're thirty:
1. Climb a mountain.
2. Drive a Ferrari.
3. Learn to scuba dive.
4. Fire a Kalashnikov.
5. Smoke a joint.
6. Stay in bed (not ill) all day.
7. Experiment with chocolate body paint.
8. Remain happy in a relationship for more than 9½ weeks.
9. Try a 'spit roast'.
10. Go to a one-garment party in a bow tie.

I was a few weeks off the dreaded Three-O and had managed only one of the above. A significant one, though. I'd actually sustained a happy relationship with an *unattached* member of the opposite sex for four months. I'd met Jan at a party in Hampstead. She was dark and pixie-ish, with a radiant face that you could happily stare at for hours. She was bright and funny and she wore suspenders to work. She was also four inches shorter than me, which was good because I'd noticed in a lift mirror the other day that my bald spot had grown from the circumference of a bottle top to a teapot lid. My fringe days were over. Let this eligible girl slip and I'd become ageing mutton on the divorcees slab.

It was late October in England. That time of year again, when the night closes in, the air is dank and Tom O'Connor is back on the telly. There was only one thing for it. Go and play away once more, and take the other half with me. We chose New Zealand because it was relaxed, you couldn't get eaten by anything and the cricket wasn't too taxing.

The last was, in fact, the understatement of the year. The

Auckland team I joined, Grafton, were a dishevelled collection of psychos, druggies, teenagers and Maoris who, despite relying on their two Test players to get them on and off the field without a fatality or the attentions of a paramedic, all got on famously. My grand aspirations of touring with the England team had materialized into taking the field with this motley crew:

1. Phil Horne – Test batsman and all round good bloke.
2. Bruce Aitken – odd jobman and dosser who lived in his van.
3. Matt Horne – teenage potential test player, brother of Phil.
4. Blair Webby – dreamy school teacher and Woodbine king.
5. Ian Fisher – punchy all rounder and minor hell-raiser.
6. Wally Kiata – strongarm Maori taxi driver.
7. Me.
8. Mark Elia – fast bowler and international rugby player with muscles of steel.
9. Scotty Fuller – chirpy, cheeky wicketkeeper (aren't they all?).
10. Willie Watson – wisecracking Test bowler with strangled-cat lbw appeal.
11. John 'Tube' MacIntyre – ageing, feisty left-arm spinner who produced native kokako bird call when annoyed or inebriated.

12th man (self-appointed): Lord Ted – 60-year-old midget who claimed to have batted for Derbyshire, bedded Fiona Richmond and ridden Princess Margaret's horse. 'What, her rocking horse?' was the standard response.

They played on a ropy recreation ground by Auckland's main motorway and the clubhouse was so broken down the tramps slept outside it. There were holes in the ceiling and the floor was littered with broken glass, chip wrappings and extinguished spliffs. There was a snack bar across the road, but when lunchtime came, half the team preferred wacky-backy to seeking any solid sustenance. It was certainly a new take on sharing a joint for Sunday lunch, and the clammy air in the 'dressing room' made me feel rather queasy. One or two were still puffing away as we walked back on the field.

This all took the pressure off me. They didn't expect much from anyone, particularly during the afternoon when several team members were only semi-conscious. The sheer fact that I had a newish bat, a pair of decent pads and could negotiate the heavily populated outfield (lots of interlocking games, as usual in New Zealand) without getting lost or arrested, vastly improved their chances.

Amazingly, we started to win games, and it was all rather fun. They were such an unprepossessing lot and other teams seemed to regard us as a bit of a joke and weren't as on their guard as they should have been. The thing is there was a higher level of natural fitness than you'd associate with English amateurs, and the genuine talent and enthusiasm that lay beneath the larking about, flourished in its liberated setting. The opposition just got more and more wound up.

I'll give you an example. A useful neighbouring team, Parnell, watered their pitch to make it unreliable. The Horne brothers battled hard for fifties, while their befuddled partners Aitken and Webby played and missed and were so slack-gripped their edges failed to carry to anyone. The bowlers were getting increasingly irritated and eventually lost control. Wally, the big Maori taxi driver came in and swung the willow gaily and that made them even madder. We got 200 on a 150 pitch, and then exhausted the oppo after the day's play with a game of touch rugby. Mark Elia, a centre in the Kiwi rugby league side come winter, left everyone in his wake.

We had a heavy night, accompanied by some of Parnell's players. Wally initiated a number of drinking games, most of which he lost. Twice running out of money when it was his round, he nipped out in his cab for fifteen minutes, picked up a couple of fares, then came straight back to the bar to spend it. At about 3a.m. he ferried the stragglers home. (NZ drivers' night-time philosophy seemed to be the drunker you were, the less pain you were likely to feel when you crashed.)

The next morning we turned up only twenty minutes before the start of the second day's play. The wicket had dried out and Parnell thought they'd get 200 easily. They lost a couple of wickets to the new ball, but their ginger-haired captain was looking solid and in control. Ian Fisher, whose steady medium-paced bowling was not in keeping with his irascible personality, was working himself into a lather about something. He started abusing the batsman, calling him 'chicken shit', a 'cack-handed prick' and 'peanut head'. We were wetting ourselves in the slips as the batsman's hackles rose.

When Fisher, who bowled from very close to the stumps, accidentally clipped the wicket at his end with his hand, the ball spilled out and trickled into the outfield. The mid-wicket fielder was about to pick it up and throw it back, but in a fit of pique the batsman strode after it shouting 'HANDS OFF, THAT'S MINE!' Obviously imagining the stationary ball was Fisher's head, he swiped furiously at it, but only succeeded in taking a huge divot. The ball dribbled to within easy reach of square leg

170

who swiftly returned it to the wicketkeeper. The batsman, stranded some way from his crease, was run out by yards. His mood wasn't enhanced by our helpless laughter, and he clanged his bat angrily on a pavilion support as he went off, slightly damaging both.

Fisher was sent off himself soon afterwards for mooning, but he had broken Parnell's resolve and they capitulated. Their running between the wickets was also hampered by hangovers and various minor injuries from the touch rugby, and they were all out for 163. They bolshily closed the bar when the game was over. It was probably just as well. Punches would have been exchanged, rather than handshakes. New Zealanders are basically docile, intelligent people. Sport brings out their Scottish genes.

Joined at the Hip

There was no such antagonism in our Auckland household. Jan and I were staying with Grant, my Mr Puniverse friend, and his wife, and if anyone got too naggy or irritable he'd put on one of his Tom Waits or Neil Young records. The spectre of that toneless drivel was enough to keep the conversation light and fresh. We took it in turns to cook meals, picked all the vegetables from the garden, ate home-made bread and scones, and recycled everything from bottles to flapjack wrappers. It was like a running episode of *The Good Life*.

It was the first time I'd co-habited with a girlfriend and at first I quite liked it. I didn't have to leave spare items of underwear round at her place, there were no sharp, unfamiliar objects to bump into on 4a.m. forays to a strange bathroom, and there was someone to tidy up your clothes and make the bed. She came to the park and helped me sort out my festering no ball problem, and encouraged me to swim-train at the city baths every day where I was regularly lapped by a bloke with no legs.

Jan and I were well matched – equally unpunctual and disorganized, with catholic tastes in food and people and the attention span of a gnat. She even still laughed at jokes she'd already heard me tell forty-eight times. She was great looking and admired by everyone, occasionally wild and usually a little bit scatty. I knew she was the only one for me.

It felt like a proper relationship, and in spite of all the 'You're under the thumb now then' and 'Got a pass out tonight have you?' comments, it didn't feel too bad. It beat the hell out of the dating game, that's for sure. I was even beginning to think marriage was rather an enticing prospect, and enthusiastically volunteered to help Craig, a Yorkshire mate whose family had migrated to New Zealand, and his dad erect a marquee for his sister's nuptials.

We were screwing in the final bolts to the metal frame, when a neighbour stuck his head over the fence. 'What're you having, a hanging or a wedding?' the neighbour asked.

'What's the bloody difference?' said Craig's father, morbidly. It still didn't put me off the idea and I quoted them a line from *The Rainbow*, which I was reading at the time.

'According to D. H. Lawrence,' I said, 'marriage is "the new superfine bliss, a peace superseding all knowledge."'

'Is 'e the lad that plays for Gloucestershire?' Craig's dad said.

While Jan, a qualified solicitor, got some temp work, I earned my keep writing on cricket and English football for the *New Zealand Herald*. The paper's apparatus, with its gummy typewriters, inky metal plates and xerox-spewing telex-machines, might have been stuck in the 1960s. So was its wage structure (I got £30 an article, less £8 tax). But it was valuable experience, and you had to start somewhere. D. H. Lawrence had some of his first stuff printed in the *Nottingham Evening Post*.

One piece I wrote reported the likelihood that Graeme Hick was about to become qualified for England. Initially, I'd been appalled that the registration rules might be changed to suit one individual (reducing the 'quarantine' period from seven years to four). But having just seen him destroy the Auckland bowling attack with 211 not out in three hours for Northern Districts, I could see the utilitarian argument. 'Ignoring Hick's commercial potential until the existing deadline of 1991,' I wrote, 'represents kicking a gift horse in the mouth. He could become the highest Test match run-scorer of all time.' Another fantastic Hughes prediction.

I also did a few radio reports for the BBC on the Australia v West Indies series. I'd watch the evening session on New Zealand TV, and phone in updates to Greater London Radio for their breakfast programme as if I was at the match. This wasn't particularly easy. Not only was I about 3000 miles away from the actual game, but also the phone was in a different room from the telly. With a system of mirrors, I could just make out what was happening, and I think I got away with it.

At this point in the late eighties, the Australians were going through a turbulent period, during which they had initiated SONG (Save Our National Game). They'd have been better off founding COST (Change Our Shit Team). Having been trounced by the West Indies, Pakistan and, before that, New Zealand, they eventually did. They brought in Steve Waugh's twin, Mark for his one day international debut. Mark promptly ran out Steve and his captain Allan Border in the space of two overs. The Waughs were the new Comptons.

Foreign Bodies
Auckland was more identifiable with the modern world than when I'd last been there. The milk wasn't quite so much like double cream, there were less people plodding around town in gum boots, and a respectable old umpire, Peter Plumley-Walker – pukka voice, handlebar moustache and all – had been found to have been dabbling in S&M. We only knew because three days after he'd failed to turn up to umpire our match, his body was found bound hand-and-foot at the bottom of a waterfall. Even an incensed Grafton bowler, denied a plumb lbw, wouldn't have gone that far. There was also a daily column in the *NZ Herald* entitled 'Today's Armed Robbery' which was often significantly larger than my articles. The neglected Polynesians, among others, were starting to throw their (very considerable) weight about.

I wondered if they couldn't direct some of this strength and aggression towards cricket. With one Grafton bowler suspended for abuse and another on Test duty, the team were a bit short of firepower. In my role as club coach, I suggested one of the Grafton lowlifes brought a couple of these islanders down to nets. There was Y'amata Tao'loadunutella (or something), a truck driver, and an enormous chap called Unga'ralla Iswalloa'tunavegemite who told me he was a warehouseman. Or maybe he just said warehouse. I've certainly seen smaller garden sheds. Jonah Lomu would have been the titch of the family. They played a primitive form of the game in Fiji which seemed to be dominated by eating. Not much different from English cricket, then. Their appetites were even more extensive than their names.

I was nominated to bat against them. 'It was your idea,' the others said. It was a most unpleasant experience. They unleashed the ball at enormous speed, which would have been half-acceptable if it had been allied to a reasonable aim. But one would be a very high bouncer, the next a hand-to-head missile, another would shoot into the side netting, and rebound at right angles off a net pole and shave your chin. It was like facing Courtney Walsh bowling in roller skates. The worst part was they thought my leaping and diving and wincing was just a normal part of the game. They even laughed. A 5ft. 9in. runt pitted against two 6ft. 5in. bears, I had no choice but to humour them.

'Thanks,' I said, as I edged past them at the end.

'No problem, it was great, ay,' said Unga'ralla, the less-scarred of the two, and slapped me cheerily on the shoulder blade, exactly at the point where I'd been hit by a beamer five minutes before. For the rest of the cricket world's sake, I hope the Pacific islanders never learn the finer points of the game or they will trample on orthodox technique in the same fashion as Lomu has done in rugby. For the moment, one of the pleasures of cricket is that Big is often Ugly, and Small (Lara, Tendulkar) can be Beautiful.

There was a weekend lull in club matches while the Kiwis played a Test against Pakistan in Auckland. Mr Puniverse's house was only fifty yards from the Eden park ground so I went every day. It was a sour affair. Pakistan ground out 600, consigning themselves to trying to bowl New Zealand out twice, which they singularly failed to do. On the last day, frustration crept in and Salim Malik could be seen (and lip-read) regularly taunting the square leg umpire, Brian Aldridge, with anything he could think of – bad decisions, poor dress sense, ignorance of the

Koran. It was extreme petulance and Aldridge frequently walked over and complained to Imran, but the Pakistan captain just shrugged and said haughtily that there wasn't anything he could do.

The match petered out into a dull draw. Four days later there was a one day international between the same teams in Christchurch. I watched it on TV. Aldridge was again officiating, and when Salim walked in, he politely gave him his guard. After patting back a couple of straight balls, Salim attempted to work one away that was veering well down the legside. He missed and it grazed his pad. The bowler grunted, more in annoyance of his misdirected delivery than anything else, and Salim re-marked his guard. When he looked up, he was staring at a raised index finger. Aldridge had got his own back in the only way he knew and given him out. Salim lingered in slack-jawed astonishment (as did the bowler) but he had to go. He marched off in high dudgeon. It wasn't, of course, his last tangle with authority.

The match was followed immediately on TV by 'My dear old thing' . . . Henry Blofeld's regular Tuesday night interview. The Kiwis were obsessed with Blowers, giving him prime-time television chat shows, radio phone-in programmes and newspaper columns. His voice could even be heard on the telephone network when you were put on hold by an airline or hotel: 'My dear old thing, it's just not cricket if you don't try the exquisite food, exceptional wines and immaculate service of the Park Royal hotels . . . in Christchurch, Wellington, Auckland or Dunedin. So play a straight bat and choose Park Royals – where you can have your chocolate cake and eat it . . . ' There seemed to be no escape from his clichéd, dandy image of fusty old England and it made me want to scream. I switched the TV off in a huff. It didn't help that the *NZ Herald* had cut my comprehensively researched feature about world cricket's dearth of spinners for a story about the technique of an Auckland bowls champion.

Xanadu?

Still, I was enjoying the cricket and I was in harmony with a girl. I sensed, too, on my second visit, that New Zealand could be an idyllic place to live. The weather was warm enough to exist in T-shirt and shorts, there was glittering sea everywhere you looked, the people didn't bite and neither, it seemed, did the insect population. I could buy a house here for the price of a London parking bay, play for the Auckland provincial side and perhaps, in time, be called up for New Zealand. (Richard Hadlee was on his last legs and it was still Ilford 2nd XI at the other end.) It was a tempting prospect.

I couldn't be certain, though, until I'd seen a bit more of the country. In the Christmas break, Jan and I did a break-neck drive round both North and South islands. We did all the touristy things – white-water rafted, bungee-jumped, scuba-dived, trekked through mountains with over-enthusiastic Americans and droning Danes. It sounds exciting, but somehow it felt like we were riding through a giant, natural theme park.

On a lonely mountain road, we came across a sweating, bearded hitchhiker in jeans, lumberjack shirt and bobble hat. 'I've just been trying to climb Mount Cook,' he said, 'but I got blown off a ridge three times at 12,000ft. so I thought I better come down.' He, to my mind, was the epitome of a New Zealander. Individual, indomitable and slightly insane.

I continued my beach recce. There were some amazing stretches of sand on the South Island but there wasn't a soul on them. With good reason. As soon as you had spread your towel out and taken off your top you were toast. Sand flies gathered for their feast, and within seconds there were little black dots on your legs, arms, and feet, and a sensation of tiny pin-pricks. You could kill them easily, but by then the damage was done. Within an hour the bites became intolerably itchy bumps, and they didn't heal for days, sometimes weeks. In the meantime you couldn't sleep at night for scratching. It was like lying in a bed full of grit. It sent you delirious. I promise you, if I was marooned on a beach with sand flies and the sea was shark-infested, I'd dive in the water.

On the Coramandel peninsula, a jagged finger of land jutting off the North Island two hours from Auckland, the beaches were glorious and the sand flies non-existent. Unfortunately there were no well-adjusted human beings either. This was the land of beach bums and beatniks that time forgot. A sort of southern hemisphere Cornwall. The buildings were tumbledown, the pony-tailed inhabitants wore flower-power clothes and Jesus sandals and drove clapped-out Corsairs, and cannabis grew wild by the side of the road. Basically everyone was permanently stoned.

Parched, you pushed into a corner store through the floor-length bead curtains, and, before being overcome by the smell of joss sticks, asked for a Coke. A hippy, like Neil in *The Young Ones*, barely awake, muttered, 'Aw, dunno, think we might have had some a while ago,' and carried on plaiting his hair.

'Well can I have one then?' I asked.

'What?'

'A *Coke!*'

'Oh, er, hang on then. Just a minute.' He disappeared behind a red velvet throw, returning a considerable time later, expressionless. 'Yes?' he said, blankly.

The impossibility during a hot two-hour drive on

rutted, dirt roads of finding anyone vaguely compos mentis or anything edible other than lentil burgers sent the Coramandel beach-rating plummeting somewhat. The water on the east coast here was calm and blue, the sand virginal and fringed with big-leafed ferns, there was no sound except the sweeesh of the waves and the occasional screech of a gull. You could stare at the sea and the sky and the forested islands on the horizon and imagine this scene hadn't changed for a thousand years. Unfortunately, the lure of such places (Lamu on the Kenyan coast, remote islands off Thailand, north Norfolk) is tarnished because the people are a bit ga ga.

Our round-New Zealand jaunt was abruptly terminated on the outskirts of Auckland. A mangled old Holden rammed into the back of us at an intersection as we waited for the lights to turn green. Our car was catapulted almost right across the junction. After the initial shock, I realized we were completely unscathed. I climbed out through the open side window, just in time to see the Samoan occupants of the other car disappearing into some bushes. I stuck my head inside their vehicle. I reeled back from the stench of alcohol and marijuana, impaling my head on a jagged piece of metal in the process, which required four stitches. It was final cast-iron evidence that dope and me do not get on.

I had in the course of the previous month, however, filled in most of the gaps on the things-to-do-before-you're-thirty list. I'd

1. Climbed a mountain – Mt Aspiring (3027m) in Fjordland, South Island.
2. Driven a Ferrari – well, I hadn't actually, but I'd got our Toyota up to 138m.p.h., wind assisted, on a bit of deserted road.
3. Learned to scuba dive.

4. Fired a Kalashnikov. OK, I didn't manage that one, but I'd bowled a few hand grenades on exploding wickets.

5. Smoked a joint.

6. Stayed in bed all day – after smoking a joint.

7. Experimented with chocolate body paint – does spilling your hot cocoa down your girlfriend count?

8. Remained stable in a relationship for more than a year (despite 7. above).

9. Tried a 'spit roast' – well not exactly, but some randy Danes did apparently have one near us in an open-plan mountain hut. I slept through it.

10. I had *not* gone to a one-garment party in a bow tie. The only person who owned a bow tie in New Zealand was Henry Blofeld.

It'd been a successful six months. In addition to the physical and personal achievements, I'd also helped Grafton gain promotion to the Auckland first division, and made plans to return. New Zealand had a lot going for it, not least the fact that there were only 2,999,999 other people vying for your (fresh) air, rather than 56,930,199 other mouths gagging on the UK's unsavoury mix of carbon monoxide and curry-and-lager-laced methane. My powers in county cricket seemed to be waning, but I could survive long enough to earn a benefit year. For the price of a terraced house in Chiswick I could buy a waterfront job in Auckland with pool, sundeck and imitation-marble bathroom . . .

10.
Aisle Altar
Hymn

Suspended Animation

Emigration to New Zealand seemed an even more attractive idea after a week of unremittingly grey skies back in English spring, and a Lloyds cashpoint machine gobbling my card because having been away for the winter I'd forgotten my pin number. A letter from some Auckland acquaintances I'd not seen since before Christmas, brought me to my senses. 'It's been a busy few months,' they wrote. 'John's been putting up shelves in Tom's bedroom, I've trimmed the privet hedge and when we had two Australian friends to dinner, I cooked them a real Kiwi meal – New Zealand lamb, boiled potatoes and cabbage.' New Zealand, I realised, was just too unseasoned and small-town for my liking.

Somehow, the time there had done me good though. It may have been the winter relaxation or the swimming training or the no ball eradication or my domestic stability. Whatever, I had my best-ever county season in 1989. I was 16th in the national bowling averages, above all but two of the nineteen bowlers England had forlornly tried against the Aussies that summer (England used twenty-nine players in the series and lost 4–0). English cricket had nose-dived, but my life was soaring.

There were three winter tours at the beginning of 1990. England to the West Indies, England A to Zimbabwe and Mike Gatting's 'rebel' team to South Africa. I thought I was a certainty for one. The time was right for my arrival on the international scene. I'd grafted the styles and skills of six cricketing nations on to my own game, and I thought I had something for every situation.

Except, as it turned out, the most important ones. I'd fine-tuned my variations of pace on the range of surfaces in Australia, New Zealand and South Africa in particular, adapting the skills of the Hadlees and le Rouxs and Lillees that I'd seen at first hand. I'd perfected the slower delivery. No one could spot it. Especially in the last over of the Nat West final at Lord's. Warwickshire's Neil Smith smote it out of the ground. The ball was lost and so was the match.

The Nat West final is the county cricketer's showpiece, a chance for them to demonstrate their wares to a wider audience, and, perhaps, the national selectors. There have been numerous instances of players' performances there earning them a tour place. I'd had the opposite experience. Conceding ten off that last over was confirmation, if anybody needed it, that I wasn't suitable for promotion, and probably never would be. I didn't make any of the tour parties.

The incident sat heavily on my mind for a while. It felt like all my life's endeavour had been scuppered by one ball. All those visions of taking the field in an England touring sweater, and headlines in the *Sun* 'Windies blown apart by Hurricane Hughes' and the right to put Middlesex *and England* after my name on a sponsored car, had gone up in smoke.

Then I got a letter from Middlesex with a bonus of £3500, a new three-year contract and confirmation of my benefit year in 1991 and I felt like someone again. I went out and bought Jan an engagement ring and proposed to her on the upper deck of a 65 bus going to Kew Gardens. I had slight lingering doubts (she didn't look like Meg Ryan). So did she (I was no Dennis Quaid). But she accepted immediately and we settled on a spring wedding date. I was so contented I said 'I love you' back. Twice.

There was quite a lot to organize so I stayed home for the winter. I hadn't had pale forearms or worn a thick polo neck for eight years. It was quite a novelty. I went to foggy rugby grounds, set a friend's garden gate alight with a Catherine wheel and chundered on haggis at a Burns night. I played park football on Sunday mornings as a hangover cure and didn't notice the dog shit.

At home I threw out the Kiwi lodgers and the Kim Basinger posters and I planted tomatoes in the garden. I volunteered for the camp bed at my prospective in-laws and entertained their grandchildren. I still broke things and spilt my food and tended to wear garish shorts around the house in memory of summer, but Jan hoped (and thought) I'd change. On 31 March 1990 we walked up the aisle as planned.

You may recall from *A Lot of Hard Yakka* the early hiccup in our new life together. I slept with the chief bridesmaid on my wedding night. The festivities ended up at a friend's house, and when I discovered Jan had crashed out in the front bedroom with a girlfriend, I got into the spare bed, fully clothed. When I woke up, the bridesmaid was asleep next to me. She also happened to be my sister.

But that was quickly forgotten, and the first summer of married bliss went well. We didn't argue about the washing up or who'd put the rubbish out or how much to pay into the joint account, I helped fasten her suspenders for work and she sewed up the hem of my whites. I phoned her every other night on away trips. We had parallel music tastes (Mendelssohn, Springsteen, Everything But The Girl), liked the same spiciness in food, read the same novel (*Metroland* by Julian Barnes) simultaneously. Everyone said it was right because we had so much in common.

Middlesex, with my irregular assistance, won the county championship for the fourth time in ten years. It was an odd season of straw-coloured pitches, seamless, unpolishable balls and ridiculous scores – Lancashire replied to Surrey's 707 at the Oval with 863 all out. But Middlesex had a battery of fast bowlers, Phil Tufnell to get under opponents' skin, and 2400 runs from the West Indian Desmond Haynes, whose physical and verbal presence flattened anything in its course.

I had a new wife, a £3500 win bonus and the promise of a lucrative benefit year and I was going to live happily ever after.

Until English winter set in. That's when the trouble started. I couldn't cope with two in a row. Draughty October gave way to dreary November, December was the dregs. I was visualizing the open-air concerts and the beach-barbecues and the lissom bronzed legs, while we were having our DIY disagreements and where-are-we-going-for-Christmas disputes and she was doing the ironing in her baggy tracksuit bottoms.

I was mostly consumed organising my benefit, booking

venues, cold-calling advertisers, sending out mailshots. The only paid work I got was some football reporting for Greater London Radio. One Saturday I was reading out my match analysis at Fulham after the game, when someone turned the floodlights out, plunging the ground into pitch darkness. I stumbled through the rest of the live report, getting most of the names wrong.

Several irate supporters rang in asking what bloody match the reporter had been watching. I was withdrawn from reporting duties and the following Saturday given a 'safer' assignment, to read the sports news on Chris Evans' programme, instead. It was all rather frenetic just before going on air and I accidentally spilt coffee all over his script. He flipped and said people who couldn't hold their drink were bad enough, but people who couldn't hold their coffee were just imbeciles. I wasn't asked to work Saturdays after that.

Jan was irked by my clumsiness and my lack of interesting (i.e. non-cricketing) friends and my habit of daubing my face in Ambre Solaire to ward off winter blues. She'd got used to me being away playing all summer and now I was under her feet all winter: a fly-by-night turned parasite. The 'lure' of being married to a sportsman, ha, ha, had started to wear thin. She stayed at work later and reacted tetchily to me leaving a dirty plate lying around or failing to hang up her dry cleaning properly.

We were both constantly late for everything, and people started giving us false meeting times half-an-hour early. Wise to that, we started allowing for it and were later than ever. We scrapped over our shared copy of *A History of the World in 10½ Chapters*, and cocked-up dinner-parties for the organisers of the benefit ferret-racing evening because we both thought the other was cooking.

Stress levels were building up, the relationship was imploding. A few months after people had said it was right because we were so similar, they were saying it was wrong *because we were so similar*. In early summer 1991, fourteen months after marrying, we agreed, amicably, to separate. I'd had it with suspenders by then, anyway.

After the private pain and the public embarrassment ('Wot, your missus shagging a decent-looking bloke now is she?' was a typical reaction in the Middlesex dressing room) there was more private pain and public embarrassment ('If you top yourself can I have your sponsored car?') Despite all the years of trial and error, I wasn't prepared for a knock this hard. I spent most of the season injured, mainly in the head, and was not much good to anyone (except Neil, my benefit treasurer, if I presented with him a fat cheque).

Eventually, following a lousy summer of self-analysis and spoilt analyses, I began to look more positively on the situation. It was better to have tried and failed, than not tried at all; nothing ventured, nothing gained; a bird out of the hand leads to two in the bush, etc. etc. What neither of us had understood I suppose, is that marriage is a sort of death. It's the end of your old self, the start of something new. You can't just carry on, selfishly, like you did before. You've got to recreate yourself, it's a different life. Maybe the New Zealand bloke looking over the fence was right: a wedding *was* a bit like a hanging.

Cold Blooded Pursuit

My future had been dashed on the rocks of domesticity. I had to relaunch myself. After a winter tidying up the benefit, I signed for a new county (Durham), with a new personality. Steady and professional during the day, giddy and frivolous at night. For two summers I plied the straight and narrow on the field, went a bit mad off it.

Ian Botham, who'd also joined Durham, called me 'Pluto'. He said I was on another planet. I might well have been, but time was running out on all counts. The pace of my bowling had declined to barely above medium, the knee joints crackled like bowls of Rice Krispies, the bald spot had gone from Jaffa Cake size to individual quiche. The glint off it was almost blinding the prey.

There was plenty of fish in the sea up north, but females' attitudes seemed to have changed in the years since I'd last had a dip in open water. They didn't linger around, hoping for a morsel or two if they were lucky. They knew what they wanted and how to get it. The trout had metamorphosed into piranhas. I was chewed up and spat out. I quite enjoyed it in a masochistic sort of way.

On the playing side, Durham was two years of fun and fruitlessness. It was exciting being in on the birth of a new county, but the baby was a slow learner. Promising positions were continuously squandered through inexperience. The wily nous of other teams told in the end. Two seasons running we were grubbing around with a wooden spoon and egg on our faces.

I couldn't go on like this. My body sounded like faulty plumbing and the scars – mental and physical – were mounting. Durham was great, but for me it was a cul-de-sac and anyway, it was freezing. I retired from county cricket and the endless circuit of neon-lit north east bars, secured some rugby reporting with *The Independent*, and re-entered the chase down south.

I had mixed results. I enjoyed covering rugby despite finding it a rough and primitive sport. It was the equal of some of the houses I ended up in. During the winter I went out with a girl whose address was 868 the North Circular and another who lived at 499 the Great West Road (I can hear the estate agent's blurb now – 'enchanting period cottage in light, spacious setting beside Kew Gardens and conveniently located for all transport amenities'). Both their bedrooms overlooked six lanes of traffic, which thundered and screeched all night. Going to bed was like a peep show crossed with a Formula 1 arcade game. After foreplay, I just about managed to stop myself from saying 'Now, d'you want four star or unleaded?'

I missed the warm outdoor life and the adrenaline of playing sport, and to cheer myself up I joined a posh new gym, the Harbour Club in Chelsea. My well-connected friend Alistair was a member and did some promotional work there. I'd get some exercise and he'd introduce me to the right kind of girl – smart, lively, affluent, knew most of the answers on *A Question of Sport*. He did his best, but the women were far too fixated on their calorie-burning monitors and their rippling, black personal trainers to notice me killing myself on the rowing machine.

Instead, we played tennis on their indoor courts. It was good to get back into some earthy, competitive ball game rather than pretending not to look at women looking at themselves in the mirror lifting 2oz. dumbbells. In fact, during our matches I forgot about women completely. It was a refreshing sensation.

We were knocking up one morning when a slender, statuesque blonde crossed over from an empty court. 'Hi Alistair,' she trilled. 'Listen, my coach has gone and I've got a few minutes to kill. Could we have a threeway?'

'Sure,' he replied, and waved her over. 'This is Simon.'

'Hi, Simon,' the girl said sweetly, and extended a dainty hand. It was Princess Diana. I was startled by how tall she was.

A 'threeway' with the most desirable woman in the world! Now you're talking. An odd image crossed my mind of the Queen in full regalia looking disdainfully down on our tame strokes from atop an ornate umpire's chair and exclaiming 'Dunce!' For approximately four minutes and 43 seconds I partnered Di as she practically assaulted the ball, almost as if she was venting her frustration on it. I noticed her tanned, sinewy arms as she played vigorous forehands, the sleekness of her limbs, admired her athleticism. She had been transplanted from a Mills and Boon novel. I could see what all the fuss was about. I'd certainly make a fuss of her if she were mine.

She said 'Shot!' to me once and I went slightly weak(er) at the knees. Then her mobile rang and she looked a bit flustered and said she had to go. I wondered if it was Squidgygate Bloke. I caught sight of the huge rock on her left hand as she replaced the phone in her black Prada bag and realised that if I fussed around women like that, I'd soon have the bailiffs round.

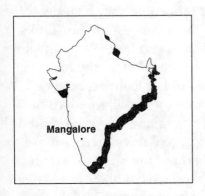

Mangalore

11.
India

Long Distance Training

I was getting nowhere fast. And expensively. The gym subscription alone was £1500, plus all the meals and odd flyaway weekends I was treating girlfriends to. Ridiculous isn't it that the pursuit of the perfect partner can consume your life's savings, yet going the whole hog and getting married in church costs a paltry £60. Set against that, a decree absolute is only £21.50, but the humiliation is unquantifiable, never mind the fuss of dividing up the (unused) Wedgwood dinner service.

I still had some Asian friends from my first trip to Sri Lanka, and I began to see some advantages, for men, in their ancient system. Concentrate on your study or work, be a devoted Hindu/Christian/Muslim, while other people found you a wife. Free. Arranged marriages saved a lot of money, time and heartache, and you didn't discover the person's unsavoury habits before you'd even bought the engagement ring. There were no preconceptions. Asian newly-weds had no baggage.

I had the chance to see the system at first hand. Dilip, my old cricketing sidekick, whose family I'd stayed with in Colombo on my first overseas venture, was getting hitched. I was stunned when I heard the news. The only woman I'd ever seen in Dilip's company was his mother.

'Who to?' I asked, rather too incredulously.

'I don't know yet,' he said on a crackly phone line from Bangalore. He had several candidates to see in Mangalore, his mother's home town, that weekend. The date for the wedding had already been set, though, and I was cordially invited as a 'special guest.'

I didn't hesitate to accept. His wedding coincided conveniently with the start of England's 1993 tour of India. I arranged to cover some of it for the *Sunday Independent*, who seemed to have liked some of my rugby articles. Also, I'd toured India before and I loved the place. It was hot, the food was delicious, and as soon as the people discovered you were an English cricketer, they worshipped you. It was the ideal escape from the trials and tribulations of being a floundering thirty-something male in post-feminist Britain.

It was quite a journey. I flew to Bombay, endured a white-knuckle taxi ride around the airport between international and domestic that was straight out of *The Italian Job*, and boarded a flight for Delhi. Then another to Madras. I wanted to do the last leg by rail.

I had booked my Madras to Mangalore train tickets in Wembley. That's right Wembley, Middlesex. Some weeks before I was due to travel, I sat in a shabby office just off the high road, the twin towers just visible, watching the diminutive Mr Dandipani laboriously writing down my requirements. 'There's the 12.26p.m. express from Madras to Bangalore,' he said, staring into space. 'Takes seven hours twenty minutes. On a Thursday and a Sunday that connects with the 8.42p.m. fast passenger service from Bangalore to Mangalore. Takes fifteen and a quarter hours. You'll be there at 11.36 the following morning. Second class £32, first class fan £48, first class air con £54.' He studied an unsightly damp patch on the wall. 'Or you could take the 4.45p.m. Brindavan express from Madras. Takes six hours ten minutes. But you'll have to spend a night in Bangalore. Which shall I book, sir?'

He reeled practically all this off in one breath without once consulting a timetable or a computer screen. Everyone I've encountered since who's been to him reported the same thing, for a multitude of routes. Mr Dandipani had, apparently, consigned the schedules of the entire 60,000k.m. Indian railway network to memory. I chose the 12.26 option, handed over my £48 and he gave me a hand-written receipt with my train times on it. I was certain I'd been conned, but I kept the slip anyway.

I arrived at a besieged Madras station two months later in good time. I showed my receipt to a harassed supervisor and he moved me towards the booking office. There was a queue of about 900 at each window, most apparently lugging all their worldly belongings in a jute sack. My heart sank. It was clear I'd never get on the train, and as the only white person in the queue, I was pestered by a host of beggars, peanut roasters, *chai* vendors, cigarette sellers, shoe-shiners and porters. 'Carry your bag sah'b, carry your bag!'

I was cursing Mr Dandipani and my conspicuousness when a man in train conductor's garb came up and asked me where I was going. He pored over my crumpled receipt and then said 'Platform 31, staircase 24, coach DD.'

It sounded like a woman's vital statistics. I weaved through the chaos of lost children, wandering animals and men humping fridges, following his instructions.

I walked across a long wooden overpass and looked down on the trains and platforms and the maze of tracks below. It made Clapham Junction resemble Llandudno Halt. I fought my way through the shouting, betel juice-gobbing melée on the relevant staircase and walked along a battered, destination-less train with what seemed like about fifty carriages. I stopped at one with a fading DD painted on the side. Below it hung a clipboard with two sheets of names written in neat italics. Entered beside the words 'Compartment 12, seat 57' was 'Mr SP Huges.' And the seat was vacant, though the 15" television carried by the monk next to me partly rested on my leg.

The 'express' creaked into motion on the dot of 12.26, and though it rarely exceeded 30m.p.h. for about seven hours, it did arrive on time in Bangalore. During the journey I dipped into a section about Hinduism in my Indian travel guide, and was interested in the concept of influencing your rebirth. I imagined I'd come back as someone important – a landowner, a judge or Melvyn Bragg. But then I totted up all my bad *karma* – the failed relationships, the two timing, the abuse of various international telephone systems, the ruination of twenty thousand Middlesex supporters' hopes in the 1989 Nat West final. The only good *karma* I could think of was my tolerance of the monk's TV on my leg. I downgraded my reincarnation to a willing labrador.

I found the connecting train to Mangalore easily, and it too listed my name, this time spelled correctly, on the outside of a sleeping compartment. An attendant directed me to a counter where I could collect my bedding and pillows, wrapped in cellophane, also with my name on.

The train again departed and arrived exactly on schedule. I half imagined Dandipani controlled the signals from his room in Wembley as well.

After two days' travelling (which felt like two months), I'd arrived in Mangalore, together with other visitors from far and wide. Dilip's family had invited so many wedding guests, they'd commandeered an entire five-storey hotel to accommodate them all. Asians don't do weddings by halves.

A Good Arrangement

Dilip and his bride-to-be had set eyes on each other before the big day. Briefly. A week or so earlier, Dilip had been stationed in a private room of a hotel, as a dozen potential partners were wheeled in one by one for him to choose from. He'd whittled it down to three for a second assessment, and after final consultation with his father, had finally decided on Gwen, an affectionate dental student.

It might sound more like a job interview, but this is the way people pair off in India. And, perusing the *Hindustan Times* on the morning of the wedding, I was amazed to find fifteen pages of people advertising themselves for marriage. Most were pretty standard:

Suitable alliance for well settled, charming Mathur girl, 25/veg/tall/fair complexion/born Feb 67, teacher well-versed in House hold. Father gazetted officer, brother MNC manager. Simple early marriage. Caste no bar. Reply to . . .

But there was also the occasional odd one:

Life-companion for 28 year old, good looking boy, in decent job, suffering from sexual disorder, ie., acute premature ejaculation. Girl should either be suffering from same disease or is not interested in sex otherwise.

The ceremony itself took place on a small parade ground. Twelve hundred guests sat at oblong trestle tables munching bhajis and making small talk or watching their children skirmishing in the dust. While we waited for something to happen, I chatted to the local marriage fixer, a Mr Gohel. 'I like to call it arranged love,' he said whimsically. 'Romance clouds your judgement. In the west you all think marriage is going to be a moonlight sonata and that life will be a rainbow. There are no illusions in Indian arranged marriages, and you might fall in love after a few years.' Whereas, in my experience, western marriages were the total opposite.

The bride and bridegroom eventually appeared on a raised platform, accompanied by about fifty relatives who totally obscured any clear view of the couple. Some twangly music played and then everybody stood up, I assumed to sing, but then they all made their way to a line of booths to load up their plates with a vast array of steaming curries. I was licking my lips in anticipation of the feast, but as I headed towards a huge urn of simmering prawns, some third-uncle-twice-removed took me by the arm and led me to the platform. 'You can give your speech now,' he said.

Public speaking is difficult enough at the best of times, never mind when there's a crackly PA and you've had precisely thirty seconds warning before addressing 1000 Indians, virtually all of whom are either noisily refilling their plates or chewing on marinated lamb shanks. I racked my brains for appropriate stories.

I told them the one about Mike Gatting in Bombay

being asked to go a bit wider at slip and Chris Cowdrey saying 'If Gatt goes any wider he'll burst.'

Dead silence.

I told them why Pakistani bowlers get so many lbw decisions back home, because when a ball raps a batsman on the pads they shout 'Alla galla hie?!' which is Urdu for 'Where's Allah?!' and the umpire immediately sticks his finger up towards the heavens.

Barely a murmur.

I told them my fail-safe, the one that always gets them rolling in the aisles, about the time I was walking off the field with the England captain Mike Brearley when a kid came up and excitedly asked for his autograph, and he obliged and then the boy dutifully handed me the book and a pencil and I signed. The little bugger looked at what I'd written for a second, and then just rubbed it out.

No reaction except a 'Sunil, come back here!' from the back to an escaping four-year-old.

Desperately trying to think of a tale that might amuse them, I played for time by telling them that when we were kids, Dilip and I used to muck about playing cricket in the car park beside his London flat and one day he smacked the tennis ball on to the roof of the flats and we were just going to get it when his dad appeared in the doorway angrily waving an umbrella.

Uproarious laughter. It didn't die down for some time, after which I left the podium to hysterical cheering.

The reception went on late into the evening, until it seemed, the entire town had met the couple and a whole pack of stray dogs was scrapping over leftovers beneath the tables. Then, the following day, the bride and groom were wheeled out again at lunchtime for a legion of family and relatives to give them a final pat on the back/pep talk. By now Dilip's sixty-eight-year-old father, Benji, had met, or introduced to each other, about 1500 distant cousins and friends. It was all too much and he had a heart attack and tragically died. As the family gained a member, it simultaneously lost one too. That – bearing in mind that there is a birth or death on the sub-continent every six seconds – is India.

Runs and Wiggles . . .

I had an overnight stop in Bangalore, en route from Dilip's wedding in south India to the England team's HQ in the north. Their 1993 tour was just about to start. Bangalore is a green, spacious city, with wide, relatively uncongested streets. The buildings are mainly squat, white-washed affairs, many at the time plastered with huge billboard-images of the Indian captain Mohammed Azharuddin. His face stared out at you from everywhere, beaming mischievously. I thought how benign this image was compared to the reality of actually bowling at him, backed by 75,000 infatuated Indians. I wondered how England's bowlers were planning to restrain his flashing blade in the forthcoming Test series. Hopefully, they'd do so more effectively than I had a few years earlier.

I had been on a charity-fund-raising tour to India in the late eighties with the International Ambassadors, a Christian-orientated side captained by Vic Marks. It was the one and only cricket team I'd played in that had prayer-meetings before matches and broke into a hymn on coach trips. My only real qualification was once doing a year's stint as a church organist/choir master in Ealing, deputizing for an unreliable chap who used to nip outside the vestry for a fag during the sermon, and be perpetually late back.

There are two things constantly on your mind on cricket tours to India. Food and toilets. They sort of merge into each other. They served curry for breakfast before our first match in the Bangalore Test stadium. I decided against it, not wanting to feel 'loose' if we were fielding first. We were, and Azharuddin, guesting for the opposition, strode in at no. 4 and rattled up a quickfire 50. Running in to bowl to him on an empty stomach made me feel exceptionally queasy. I had to leave the field before lunch. They began assembling it in the dressing room at 11a.m., erecting several trestle tables and covering them with crisply-laundered white cloths, then wheeling in gas cylinders and placing the burners on the tables. There were also warming plates, and a wood roti oven like a beer barrel. Half an hour before the interval, an array of bubbling pots was giving off an intoxicating aroma of pungent spices, and someone had placed their sweaty batting gloves in the mouth of the roti oven to dry.

Six waiters dished up at 12.15 precisely. There was chicken tikka, mutton biryani, lamb rogan josh, chicken korma, spicy baked fish, dhal which was more like lentil soup, matter-paneer (curd cheese and peas), several other vegetable dishes, a bowl of raita, a tray of rotis and more than enough rice to feed the population of Vietnam. For dessert there were five different sorts of fruit and endless tubs of runny vanilla ice cream. It was like the Sunday lunch 'pig out' special at your local Raj Palace – 'All you can eat for £6.50.' The only things missing were the mints and the 'refreshing tissue.'

You constantly hear stories of visiting Test teams all going down with Delhi belly or some other lurgy, usually labelled as a stomach bug. Believe none of them. It's just over-eating at lunchtime. And it's all part of the cunning Indian plan. I know because I was once invited into the Indian team's dressing room during the lunch interval in Calcutta. All they were eating were samosas and fruit.

What you don't suffer in India, though, is that terrible rear-end burning after a curry, as if your backside is a spaceship on re-entry. The food in India is spicy, but actually not as throat-cauterisingly hot as your local Tandoori Nights would have you believe, and usually smothered in soothing yoghurt. Vindaloo is just a Bangladeshi invention to mask the stale leftovers in the sauce and make you buy gallons of lager to cool down.

This doesn't mean, of course, that it isn't in one end and out the other rather quicker than you expect. I'll give you an example. After the Bangalore match on that eighties trip, we drove through the Nilgiri mountains to the 'shirting and suiting' city of Coimbatore. There was a brief prayer meeting, after which our liaison man said he had organised 'a practice match' in a small nearby village the next day, against a few local players. It *sounded* like a leisurely day, and I had a big breakfast before we left.

The journey took two hours along uneven roads through palm and paddy. In the dusty town of Udamalpet, there were lots of people in the main street, all heading in the same direction. We drove under a large banner saying 'UDAMALPET WELCOMES CHEERFUL ENGLISH CRICKETERS' and into the park-ground. Through a police cordon. At least 10,000 people were already seated in temporary wooden stands and more were streaming in. This was our 'practice' match.

I didn't mind about that. Of far more concern was the apparent lack of a toilet. Absolutely the first thing you do on arrival at any Indian cricket ground is check location, paper supplies and flushability of the nearest lavatory. One equipped with a seat, a door, a working cistern and a full bog-roll is a genuine collector's item. A lock is an irrelevance as, invariably, there's no time to fasten it.

Sudden cramps are a perpetual risk, and you need to know that you can make it from field/dressing room to pan in under fifteen seconds.

Here at Udamalpet there was no sign of a shed or a cubicle or a lean-to. The changing 'room' was a large covered sand pit enclosed by waist-high wicker-work. The rest of the ground was all temporary seating. There was nowhere to hide. Indian sod's law decrees it's at times like this you're desperate to go.

Now I'm just about OK with camp toilets, portaloos or holes in the floor in French *pensions*. I don't like my girlfriend/wife walking in when I'm sitting comfortably, but I put up with it. I do however draw the line at squatting down in front of your team-mates in a clammy sand pit, backside beneath the wicker partition visible to half of India.

It did have one beneficial effect. It meant I couldn't give a toss when, having taken the field, we were informed over the tannoy that the opening batsmen would be Kris Srikkanth and Mohinder Amarnath, to be followed by Vengsarkar, Azharuddin, Sandip Patil and Kapil Dev. The 'practice' XI we were playing was virtually the Indian team. I didn't even notice Srikkanth crashing sixteen off my first over. All I was thinking about was bowel control.

I had no nerves, and it ensured I eased rather than rushed to the wicket. I soon got rid of Srikkanth (admittedly caught long off) and finished with four wickets. Following that experience, if I ever found myself rushing anxiously through my run-up in a county game, I always envisaged bowling at khazi-less Udamalpet, and a more controlled service was soon restored. It was probably the most useful thing I picked up from Indian cricket.

You certainly learn to expect the unexpected. The day

after the Udamalpet match, we were due to play a floodlit match in Coimbatore billed as a one day 'international', despite the fact that our only Test player was Vic Marks, and he was ill. At 2p.m. our coach was met outside the Coimbatore hotel by a police escort of two trucks, three vans, an armoured car and ten outriders. Anyone would think we had the Pope in our team. We made tortuous progress to an athletics stadium, largely due to the congestion caused by our cortège.

Thousands of people were milling about around the stadium and the trucks and vans got stuck in the melée. Lines of onlookers stood outside the gates, banging happily on the side of the coach yelling 'Iron Bottom!' and 'Geoff Boycott!' and waving scraps of paper, rupee notes, even leaves for us to sign. Inside, a crowd of 40,000 were sitting noisily waiting for the match to start.

This time at least there was a building to change in, though it was actually an annexe of the district telephone exchange, which bordered the ground. Our kit was spread around between piles of redundant cable and boxes of connectors. The Indians had a canvas tent tacked on to the side.

The match was an enormous success, with explosive batting all round and a barrel-load of sixes. It was a real exhibition. I marvelled at the Indians' quick arms and nimble feet. With often tiny physiques they were still able to hit the ball with considerable power. But instead of crunching it back from where it had come, in our rigid, lead-booted way, they skipped daintily about the crease, slashing, slicing and sweeping. It was Indian dance to English square bashing.

Again, Azharuddin's batting was a cut above the others. He whipped decent balls to unlikely corners with a rapid swish of his arms. It was like bowling at a revolving door. His wrists seemed to be rubberised, and he wielded the bat like a switch blade. He waited, motionless, so long for each ball to arrive, you thought he hadn't seen it. You were about to yell triumphantly for a plumb lbw when a blur of willow flashed the ball past the square leg umpire's left shin. You'd stare at him aghast at the outrageousness of the stroke, and he'd wiggle his head in that idiosyncratic Indian way, and shrug apologetically.

I always had trouble with the Indian head wiggle. 'Yes', 'no', 'thank you' and 'sorry' are all roughly the same side-to-side motion. The only way of telling is by looking at the raised/lowered eyebrows. When Azharuddin is flogging some poor mortal's bowling, I reckon he is saying both 'sorry' and 'thank you' simultaneously.

Rude Awakenings
I hoped Gooch's '93 team wouldn't see too much of Azhar's contented wiggle, but by then he had a lot to be contented about. He was the idol of 900 million people, a rupee billionaire at the peak of his powers with a film star girlfriend. He had the pick of the delicious Indian female crop. Wandering around Bangalore, I looked at all the stylish, trouser-suited women going about their business in this software-orientated city – a sort of silicon valley of Asia – and wondered whether western *laissez faire* had penetrated their moral values as well as their dress styles. Did Indian women flirt and have one-night stands? Was there a Bombay branch of the Chippendales?

I stood in a non-moving queue for the X-ray machine at Bangalore airport. I was waiting to fly to Delhi. So was the delicate vision in front of me, a luminous, mid twenties Indian girl in black denim. We got talking and after I'd aired the fact that I was 'joining' the England cricket team, she told me she was going to Delhi, on business, for the first time. The flight was getting in late and she wasn't sure if she had a hotel room.

'Oh,' I said, pretending I hadn't taken it in, while feverishly contemplating my next move.

Three hours later, collecting my bags in Delhi airport, I accidentally-on-purpose bumped into her again. She looked lost.

'My hotel's only ten minutes from here, you can book somewhere from there if you like,' I said, fully expecting a blank refusal.

'OK,' she said. 'Thanks.'

We got to the Taj Palace, a glitzy five-star place with a lobby the size of Trafalgar Square, at around 11.30p.m. I suggested she phoned from my room. Once inside I looked at my watch, and at her pretty, flustered face and glanced pointedly at the second bed.

'Look it's late,' I said, 'you don't want to be trying to book a hotel now. Why don't you sort it out tomorrow and kip here for one night?'

She stayed five. I don't know why. I guess it was mainly curiosity. Sunita took time to open up but eventually she talked about her strict Hindu upbringing, and the freedom of having a well-paid job and how confusing it all was. Her mother and father had had an arranged marriage and she knew some of the safe, studious men they had in mind for her. She had just seen *When Harry Met Sally*, (dubbed into Hindi) and thought finding a partner was better the western way.

The first morning-after she also said I looked like Billy Crystal, which, considering I had only ten per cent of his hair covering despite being fifteen years younger, I thought unlikely. She certainly didn't look like a duskier Meg Ryan, but fake orgasms do sound the same in India as they do in America. Or England for that matter.

She stayed in the room most of the time, apart from when she had business meetings. She was embarrassed to venture out into the foyer with me, and as time went by, I was, with her. She was all over me whenever I returned, and increasingly resembled a kid who had never been allowed out, being let loose in an adventure playground. It was exhausting. I began to avoid going back upstairs until it was quite late and was rather relieved when she finally flew home.

It was wet in Delhi that week and for several days the England players had nothing much to do. I sat around with them in the lobby. After a spot of training in the hotel gym, Graham Gooch was immersed in *Fatherland* by Robert Harris, Graeme Hick read something from the Wilbur Smith stable. Phil Tufnell was talking spin tactics with Vic Marks, now cricket correspondent of the *Observer*. 'It's a whole new ball game out here,' Tuffers was saying, having received some rough treatment in a couple of the early matches. 'They're good at playing my sort of stuff. I can't just throw up a few loopy-doopies like I do to the West Indians.'

Amongst the remains of a late breakfast, Robin Smith (chairman) and Neil Fairbrother (chief sneak) were having a Fines Committee meeting. The coach Keith Fletcher was the prime target, for taking drinks onto the field in blue tracksuit bottoms, and for rabbiting so much at dinner the previous night that Clem Driver, the scorer, had been forced to turn his hearing aid off.

Devon Malcolm and Chris Lewis were in the gym, and the newcomers to the England party – Richard Blakey, Paul Taylor and Ian Salisbury – were rehearsing a 'sketch' for their initiation ceremony on Monday night. Dermot Reeve, super 8 in one hand, hairbrush in the other, was filming them for his tour video diary, screened once a week in the team room. Only Michael Atherton had ventured far afield, visiting the Taj Mahal the hard way – by taxi – a ten-hour round trip.

Evenings were spent either in the Taj or Sheraton over the road, or mostly at the British High Commission, where, in surroundings like a university campus, you could play snooker, join in karaoke nights, eat steak, egg and chips and drink draught Boddingtons. Take it from me, the only real hardship for an England player in India is on the field.

There they were suffering. In their first match against Delhi they'd choked on thick black smoke issuing from a clay chimney as well as on the accuracy of the local spinners. In the second, at Ahmedebad, a crummy, polluted city, unrest and firecrackers amongst a boisterous crowd had made concentration difficult. In the third, on Delhi's dilapidated Test ground, Navjot Siddhu had carried out a calculated and brutal assault on the spinners, Emburey and Tufnell, which had badly dented their confidence. And there was a large rat in the dressing room. 'Stamp on it!' someone shouted. 'Don't do that,' the chief dressing room attendant cried, 'he's one of our oldest members.'

Cricket in India is a test of character as much as skill and England were failing it. They had trained hard for the tour in the sanitized surroundings of Lilleshall sports centre, yet no amount of practice or physical jerks could prepare you for India's idiosyncrasies. Off the field you were stared at as if you were a gargoyle with three heads. On it you could get harassed and heckled and pelted with fruit.

In my playing experience, I had found it better to joke with the crowd or juggle with the fruit, than get all antagonistic. Winning the spectators over, which is quite easily done especially if you lapse easily into idiocy, disperses the siege mentality some teams feel and suddenly it seems a friendlier place. The way to survive the sub-continent when things don't go quite to plan is to smile and shrug. England just whined and whinged.

Erratic Behaviour

It was hard to moan about the next venue, Jaipur, a short flight south. The team (and press) were housed in a spectacular hotel, a converted Maharajah's palace, much of it made of marble, in its own spacious grounds with manicured lawns and strolling peacocks. The rooms were arranged round the main courtyard, most split-level with white wooden shutters and tapestries and little balconies. Some had four poster beds. Outside each, a personal bearer in a white tunic sat patiently, jumping to attention when you emerged. The main bar had thirty different whiskies and was decorated with moose heads and guns in display cases. We could have been at Gleneagles.

About 90,000 turned up for the one day international against England in Jaipur, only about a third of them with tickets. *Lathi*-wielding cops beat back the gate-crashers, bangers were let off and missiles had been made out of a splintering sign saying 'No weapons inside.' The whole stadium was shrouded in a fog of smoke and dust. This made finding your seat considerably harder, especially if it was already taken. About twelve people were occupying the place I'd been allocated. It was easier to go somewhere else than get them to move. I finished up sitting next to the photographers round the boundary.

Five yards from the field, you certainly got a vivid reminder of how daunting it can be to play India at home. The schoolboy prodigies Sachin Tendulkar and Vinod Kambli shredded the England attack. Each boundary was greeted with a hail of fruit raining down on the hapless fielder (and us) and a cacophony of cheering and explosions and rattling of the metal fences. Trying to communicate with his team, poor Gooch, with his thin, reedy voice, couldn't make himself heard. The first prerequisite for the next England captain to tour India is that he should have a loud, booming voice.

From Jaipur, the tour party flew to Calcutta, via Chandigarh. I went overland to Delhi via Agra. I just had to see the Taj Mahal. The six-hour train journey was torture. There were no carriage doors and no glass in the windows and the roof was full of holes, through which acrid diesel fumes blew. The sun was just rising and it was 3°C outside. The wind-chill factor made it about minus 30°C.

It had never occurred to me that parts of mainland India got cold. You only had this mental picture of dust and heat haze and everyone in thin cotton clothes. I hadn't brought a single jumper. All the other passengers were dressed like sherpas, wrapped in shawls and scarves and woolly hats. I was in a T-shirt and shorts. Once the train had clanked into action and a Himalayan draught began whistling round the carriage, I began putting on all the T-shirts (6), pairs of trousers (2) and layers of socks (4) that I had. It was still perishing. Seeing groups of men on platforms shrouded in clothes, huddled round braziers of hot coals, just made it worse. Not on the ski slopes of France nor the winter tarmac of Moscow have I ever been colder.

Arriving at Agra, I was besieged by hawkers. They are all over you like paparazzi round soap stars. At least being in a huddle warmed me up. To see the Taj is worth all this hassle times ten. The gleaming white marble dome against the blue sky, the perfect symmetry of the structure and its accompanying minarets, is spell binding. Even the palm trees in the manicured gardens appear to be identical. I'd have to add the Taj to my list of irresistible man-made objects – the Chrysler Building, Concorde, Sydney Opera House, Liz Hurley – that you can't take your eye off. It's totally mesmerising. And it's fascinating *inside*.

I made the mistake of returning to Delhi by car. I thought it would be warmer and the taxi fare was only £8. But it nearly cost me my life. It was three and a half hours of spot-the-non-suicidal-driver (about three in all.) Which side of the road do they drive on in India? The answer is your side. From the opposite direction. Overloaded trucks, horns blaring, bore down on us, their cargo apparently travelling at an uncontrollable tangent to the wheels. There was no option but to pull off on to the ragged edge of the tarmac. Ditto the streams of listing, supercrowded buses. Sometimes the on-coming traffic was three vehicles wide. It was growing dark, but none of them had any lights, except the Christmas-tree variety hung round the edge of the windscreen.

My own driver played his part, once attempting to overtake a van that was already overtaking a truck that was swerving round a goat, on a blind corner. He wouldn't have heard my vehement reproaching, as his palm was permanently on the horn (or Egyptian Brake Pedal, as it is known in many Third World countries.) He sat forward in his seat, peering out of his filthy windscreen, partly blinded by the reflective tinsel draped across the dashboard. A picture of his wife and kids, suspended from the broken rear-view mirror, swung in and out of his eyeline. He gripped the wheel tightly, wrenching it abruptly from one side to the other, as if he was playing some kind of sadistic sport. If you think you've seen some classic carve-ups in Rome or on the Paris *periphérique*, you've seen nothing. Indians don't drive, they *scythe*.

The more I thought about it, the more I realised that Indian driving was like their cricket. Their batting was cheeky, pushy, risky, there was a general absence of braking. It was erratic and balls, like cars, had a habit of shooting off at odd angles. The hullabaloo their fielders made as they swarmed round the bat was no different to the chaos and commotion on the roads. In fact the rules about horning and appealing were identical.

Only appeal/horn:
1. If a pad/car is in the way
2. If a pad/car isn't in the way
3. If the umpire is stressed/the roads are busy
4. If the umpire is calm/the roads are empty
5. At all other times

Into the Abyss
With daytime smog and nighttime power cuts, Calcutta, the venue for the first 1993 Test, remained something of a black hole. England fell straight into it, and never properly resurfaced. It was all very well Ted Dexter, the chairman of selectors, commissioning a study into whether the air pollution was contributing to the ill-health of the players. It was the selectors who seemed to have their heads in the clouds. On a dry, bare pitch, England chose four seamers, India picked three spinners. Once India won the toss and batted, the match was a foregone conclusion.

The Essex contingent, Gooch and Fletcher, claimed the pitch was reminiscent of a Chelmsford strip in late-summer, arguing that it helped all kinds of bowlers. They were really covering up for the fact that the self-belief of Emburey and Tufnell was in tatters after their savaging in previous matches. 'I told Goochie I don't feel all that confident about my bowling at the moment,' Emburey mumbled to me in the hotel foyer on the eve of the Test. I sympathised, but if I'd have informed the captain every time I felt like that, I'd never have made it on to the field.

My worst fears were realized. Azharuddin made a typically uninhibited hundred on the first day and the head wiggle was much in evidence. At times the ball pinged off his bat as if it was in a pin-ball machine. His chancy method represented quite a contrast from the elegant, classical style of the nineteen-year-old Tendulkar, already the scorer of six Test centuries. England had no answer to either.

At least the Indian tail was swiftly amputated on the second day. I notched the last four wickets. Well OK, that's a half-truth. I recorded them in the official score-book. When Clem Driver, the England scorer, was taken ill (probably knowing what was in store) I voluntarily stood in for the rest of the day. It finished with England five down for 88. I just wasn't destined to make a positive contribution to England's cause, even with a pencil.

You can walk to the Eden Gardens ground from the Oberoi Grand hotel across the Maidan. This vast swathe of parched grass underlines just how sports-mad the Bengalis are. Everywhere it is littered with impromptu games of cricket – splintering bat flayed unhesitatingly at pock-marked rubber ball – or football, or polo or a crowd gathered round to watch *kushtia*, bare-torsoed adolescents wrestling. Fortune tellers with card-picking parrots in cages inform you that 'India will win by eight wickets,' though you didn't need to be a clairvoyant to predict that.

By the end of the fourth day, India had bowled out England twice and needed only 43 more to win, with all second innings wickets intact and England couldn't wait to get out of Calcutta. I, however, had grown fond of the place. I loved the grand Victorian buildings peering through the smog, the huge bowl of the cricket ground filled with 75,000 thrilled supporters, the fantastic array of spicy food morsels for sale on the Maidan – the best lunch spread in the cricket world. I loved the cheerfulness of the people, making light of their poverty and squalor. I loved the fact that you could escape the chaos of the streets by riding Calcutta's underground, where there was no graffiti and hardly a scrap of litter to be found, and at Park Station there were TVs erected on the platform showing a video of the 1992 FA cup final between Liverpool and Sunderland.

I stood transfixed on the Howrah bridge, a great Meccano set of steel across the Hooghly river, watching the never-ending trudge of pedestrians filing across. Half a million people use the bridge every day, most ferrying goods to shops on foot because the trucks and cars and bullock carts trying to cross are stuck in perpetual grid-lock. I saw one man carrying a box the size of a garage on his head. He balanced it in place with one hand, while he pressed a transistor tuned to the cricket to his ear with the other. It seemed to give him extra strength. In India cricket refreshes the parts other creeds cannot reach.

Watching that scene, I understood why Indians are almost always smiling and outwardly happy. It's because their life is slow and largely unmechanized and they accept that and don't try to pack everything into a day. They don't have huge aspirations. They take pleasure and pride in fairly simple tasks (including beating England at cricket). The curse of the technological age is that we, with all our dishwashers and microwaveable food and Black and Deckers and automatic car washes, get totally stressed out trying to do too much at once. Basically, we're totally contrasting peoples. Indians are extremely bothered about cricket, and not particularly about life. The English are precisely the opposite.

I didn't attend the fifth day of the Test. The match was good as over, my *Sunday Independent* work was complete, and after six weeks in India I was ready for home. The only day off I'd had from travelling, wedding functions or writing cricket articles was spent on a windy, driftwood-strewn Mangalore beach reeking of dead fish. At Calcutta airport, I climbed aboard the 9.30a.m. Air India departure to Heathrow, just about the time the Indian openers resumed their pursuit of a total of 79 for victory. The jet climbed above the smog line, and was just levelling off as a voice crackled over the tannoy. 'Good morning ladies and gentlemen, this is your captain Rajesh Gupta speaking. We are now cruising at an altitude of 33,000 feet with a land speed of 540 miles an hour. The outside temperature is minus 60 degrees centigrade. The journey time to London is 10 hrs and 30 mins . . . And the score from Eden Gardens is India 57 for one, Prabhakar bowled Hick 13, Siddhu not out 35. India needs 22 for a great win . . . I hope you enjoy the flight.'

The Score

People		Beaches		Cricket		Catches		Total
6	+	3	+	8	×	1	=	17

12.
West Indies

Do's and Don'ts

After the 1993 Calcutta defeat, England lost ten of the next twelve Tests, and played predominantly catch-up cricket for the next five years. Australia, when trapped in a similar vortex in the mid eighties, promoted the game heavily and introduced their cricket academy. England, apart from a bit of superficial tinkering with the county championship, took little action. As usual, the powerlesses-that-be relied on the cycle of fortune turning things around.

In my Brentford bird-free zone, I took the opposite path. I joined two dating agencies. One paired me with Christine, a pot-holer with an incipient moustache. Over a Thai meal, she bored me rigid with tales of crawling about down sink holes at Malham Tarn. Her woolly jumper had that strange wet animal smell. I added her to the slobs and slags and Russian air-hostesses on my list of DWNs.

The other agency, Dinner Dates, brought sixteen men and sixteen women together at a dire establishment called Elephant on the River. It was Garfunkels with candles. There were four tables of eight and after each course, the men changed tables. I ended up sitting next to Elaine, a well-built Irish environmental health officer. When the Manhattan Transfer-cover band had wound up, she said, 'I'll buy yew a drenk if yew like.'

We went to a club. She didn't want to dance, just swig brandy. After several she said, 'I'll gif yew a left home if yew like.'

She came in for coffee. We watched a video.

'I need de batroom' she said.

She didn't come back for twenty minutes. I found her upstairs in my bed, naked. 'Yew can make love to me if yew like,' she said.

I escaped to the spare room and locked the door and added 'Irish environmental health officers' to my list of DWNs, which was lengthening alarmingly.

You would have thought by now, after all these escapades, I would have a vague understanding of womankind. In fact I was as mystified as ever. I'd hunted high and low and far and wide for the right girl, the DW who actually liked me and all my foibles, and I'd ended up with injured pride, a plummeting bank balance and drawers full of unused condoms. I didn't know where to look any more.

Perhaps I was trying too hard. I decided I'd purge my worries about sex, love and marriage by spending the winter of 1994 watching England on tour in the Caribbean. Pure, unadulterated indulgence. Quite apart from the hot sun and postcard-perfect beaches, the West Indies always held a fascination for me that had been only heightened by a brief trip to Barbados in 1987. I was intrigued to know how islands with less than 100,000 inhabitants could produce such a succession of brilliant match winners, how dynamic players like Collis King and Sylvester Clarke unleashed such potent skills fuelled only by rum and Red Stripe. Whether it was true about Malibu that 'when it pour, the sun shine'. I secretly wished I'd been born a West Indian.

They were still the kings of world cricket. They hadn't lost a Test series since my travels had begun in 1980. Their play might plumb the depths as well as scale the heights and it always made compulsive watching. In early January I booked myself on a two-month 'budget' supporters' tour taking in four Test matches and six islands. Eight weeks in the Caribbean with no strings attached. A sort of bumper episode of *Wish You Were Here*!

Before I left I threw a 'bad Christmas present' party at home. You brought one and left with another. In the Swinging Sixties it would have been wives. In the Consumerist Nineties it was dalmatian lavatory brush holders. I threw a load of dross into the mix. It was a final attempt to clear out the remaining flotsam in my life – the knick-knacks and kitsch souvenirs and bottles of undrunk Pimms I'd inherited from my benefit year. I cooked an enormous fish curry with enough chilli to blow up Birmingham and conned a hundred beers out of a friend who was a Guinness rep. This was going to be a party to remember.

It was. About 8.30p.m. my PR friend Jane arrived with a girlfriend in a black sweater and flares. Initially I thought PW. Within half an hour she was DDW. She had more than a passing resemblance to Helena Christensen, she was at least fifteen times more intelligent than me and she laughed when I made a plastic spider jump up someone's skirt. When she then ripped my mug tree off the kitchen wall, saying it was typical bachelor tat, I realised this was the sort of woman I needed. Someone who had swept in almost behind my back and would give my whole existence a good spring clean.

'Fancy spending a couple of weeks with me in the Caribbean?' I suddenly ventured casually.

'Too right I do,' she said. And that was that.

Well, not quite. Having endlessly circled the world like a wayward satellite, been in and out of love more times than Miss Piggy and then met a potential soul mate on my own front doorstep, I couldn't just dive in head first. I had to do a spot of paddling first. Over the next ten days we went out twice for dinner – during which we discovered our shared fear of electricity pylons and shared love of the Sex Pistols' version of *My Way* and she called me a div brain – and *then* I dived in. I booked a Friday night at Blakes hotel.

Blakes is the kind of place James Bond might take Pussy Galore if he was in London. Nestling in an unprepossessing street just off the Brompton Road, it's discreetly luxurious, with black and gilt decor, a black marble bathroom, a huge four poster bed covered with velvet cushions and a CD player hidden in a large ornate wardrobe. It was a totally seductive environment, until you saw the room service menu. The club sandwiches were £15. Each. We couldn't afford to eat anything else. It didn't matter a jot. A place like this makes women take leave of their senses. By Saturday morning Tanya and I were virtually married.

I Will

Timing – being in the right place at the right moment – equals harmony. I never had it, not in batting, nor in my brief term as a choir master, nor in relationships. A day after really connecting with a desirable, clever, funny, *available* girl, I was on an ugly, smelly, over-crowded Kenyan Airways flight to Nairobi. For practically the first time ever, I did not want to be sunning myself out of England in February. My first assignment for the *Daily Telegraph* – covering a tin-pot tournament in Kenya (the world cup for non-Test playing countries) – could not have come at a worse time.

I barely noticed the see-sawing matches under a cloud-less sky, or the Masai tribesman performing traditional dances in the hotel foyer, or the incessant clanking of building work outside my room, or even the leggy Dutch air-hostesses stretched out by the pool below. All I could think about was the girl who understood Fermat's Last Theorem, and loved Prokofiev and Prince and prawn vindaloo, and laughed when I deliberately fell off my chair.

After three days of long-distance pillow-talk, which at £7 a minute was running up a humungus phone bill, I knew this was it. A neon sign was flashing in my head saying 'Closure!' She'd hit my G-spot. It's the same sensation you get when you melt a blistering drive 300 yards dead straight, or scorch a thirty-yard volley into the top corner, or rip up the off stump with a booming outswinger. It happens once or twice in most of our lifetimes. And then it's gone and you're back to the slicing and the scuffing and spearing balls down the legside, and wishing you could've bottled that special feeling to have every morning with your muesli.

This was one of those bottling moments (the fact that I hate muesli is irrelevant). I acted on impulse. I faxed her a proposal of marriage. 'Fancy getting hitched sometime in June?' I wrote. Half an hour later I got a fax back. One word was written in huge capital letters, right across the page.

'YES.'

We had known each other eighteen days.

Corridors of Power

Before the wedding, the honeymoon in the West Indies. Naturally. I went out on my own beforehand to see some cricket as planned. I suppose you could call it a stag month. Georgetown, Guyana was the first port of call. Or it was supposed to be. My flight to Barbados was delayed by a bomb in London and I missed the Georgetown connection. There wasn't another one for two days.

There were some furrowed brows in the Barbados baggage hall. David Gower and Paul Allott were commentating on the Guyana Test, John Emburey was acting as England bowling coach and I was writing some columns for the *Telegraph*. The match began in twenty-four hours and Guyana was 1000 miles away. We'd checked all the airlines and seen all the shaking heads and resigned ourselves to watching the first two days on telly. We were just debating which hotel to book into when a local man in a white open-necked shirt approached us.

'It's Gower ain't it?'

'Er, could be,' said Gower.

'What you doin' here, man?' he went on. 'Test's in Guyana.'

'Well that's just the problem,' Gower said. 'The Test's in Guyana, and so's our plane.'

'Hey, we can't have a man like you not at de Test,' the guy said. 'I'll take y'all.'

He jangled a set of keys in his pocket and led the way through a side door, bypassing immigration, X-rays, all that sort of nonsense, onto the tarmac. Three jumbos were parked outside, and two smaller jets. There were no other planes in sight until we rounded the last jumbo. Obscured behind its back wheels was a tiny, unmarked craft with a single propeller and six seats. It was like a transit van with wings. We clambered in and sat with our bags on our knees as he cranked the engine up.

The sun was setting, and forty minutes into the flight night had fallen. There was no light in the cabin, except the illuminated pilot's instruments. We sat in the pitch dark not talking much. After about an hour, the pilot spoke.

'Shit, where we goin' again?' he said.

'Guyana,' someone replied.

'Oh yeah, right,' he mumbled, switching on a torch. He perused a map, then banked the plane sharply to the right. Land soon appeared below, and then an airport. We taxied off the runway and I saw a sign saying 'Welcome to Port of Spain.' We had landed in Trinidad.

'Can't land in Georgetown at night, man,' he said. 'Stay here and I'll take you in the morning.'

He was as good as his word. We took off at eight and within half an hour were flying along the coast of South America. Getting lower over Guyana, you could see water everywhere. Little florets of broccoli poked up out of it. Trees. We landed at Georgetown's tumbledown airport, and the pilot dropped us at the terminal.

'Enjoy!' he said, beaming. Then he turned the plane round and was gone. We never found out his name nor who he worked for and we never paid him a cent. Only in the West Indies, with its scattered layout and vague security and adulation of great Test cricketers, could this have happened.

The Bourda ground is attractive in a quaint kind of way.

The old wooden pavilion stands to one side on stilts, like many Georgetown buildings (the town is below sea level) and the other enclosures are topped with red or green tin roofs. It's backed by palm trees from which spectators really do hang for a good, free view. The public stand is a real melting pot of fine-boned Afro-Indian faces and the atmosphere is heavy with humidity and the sounds of impassioned spectators. Outside haggard coconut salesmen bray and buses parp. It feels like the tropics. I liked it.

Not many of the England players did, though. There were no practice facilities and they mistrusted the pie-crust pitch and the rutted outfield and when the West Indies batted, they had to keep picking the ball out of the smelly dyke that ran around the boundary. They were already disgruntled by having to share their poky, triangular hotel rooms with each other and the odd cockroach, yet stayed put because they felt the food in outside restaurants was too ropey to risk. Only Atherton, Smith and Tufnell ventured out much, and in the latter two cases they tended to go to the other extreme.

So by night they suffered self-inflicted imprisonment and by day they were manacled by the West Indians' four-pronged pace attack, probing down a relentless corridor. You looked at the England team man for man, and you could see that overall they were too mollycoddled and self-satisfied to put up much of a fight, and that was partly county cricket's pampering fault.

I suppose you also had to feel for the England batsmen up against Ambrose, Walsh and the two Benjamins – fearsome speedsters all – knowing that the ammunition was being returned by Lewis, Fraser, Igglesden and Salisbury. With due respect to Fraser, this was cannons against peashooters. Lara made a hundred, Chanderpaul, the local teenage débutante, added an impudent fifty.

Having won the Jamaica Test, West Indies were heading for a 2–0 lead in the series.

England players often imply these overseas tours are glum rather than glam because there's never any time to sightsee. There is if you make half an effort. On the rest day in Guyana, a few snappers and journos boarded a launch and motored inland up the wide, copper-coloured Demerara river. We branched off up a small inlet and were soon in thick rain forest. The trees hemmed us in and shaded us from the sun. It was cool and tranquil. It could have been deepest Amazonia.

There was a village in a small clearing and we moored and went ashore. Here, about 200 miles from the Brazilian border, you expected to see lots of miniature Peles running around showing off enviable dribbling skills and shouting 'GOOOAAAAALLL! In fact, there were little kids mucking about with a ball, but they were playing cricket not football. The wicket was the base of a palm tree, two bowlers alternated from the same end with a half-eaten rubber ball which leapt or crept off the uneven ground, and there were about twenty enthusiastic fielders. You batted on until you were out. I lasted six balls.

A tiny lad, knee-high to a Guyanese cockroach, hooked and cut fearlessly, dabbed and glided other deliveries, reacting nimbly to the misbehaviour of the ball. He wielded a bat that was far too big for him for nigh on half an hour. I bowled a few at him, getting quicker and quicker until I let one go flat out. He uppercut it into a wooden school hut. 'Come on sir, bowl one really fast,' the fielders shouted.

Chanderpaul had himself learnt to play in such surroundings, and you could see it in his batting. Neat, dapper, resourceful and totally uninhibited. He larrupped his fourth ball in Test cricket through extra cover for four, and continued to play as if he was with his mates beside a creek. Yet if he'd been English, his grotesque hunch at the crease would have been dissected, his cranky grip disrupted and his natural game destroyed. It's all style over substance, English cricket.

We continued on up the tributary, arriving eventually at a place where the river widened into a sort of bulb shape. There was a landing stage and a huge timber retreat built on top of a low hill. We spent a few hours there, eating a delicious fish lunch, lounging around in hammocks or basket chairs under silent fans. All you could see was the water and the tall grasses and the forest beyond. Later, when it had got cooler, we canoed around a flooded meadow teeming with bird life, before cruising back to Georgetown. This is the pleasurable, tantalizing part of the Caribbean touring cricketers rarely see.

The beach by the players' hotel was strewn with boulders and assaulted by a mucky sea, so they'd remained by the pool most of the day, grumbling about the humidity and the steak sandwiches and the caustic newspaper reports (Colin Croft had suggested in the *Guyana Chronicle* that Graeme Hick was a coward and 'should be sent home.') None had come on our trip, but I felt if some had done it might have been enlightening and alleviated their stress. If nothing else, on that clearing-by-the-water they could at least have faced some local bowlers who were under 6ft. 4in.

Lofty Heights
The tour moved on to Trinidad. Port of Spain doesn't fit the stereotyped image of the blissful, recuperative Caribbean at all. Hemmed in by hills, it's a polyglot with criminal tendencies that doesn't have a beach or a pretty

harbour, and the main modes of transport are not Escorts or Mokes but long, throbbing, old limousines. It feels more like El Salvador with an accompanying gun-toting culture. Even Lara, the national hero, was mugged and all his gear stolen, though when the thieves discovered his identity, they returned it.

Both teams stayed at the Hilton, which seemed safe enough atop a cliff overlooking the Queens' Park Savannah, and provided a caged walkway to the popular Pelican Inn. On a budget, I was obliged to share my room with a travelling England supporter, a Lancashire fan of twenty-five going on fifty who went to bed about five hours before I did wearing his blue, Mike Watkinson replica Sunday-league shirt.

If Calcutta boasts the best array of food at any Test match ground, Queen's Park Oval comes a close second. Underneath the main stand are chicken, burger and curry stalls, and best of all the biggest variety of rotis west of Shepherds Bush market. West Indian cuisine is nothing to write home about, but rotis – savoury rolled-up pancakes with a spicy meat or fish filling – are special. Here, apart from the inevitable beef and chicken rotis, they also had jerk pork, goat, prawn, cuttle fish and lobster. Great hot for lunch and also, cold, to soak up half a gallon of Red Stripe at midnight. Rotis, for me, always evoke the image of the Barbadian fast bowler Wayne Daniel bringing armfuls of them up to the Lord's dressing room for Sunday lunch, and eating them as he described his latest conquest.

The Test was surprisingly well-contested for three and a half days, and the crowd were absorbed. I was struck by the depth of their cricket knowledge, dopey-looking rastas revealing a precise appreciation of Bradman's greatest performances or the impact of Bodyline. They observed the tense struggle keenly, only occasionally imploring an obdurate Jimmy Adams to 'Givvit some licks, man!'

The match exploded into life at just after 4.30p.m. on the fourth day, when England set out to chase a gettable 194 for a victory that would have got them back in the series. Curtly Ambrose, riled by his colleagues after getting out heaving wildly, tore in to bowl, arms pumping like pistons. Atherton, surprised by the accuracy and speed of the first ball, was palpably lbw, Ramprakash, in a tizz, ran himself out off the sixth. Several overs later, Smith's stumps had been shattered by sheer pace, Hick had touched a snorter to the keeper, and Stewart's off stump was cartwheeled backwards as if it had been dynamited. With Ambrose in this mood, Thorpe and Russell were chicken feed. He had taken 6–10 in eight torrid overs, and England were 40–8.

In the post-mortems, Bob Willis described the England batting as like 'rabbits in headlights.' Willis never had to face Ambrose. I did (though not usually for very long). There can't have ever been a bowler harder to combat. He is, at 6ft. 9in., the tallest paceman that ever played Test cricket and that's the main problem, rather than pure speed. The ball is delivered from three feet above your own eyeline. You have to look up, then sharply down, as it's banged into the turf, then up again as it leaps towards your chest. Sometimes you lose sight of it for the crucial quarter of a second before it re-emerges in front of your face. That's the headlight, and you're the rabbit about to be wasted.

You know his good length ball and his rib tickler pitch only two yards apart. He's so accurate and his action is so rhythmical it's hard to distinguish them. You tell yourself it's best to try and inch forward to him, as a first line of defence. The head is willing but the legs aren't. It's not fear, but common sense. You know you might be smelling one in a minute, and you'll whiplash backwards and punch it tamely to backward short leg.

Engaging him in pleasant conversation at the non striker's end – saying 'Terribly hot, isn't it?' or admiring his three heavy gold chains – doesn't pay dividends either. In fact it makes him madder. Batting against Ambrose is like facing someone wanging down one of those super balls on to crazy paving. He could make leadshot bounce off a sandbag.

Sandbags is what England needed when the match resumed on the fifth day, but the last two wickets yielded only a further six runs, beating by just one England's lowest total of all time (in 1886). A post-match banner appeared reading: 'The Philadelphia 76ers, the San Francisco 49ers, the England 46ers.' The West Indies had taken an unassailable 3–0 lead in the series. Again.

'I understand how important it is to play my cricket hard,' Ambrose said afterwards. 'I do it for the people. They expect nothing less and we're very conscious of them whenever we take the field. Their love is very strong. It is demanding on you, but it also makes you strong.' There's a living bond between the West Indian players and the public. It fortifies the team. Materialism hadn't penetrated West Indian society yet. They were the best cricket team in the world and the success enriched the people's daily lives. Whereas our spirits were gladdened by *Noel's House Party* and *Blankety Blank*.

I took advantage of the match's early finish to try and find a decent beach. The limo-taxi had a TV in the back. The highlights of the match were on. The driver kept slowing down and craning his neck back round the headrest to see the action. When Stewart was bowled reducing England to 27–6 he said, 'Ambrose – he the minister of defence.'

I sat on Maracas beach, a pleasant cove, and watched some stringy local lads playing cricket at the surf's edge. As the wave receded they skimmed a hairless tennis ball off the thin film of water at the batsman's ribs.

Most chucked rather than bowled, and had open-chested actions, like many West Indian greats. On a sloping beach they couldn't do otherwise. Running at right angles to the gradient, they would have over-balanced if they'd adhered to the rigid MCC 'sideways-on' guidelines. Their front-on actions had evolved to avoid falling over on the sand. Then on grass, they had found it a better and less injury-prone way of bowling fast.

I had experimented with this approach myself, with promising results. Doing an open-chested Courtney Walsh impression, I'd got more pace and bounce. But it was frowned on by coaches, most of whom were indoctrinated by tradition and history. English fast bowling has been hampered for thirty years by Fred Trueman telling everyone to 'Get seydweys, lad, and bool artswing like I did.'

Enthused about my new thesis, I approached the normally taciturn Ambrose sitting on his own in the hotel snack bar, to explore it further. 'Hi Curtly, can I talk to you for a minute?' I enquired.

'What about?' he asked, barely looking up.

'You and your bowling style after that fantastic spell,' I said, assuming flattery would break the ice.

'Probably not,' he said.

'Oh . . . well how about later, after you've finished eating,' I persisted.

'Definitely not,' he said.

Disturbed Dreams

The pre-wedding honeymoon began in Grenada. It's a good place to start. A rugged coast is peppered with dazzling beaches set against a lush, mountainous backdrop. It's a calm, leisurely pace of winding lanes and brightly-coloured wooden houses, and if you crave an escapist type of life with week-old papers and an exclusive diet of conch, nutmeg and bananas, then it's for you.

Tanya arrived from Britain at 9a.m., and we transferred straight on to a small plane for a day trip with other journalists. Half an hour later we touched down at Union Island, population about twelve, half of whom ran the airport. Two were sat outside behind a low table which said 'Immigration.' One of the most annoying things about the Caribbean is its petty bureaucracy. When you go island hopping you have to take your passport, and fill in an embarkation form, and often change currency, every time you land, even if you've only 'hopped' about five miles. My wallet was already stuffed with Barbados dollars, Guyanese dollars, US dollars (for Trinidad) and Eastern Caribbean dollars (for Grenada). I could have started one of those coin-waterfalls you get in amusement arcades.

After passing 'immigration', we were led by a comatose individual to a school bus and driven approximately 200 yds at 5m.p.h. to a jetty. From there a launch took us to a sixty-foot yacht on which we spent the rest of the day. In fifteen years of following the sun, I think this was the first time I'd experienced a holiday-brochure day. Cruising the azure sea on a yacht laden with grub and grog, snoozing on deck under a parasol, dropping anchor at coral reefs or tiny atolls to swim and snorkel under a powdered sapphire sky. It was the day of our tropical imagination . . .

Until we got back to the Grenada hotel and our torsos and thighs had fully cooked. I couldn't sit down or lie on my back for three days. They don't show you that bit on *Wish You Were Here*.

England were playing a meaningless game against a Board XI in Grenada, and my journalistic attendance wasn't required. When the sunburn had calmed down, Tanya and I decided to take off and try to find our Dream Beach. The criteria was a secluded cove off the beaten track, with gently lapping, turquoise water, a distant boat or two lolling on the horizon, and clusters of palm trees cradling a virginal sweep of cocaine-white sand on which we could do things to each other with baby oil you couldn't normally do in the open air. There would be no people, and no jet skis. 'Try a nuclear test zone,' the bloke at reception suggested.

We hired a four-wheel drive and drove along the south coast, round headlands and through contentedly-ramshackle hamlets, stopping to allow a kid to bowl across the road at his father. The road climbed, and down below we could see the kind of little bays we were looking for. We stopped at a village store and were directed back two miles to an unmarked track which plunged into dense forest. The trail jackknifed between rocks and boulders, several of which we had to move to progress.

Eventually it flattened out and led to a secluded cove with gently lapping, turquoise water etc. It was at least five miles from the nearest road or house, down a practically impassable track, sheltered by thickly-wooded cliffs on either side, and clusters of palms swaying in a soft breeze. It felt like a bit of undiscovered paradise. No one would find us here. It was the beach in *Blue Lagoon* and I had my very own Brooke Shields. We laid out our towels, stripped naked and dived in the water for an 'aperitif'.

We were just starting to wade back to shore for the main course, when there was a rustling in the trees, and two small children appeared. Eight others followed behind, accompanied by parents, uncles and aunts. An entire congregation descended on our little hideaway. We lurked waist-deep in the water knowing topless/nude sunbathing is banned in the Caribbean and hoping they were on their way to somewhere else. Instead, one stuck three sticks into the sand, another produced a bat and ball and the rest spread out across the beach. The 'pitch' was directly between us and our clothes.

We couldn't really stay in the water waiting until the game had finished. It might have been a forty-over match. We had to swallow our humiliation and risk arrest to make a run for it. Just as I was making the quick dash round behind them the ball was hit in my direction and I instinctively dived and caught it. There was quite a commotion amongst the fielders. I couldn't tell whether they were cheering, laughing or cussing. It was probably the first time a streaker had ever taken a wicket. I overcame my embarrassment to bowl a couple of (wicketless) overs. When a kid of about twelve advanced up the pitch and clogged my attempted yorker into the sea, I faked an injury and escaped back to my towel.

I endured Tanya's laughter and thought it was a damn good thing I hadn't met her while this was happening to me every week on the field with all its accompanying mood swings. The game continued for a while. I was struck by the players' enthusiasm, their excellent ball sense and their genuine delight at putting one over a white man. West Indians always seem to be particularly fired-up against England. People pointed at the 'black power' thing for an explanation, their physical superiority giving them the chance to lord it over their old 'masters'.

Some said cricket appealed to a West Indian's psyche because it had all the ingredients of their music – reggae (slow, laid-back) rap (fast, aggressive) and calypso (syncopated, happy). These factors may have contributed to the West Indies' recent domination of world cricket. But sweating profusely on a scorching Grenada beach, watching a bowler amble slowly back to his mark, you saw why the sport had prospered there. Because, in the Caribbean, it's too darn hot to play football.

Pinky Winkies
Two Bajans were standing behind the nets watching England and the West Indies practise at the Bridgetown Oval.

'De rasshole Hooper . . . w'happenin man?' one said.

' 'Ima livin at de well-head, 'im alookin like a molly-booby yano,' the other replied. 'I'ma de coach, I'ma giving 'e de jook.'

'Ya man. An 'im dat Richarrrdsonnn. 'E 'ain't givin'em no licks. Whassamatta?'

'Wullos, dey tink 'e a mob o 'ton batsman, be kiss. Dem rasshole chiefs is madstaggers.'

Having shared a dressing room with Bajans for many years, listening to them chattin' breeze, I thought I had a reasonable grasp of their lingo. I had little idea of what these guys were saying. They kept nodding in agreement, but I'm not entirely sure they really knew, either. I've yet to see a West Indian look totally mystified and say to his mate, 'Hey man, speak slower. What you on about?' Maybe they're too proud to admit it.

A barrel-chested figure in a vest and shorts hobbled over to where England were practising to have a chat with Alec Stewart. It was his old Surrey colleague, the fearsome West Indian fast bowler Sylvester Clarke who had recently retired, to an entire generation of batsmen's great relief. Clarke had two lengths – short and very short – and two speeds – fast and exocet. He clanged as many helmets as he took wickets (942). More than one top county batsman suddenly developed a mysterious hamstring strain if Clarke was declared fit. He was prone to injury (as well as often neglecting to go to bed) but most people still felt it was a travesty he only played eleven times for the West Indies.

He ambled into the England nets, and despite having just staggered, in trainers and no socks, from three hours' sleep, he soon had Graham Thorpe hopping about so much, Thorpe politely asked him to leave off. Clarke retired to the bar and, knowing he was amusing company (off the field), I joined him for a drink. A TV was on in the corner broadcasting an interview with Clive Lloyd.

'Isn't that the bloke who ruined your Test career?' I asked.

'No man,' he said, and stared at his beer glass. *'That* ruined my Test career.'

(Perhaps his life too. He died suddenly in December 1999, aged 44).

Another of their great heroes, the towering Joel Garner – known locally as 'Big Bird' – was at large in the players' hotel. A female England supporter had taken a bit of a shine to him. 'Here, are you built in proportion?' she asked suggestively, admiring his 6ft. 7in. physique.

'Lady, if I were built in proportion, I'd be 8ft. 10,' Garner said.

Away from the coastal drag of hotels and mansions, Barbados is quiet and unassuming, typified by dead sugar cane plantations, gingerbread houses and wooden churches. It's a slow place where gaggles of men linger in the shade playing dominoes and the fire engines travel at

20m.p.h. Yet this mellow island, barely larger than the Isle of Wight and founder of the hammock, has produced some of the most fearsome fast bowlers in the world. Hall and Griffith began the sequence, which continued through Boyce, Holder, Garner, Daniel, Clarke, and the mercurial Malcolm Marshall. The sound of a loo flushing was usually audible before an English batsman emerged to face any of these men.

Why Barbados (and latterly Antigua) should have unearthed so many demons is hard to fathom, though the loose-limbedness of most people in the Caribbean and the lack of treacherous, slippery grass, must have been an advantage. Local circumstances certainly played their part, but Clive Lloyd identifies county cricket as the catalyst for West Indies' fast bowling might and their late-twentieth century invincibility.

'Playing in England taught all of us to be much more professional,' he said. 'With the intensity of cricket there, batting and bowling four or five times a week, you become physically and mentally fitter and learn to perform in different conditions. Being an overseas player meant you had to perform for your county. It made us harder, stronger and better.'

There for once, is English cricket in credit. Unfortunately it's been counter-productive.

Sir Garfield Sobers is Barbados's greatest icon, of course. He reigns supreme. That April (1994) his name was plastered all over Bridgetown, since it was forty years since his first Test appearance. There were special race meetings, golf days and banquets to commemorate it. They really know how to *laud* their heroes in the West Indies.

Tanya and I got tickets to a celebration night in a large concert hall. It mainly featured local personalities standing on stage delivering laborious monologues about Sobers' life, interspersed with some lame music. Sobers sat in the front row lapping it all up and came on stage towards the end to tumultuous applause. He even danced sedately to a Calypso version of 'One step forward, two steps back,' which, it occurred to me, English cricket might adopt.

Typically, England were doing their play-well-when-they've-lost-the-series bit again. They won the Barbados Test because of Stewart's two dashing centuries, Fraser's eight wickets and at least 7000 Brits, on £400 package-holidays, crammed into the ground. It was like a home game. The supporters were insurance salesmen, lift engineers and retired gas fitters from Walsall who'd traded up from their annual pilgrimage to Torremelinos. With its affordable price, all day breakfasts and cocktail happy hours, Barbados was the new Costa del Sol.

This paunchy, peeling rent-a-crowd were issued with the generic term – Winkies (Wankers Incorporated) – by the British press. They wore loud polyester leisure wear or replica football strips – the only things brighter than their reddened faces – were herded round in buses and, for the most part, moaned about the ineptitude of British sportsmen. Even Botham and Gascoigne got some flak. We really know how to *lambast* our heroes in England.

The Winkies were in full voice as England gradually got the upper hand in the Test, but they were more than matched by the Bajans, yelling their own brand of cricketing cat-calls:

'Wet him, wet him' – hit out
'Give em licks/lashes' – ditto
'Don't hide de ball' – stop bowling negatively
'Put it in de mud' – bowl him a bouncer
'He's a molly-booby' – he's a rabbit.

But as the West Indies slipped to defeat, they could only console themselves by grunting 'Dungalong batsman he,' meaning, basically, that the player was from another island. It was a side swipe at the fact that only one Bajan, Desmond Haynes, had made the team. The inter-island rivalry in the Caribbean is on a par with the mutual animosity between Australia and New Zealand (or England and France). Funny what a bit of in-between sea does to people.

Wet Dreams

Seeing England beat the West Indies in Barbados for the first time in fifty-nine years was a never-to-be-repeated experience. So was staying in a luxurious house on the island's west coast. Some fashion-industry friends of Tanya's had rented it for a fortnight and invited us to stay. The house was called The Dream, and it was. Set back from the road down a tree-lined drive, it was a whitewashed double-storey building draped in purple bougainvillaea. There was an adjacent pool and the garden gate led straight on to a private beach.

The interior of the house felt colonial, with wooden floors, tasteful antique furniture and white shutters opening on to a tiled verandah. It looked straight on to what felt like your own little tranche of the Caribbean sea. You couldn't see another dwelling anywhere. During the day, tall palms – nature's venetian blinds – filtered the sun's rays. As dusk fell the sea kaleidoscoped, twinkling turquoise, green, purple, orange, red, blue and black. It was mesmerising.

The house had five bedrooms, two maids – O'Hara and Jennifer – Armstrong, the old gardener with a rich laugh that revealed three teeth like stumps, and there were no jet skis in sight or sound. I could have happily spent the rest of my life there, swimming, diving, running on the beach. The letting agent, a fat white Bajan, brought me back to reality.

'I could happily spend the rest of my life here,' I told him.

'You can,' he said. 'The rent is £8000 a week, or you can buy it for a snip at £10m.'

This explains why most of the American and European inhabitants of Barbados are ancient and decrepit, and only occasionally seen hobbling into a waiting car. The sad fact is that by the time foreigners have accumulated enough money to live there, they are too old and lame to get out much.

Another problem with Barbados is ganja. If the locals are fond of smoking it, they're even fonder of selling it. The posher the house, the pushier they are, the more potent it is. Hash, dope, pot, grass, weed. Look, I don't know the difference between any of them. But the stuff our fashion-pack friends bought must have been skunk. It certainly smelt like one, and tasted worse. One drag and I started sweating and my face turned green and this terrible nausea swelled up inside me. I felt as if I was going to burst. Two yards from the door, I did, through my mouth. The chunder was so violent it soiled a wall and penetrated the wiring. A repaint and moderate repairs were needed. The house had probably decreased in value by £2000.

I lay in bed, a bucket at my side, watching the room spin round faster than the ceiling fan, thinking this wasn't quite 'the dream' I thought. I also realised that even if I inflicted similar damage on all the walls in the place, I still couldn't afford it.

Simply the Best
Tanya flew home after Barbados, to set about planning the

wedding. We'd known each other only six weeks, but we were definitely going to go through with it. There was absolutely no reason not to. We were totally ourselves with each other, it felt like we'd been mates for years. She was nothing like the Cameron Diaz DW I originally visualized I'd marry. She was dark-haired, fair-skinned and northern-veined and she wore chic A-line tunics rather than tight trousers or minis. That was good. I wanted to marry an eating, talking, laughing, walking, living doll, not a clothes horse. Maybe I was finally growing up.

There seemed to be a symbiosis about our relationship too. She was organised, I wasn't. She had taste, I didn't. She was rather intolerant, I was acquiescent. She'd seen every Katherine Hepburn movie, I'd seen every Laurel and Hardy film. She said batth, I said barth. She was way above my intellectual station, but marriage isn't an episode of *Mastermind*, and I was good at shoulder massages. Neither of us cared much about money. Both of us cared a lot about each other.

I popped over to Antigua for the fifth Test. It's a much poorer, more spartan place than Barbados, though it does claim to have a beach for every day of the year. Brian Lara totally dominated the match. He made 164 not out on the first day, converted it to 320 not out during the second, and broke the world Test record on the third. He said before the series, in a tone of ambition rather than arrogance, that he would make a triple hundred during it. In Antigua it seemed almost pre-destined as soon as he took guard. The wicket was flat, he had all weekend to bat and the England bowlers, to a man, wished they were back home repairing the trellis.

Lara's innings was riveting and chanceless with clean, pure shots and an amazingly consistent rate of scoring. It didn't seem to matter where the fielders were, or how many. Almost every stroke seemed laser-guided into gaps. Viv Richards, wearing a fetching green trilby with a feather in the band, watched it from the press box next to me. Occasionally a smile penetrated his slightly distant expression. When Lara flicked one nonchalantly over mid wicket, he muttered 'Shot, shot' though it sounded more like 'shat.' He said he was doing the odd bit of junior coaching in Antigua. 'If a young man have some shots, I can teach him defence,' he said. 'But ain't no good if he don't have no shots.'

It reminded me of the way Viv used to bat – blaze away when he first came in, then have a look later, once he'd asserted himself. He was the very antithesis of the MCC coaching manual and when he first came to England, people predicted he wouldn't get far because his technique was all wrong. He made just the small matter of 8540 Test runs for the West Indies, average 50.23. Not bad for a bloke who played across the line too much.

That other slouch Garfield Sobers watched his own record (365 not out) being broken by Lara with a classic cover drive, followed by a jump pull that almost caused him to fall on the stumps. The England fielders converged on Lara to congratulate him. It was the closest most of them had been to him for two days. Later Sobers made a statement in his rather know-allish way: 'It was a record that was always going to be broken, and I think Brian Lara was the only person playing who could have broken it. If you watch him play, you never see him use his pad. He hits the ball with the bat, and that's the way the game should be played.' Confucius say the simplest methods are often the best.

In the aftermath party behind the stand, numerous people were claiming credit for Lara's skill saying they had coached him or encouraged him to give himself room to hit the ball. Actually, the reason's simpler. It's because, when they learn the game in their back yards and dusty paddocks, they use such a variety of skin-piercing objects for a ball (scrunched-up Coke cans, jagged coconut shells) they make *sure* they hit it. It's no coincidence that a clip off the legs is described, in West Indian lingo, as 'come offa my sore toe.'

I savoured the atmosphere in the Antigua ground – the iron band, Chikkies disco between overs, Gravy the cross-dresser, all the whistles and trumpets. It was a celebration of the game. In the Caribbean cricket was fun, an entertainment, not the joyless, mundane pastime it had become back home. The polarised views of the bouncer put this into context. In the West Indies it was regarded as a thrilling thing, like a busty woman revealing her cleavage. Batsmen 'rose' to the challenge. In England it was seen as degrading, like a brassy woman revealing her arse. Batsmen froze to the effrontery.

During the open-air carnival the night after the third day's play, the West Indian side appeared on stage to the delight of the huge crowd. Lara sang 'Rally round the West Indies' and Ambrose and Richardson accompanied on borrowed guitars. Later, I saw the triumphant West Indies captain dripping with gold jewellery and draped with adoring girls. I thought back to Mike Gatting, stripped of the England captaincy after an (alleged) trivial dalliance with a barmaid. In Antigua, there would only be an inquisition if Richardson *wasn't* frolicking with local women. Top West Indian cricketers are bonded by two common denominators. Regional solidarity and siring five children by three different women.

When the match resumed, England admirably matched the West Indies 593–5 with exactly the same score themselves. Atherton made a hundred and so did Robin Smith. It was not a match for bowlers. Michael Holding, looking on from the commentary box said, 'Man, I'm glad I've retired.' If he, Whispering Death – the silent exterminator of batsmen – said that then I, Noisy Giver of Life, could only agree.

I was also glad to leave the Caribbean. I never thought I'd say that, but eight weeks of unremitting heat and dazzling light and interminable Calypso actually does your head in. You crave a view of a lake or a cascading waterfall and the sounds of Schubert rather than jangling soca forever drifting across another perfect palm-fringed beach towards the perpetually glittering sea. It'd be nice to have a day when you don't have to wear shades to order breakfast (and get it at lunchtime). It'd be nice to eat something other than flying fish and bananas. And, to be honest, it'd be nice to get away from a place where petrol-pump attendants and taxi-drivers say, 'We might have beaten you last time, but now we're gonna give you a damn good lickin'.'

The Score

People		Beaches		Cricket		Catches		Total
7	+	8	+	9	×	1*	=	24

*Again, I had to bend the figures a little because, if I hadn't included my wife-to-be as a 'catch' the total would have come out at 0. I'd actually rate the Caribbean on a par with Perth (34).

13.
Pakistan

From London to Lahore

Four months after meeting, Tanya and I were married in Chelsea. It was a bright, gusty day that went perfectly to plan, until the honeymoon was delayed for twelve hours because I'd mislaid my passport. I'd yakked around the world for fourteen years travelling nearly 200,000 miles largely without a hitch, only to mess up the most important journey of my life.

Luckily, I didn't mess up too much else. That summer, I tried extra hard not to do the things women hate – forget to put the loo seat down, leave little bits of washing-up undone, steal the duvet, wash your smelly running socks with her cashmere cardigans, help stick-thin girls with their luggage on the escalator. And I tried extra hard to overlook the things women do that men hate – never knowing the way anywhere, painting their nails when you're eating, keeping the duvet on in a heatwave, never being able to find anything in their overloaded handbags.

I was relaxed and stimulated and happy. Happy as a man in a Porsche 911, a woman in Harvey Nicks, a kid in a bouncy castle. I'd been bitten by the love bug.

I hadn't totally rid myself of the travel one, either. When the *Daily Telegraph* asked me to cover England's A tour to Pakistan in late 1995, I jumped at the chance. It was the one Test country I hadn't visited and Pakistan's cricketers had been the surprise package of the early nineties. It was a much discredited place, but if it was good enough for Jemima Goldsmith, one of the most eligible girls in London, then it was worth a look.

Jemima had recently tied the knot with the great Pakistan allrounder and lothario Imran Khan. Fashionable women marrying cricketers-turned-*Telegraph*-columnists was suddenly in vogue. The only difference between the Khans and the Hughes's was 362 Test wickets, assets of about £120million and the possibility of becoming Pakistan's prime minister. Not a lot really.

I bumped into them at Lahore airport when they'd just arrived back from honeymoon. While Jemima managed the bags, Imran strolled about exchanging small talk and invited me to tea. Well, he'd clattered me over the head with the ball often enough, so he owed me a gesture of goodwill.

They don't live in an outrageously glamorous house. It's a red brick villa, just off a busy main road. The living room is stashed with dark sideboards and chests, tarnished silver pots and a collection of fearsome tribal hunting knives. Also a treadmill, fixed at an alarmingly steep gradient. 'It was a wedding present,' Jemima said. 'I try to do at least twenty minutes running on it each day.' Well, she can hardly go for a jog in the local park.

The subject of ball tampering soon cropped up. Imran launched into a laborious monologue, explaining (for Jemima's benefit) how a ball swung, about the coarse outfields in Pakistan and that when bowlers roughed the ball up, they were only enhancing a natural process. He began to get quite vehement in defence of the bowler's art, ridiculing cricket's old-fashioned laws, until Jemima lifted her hand slightly. 'Shush, Imran, shush,' she said persuasively. He shushed. There was a pause while she absorbed the information. Then she said, 'Well it sounds as if the bowlers *were* unfairly altering the ball's condition.' What do women know of men's darkest secrets? Quite a lot actually.

Clearly it is Jemima's spirit, as well as her beauty and her father's wealth and power, that Imran had found so attractive. Timing was also a factor. Imran's priorities in life were once described by Garth le Roux, his South African pace partner at Sussex, as 'sex, money and cricket – in that order.' Retiring from sport seemed to reduce his testosterone-overload (I could relate to that, knowing how a successful day on the field produces an irresistible urge to immediately plant your seed somewhere) and he was ready to get hitched.

The stress of third world living – the perpetual power cuts, the unreliable phones, the constant stares – had obviously taken their toll on Jemima, but she wasn't submitting meekly. 'I deliberately haven't searched out British people in Pakistan,' she said. 'This is my home now so I want to immerse myself in the culture. That way I'll understand it quicker.'

That was vastly at odds with many of the England A team who only ventured outside the hotel to go to the ground or the nearby British High Commission, and passed up the excellent local cuisine in favour of munching on the tins of spam, processed cheese and Wagon Wheels they'd lugged from home.

Fists and Fire

I spent six weeks in Pakistan. Although there's only a twenty-five per cent literacy rate, and Imran had warned of impending anarchy if nothing was done, it felt less chaotic and more prosperous than India. Cars, buildings and people were generally in better condition. Loosely speaking, Islam is a more fundamental, all-consuming religion than Hinduism, Muslims focus on 'total sacrifice' during life – hoping, after death, to be saved rather than damned.

While Indians are naturally meeker, Pakistanis have a smash and grab approach, consistent with the fact that there's no word for 'please' in Urdu. I think it's this complete, almost blinkered, commitment to a doctrine that explains why the Pakistan cricket team is generally tougher and more successful than the Indian one, despite their coaches to-ing and fro-ing more often than National Express. It's not a matter of talent, it's a matter of attitude.

It helps that of the 60 million males in Pakistan, about 59.99 million want to be fast bowlers (the other 0.01m are double-jointed spinners). Everywhere you looked in Lahore, Islamabad or Peshawar, there were youths charging in to bowl, hair and shirt-tails flapping, on pitches and concrete paddocks. Like their heroes Wasim and Waqar, their cheeks quivered and their run ups left vapour trails, before they unleashed, with beautifully athletic actions, a vicious bouncer or a toe-crunching yorker. The taped-up tennis ball they played with swung like a boomerang once half of it had been scuffed up.

Exuberant batsmen hit out lustily in these playground games. It was pulsating stuff. This is the source of their fast bowling conveyor belt, and a young lad called Shoaib Akhtar was plucked off it rather prematurely to play in a trial against England A. He bowled a lot of fast rubbish, but you could see the raw talent, the Waqar-like approach, and an equally wandering eye when some girls appeared on the ground.

The spectators at this match in Lahore were almost exclusively men, squatting on the grass in small gaggles. During a sultry afternoon, the soporific atmosphere was suddenly broken by a violent scuffle in one of these groups. All its members scattered to other parts of the ground, before reconvening a few minutes later, all smiles. After some time I cautiously approached to find out what had happened.

'Rashid, over there, bet Fahad ten rupees that the next over would be a maiden . . .' said a man who called himself Mohammed (as about 50 per cent of men do in Pakistan, the equivalent, I suppose, of every man in Britain calling themselves Jesus or Melvyn).

'. . . There was a leg bye off the last ball and Fahad demanded his money, but Rashid wouldn't pay up. So they had a fight.'

'Who won?' I asked.

'Fahad,' Mohammed said. 'He's a policeman.'

Sports betting in Pakistan is like exceeding the speed limit in the west. Illegal and compulsory.

In a similar way to Guayana – on the South American mainland – Pakistan is a cricketing gateway that has become an outpost. While the sport's spread beyond Guyana is hampered by the surrounding countries speaking Portuguese, in Pakistan it's hampered by the surrounding Himalayas. Most of the peaks in the north are over 8000 metres, including K2, the second highest mountain in the world at 8611 metres.

We flew over them all one morning in a trip kindly facilitated by the ECB chief executive, Tim Lamb, who was out on a recce before the 1996 World Cup (England were going to be based in Pakistan). Personally, I thought he should have been investigating ground facilities or spying on players rather than gazing at mountains from a plane, but I suppose you do need some time off.

Undoubtedly Pakistan's isolation – mountains to the north and west, sea to the south and India to the east – has contributed to the individuality of the country's cricket culture. With its legion of fast bowlers and swashbuckling batsmen led by the portly Inzamam-ul-Haq, Pakistan is, in many ways, the new Caribbean. Just don't go there for a beach holiday. The only bit of sand I found (near Karachi) was littered with rabid dogs and old car tyres, and the local women were paddling in veils.

You can't get a drink, either, unless you're a sports star, a politician or staying at the Peshawar Pearl Continental, which has the only licensed bar in the country. Even there you have to pay a fee and sign a chit saying you're a registered alcoholic. What you can do in Pakistan is test out armaments. Out in the wilderness near Peshawar is Darra Adam Khei, a scruffy-looking, one-street village of two-storey wood-and-adobe buildings. It's close to the Khyber Pass, and basically beyond Pakistani law. It's a sort of Dodge City of the east. Every shop sells guns – replica AK 47s, pistols, rifles, pen-guns, even guns disguised inside a walking stick. Special agent Q would have a field day. You walk into any shop, point to something that takes your fancy, take it outside and try it.

The main street is an odd combination of mule-drawn carts, wandering camels, clanking buses and the echoing crack of gunfire. All along the road, men are shooting into the air or from special ramparts on the roof, but the buses

– belching out acrid fumes – are more of a threat to your health. I was glad I went. I fired a (replica) Kalashnikov at a nearby mountain. I missed, but at least I'd now almost completed the list of things to do before I was thirty (see p. 179). Only six years late.

The Score

It's a bit unfair to measure Pakistan using the same parameters as before, since I was now married and obviously wouldn't be making any conquests. Still, without 'catches', it actually simplifies the rating a bit, so here it is. It's not a great recommendation, though:

People		Beaches		Cricket		Total
3	+	1	+	8	=	12

14.
England v
the World

Wizard of Oz

'God, you look smart,' friends said, when they saw me in a Nicole Farhi jumper, Agnes b trousers and Patrick Cox shoes. 'Tanya's really got you sorted, hasn't she?' It was true. She had blown a rejuvenating gust through my mind and my wardrobe and people were actually starting to take me seriously. Under her guidance, I'd reinvented myself.

Cricket still played a big part in my life, of course. Apart from writing columns for the *Telegraph*, the BBC had taken me on as their Test match interviewer for the 1997 Ashes series. It would be a chance to get a really close-up view of what was going on. You didn't have to be that close to see what a mess England were in, though.

Basically, they were stuck in a rut. They flopped in the 1996 World Cup, lost a home series to Pakistan 2–0, and couldn't even win a Test or a one day international in Zimbabwe. There was no coherent strategy, with thirty-eight different players tried in one dayers and Tests during 1996, and nine different opening pairs. It was as if they had completely lost any notion of what their core values were and were flailing around hopelessly trying to find an identity.

Instead, a new order was emerging in world cricket. Sri Lanka's fearless, exuberant hitters and wily spinners had pinched the World Cup; Pakistan were winning Test series with bold, pugnacious batsmen and an attack based on searing pace from one end, and one leg spin from the other. Australia, who had recently terminated the West Indies' fifteen-year unbeaten run, used a sort of siege mentality. They surrounded the prey snapping and snarling like a pack of hyenas, until they had Warne it down. Every team except India had been cornered and crushed.

Wanting to gen up on the Australians before my big television debut, I travelled Down Under with Tanya in early 1997 to have a holiday and see their rematch with the West Indies. The old image of Oz was a strapping sheep-shearer in the outback quaffing lager round the Barbie and telling crude jokes – a life of blood, sweat and beers. The marauding fast bowler Denis Lillee, their seventies sporting hero, moustache bristling, temples throbbing, epitomized it.

Now it had been superseded by an urban scene of couples drinking cappuccinos in trendy cafés, and skate-boarding kids chilling out with their mates. Sexist macho had been eclipsed by cool grunge. Their nineties sensation, Shane Warne, a beachboy spinner with four earrings and a leisurely stroll to the stumps, was the catalyst.

Warne was a modern, accessible Australian hero symbolizing skill, success, vitality. He didn't burst blood vessels to achieve his goals but tormented opponents with a flick of the wrist and a flashing smile. He moved mountains with twirling fingers rather than toiling elbows. He could make five apparently identical deliveries all do different things. Deadliest of all is his backspinning flipper, a fiendishly difficult delivery bowled underhand as if you're swinging an incense burner. It floats through the air in smiling innocence, then skids wickedly along the ground on landing, sneaks underneath the bat and crashes into the stumps. Seeing a novice facing him is like watching a new-born foal on roller-skates.

I wanted to have a closer look at him. With the 1997 Australia-West Indies series poised at 2–1, I joined in the Aussies' squad practice the day before the crucial fourth Test at the Adelaide Oval. I bowled in the same net as Warne and the Spin Doctor, Terry Jenner, the man who had made Warne into a phenomenon, watching them plot the West Indies' downfall.

Jenner, who bowled leggies for Australia himself in the seventies, advised Warne to subtly change his angle when bowling to West Indies' dangerous left-handers. 'Go slightly wider of the crease for the odd ball,' Jenner said. 'I used to do it when I played against Sobers. You might get a miscue or an edge.' Warne practised the drill a few times.

A day later West Indies were batting in the Test. Warne was on in the seventeenth over. He went wider of the crease fourth ball to the left-handed Brian Lara, who could only ladle a simple catch to mid on. Next over, he tried the same ploy to Chanderpaul, another left-hander, and induced an edge to slip. Warne rushed up the pitch to be engulfed by excited colleagues, then turned towards the pavilion and nodded at Jenner, who was commentating on radio. 'Marvellous bowling by Warne, he planned for that,' said Jenner into his microphone, smirking. In perfect batting conditions, West Indies were bowled out for 130. Australia won the match by an innings, and with it the series.

Warne-Jenner Incorporated was a skilled industrial unit within Australia's grinding machine. They tinkered with the cogs to make the whole run smoothly. In fact, Australia's game plan was based around a series of double acts. Craft complemented graft. You'd have Slater attacking from one end, Taylor accumulating at the other. Ditto Mark Waugh and his twin Steve. Healy rabbiting and hassling behind the stumps, Taylor next to him quietly chewing gum and gobbling catches. McGrath assaulting, probing, relentlessly denying runs, bowling bouncers at the end of overs to further inhibit the scoring, Warne teasing and winkling.

To explain Australia's new world dominance, people highlighted the Australian cricket academy, the Australian's intense sense of identity and Taylor's charismatic captaincy as well as Warne's brilliance. Actually the reason was simpler. In a largely individual sport, they worked in pairs. Partnerships, they found, gave the team rigidity. It was tongue-and-grooved together. One and one made three. Not a bad metaphor for life, really.

Forgetting the Roots
Australia's skills were predictably too intense for England the following summer, and they retained the Ashes. I spent that and the subsequent season interviewing mainly-disgruntled England players, because the team

were constantly up against it. Then I lost my job. The BBC's contract to cover Test cricket had expired, and Channel 4 nicked the rights with a clever campaign. I wrote to them with some ideas, one of which was the proposal – too risqué for the BBC – to supply incisive analysis of the play *between* overs. The concept was welcomed by C4, and developed immediately.

I didn't expect becoming 'The Analyst' for the New Zealand Tests would mean being confined to a gloomy, video-tape truck for six hours a day, but I didn't mind. Actually, I enjoyed it. What bothered me much more was the way England were playing. It confronted me several times an hour. From seventeen different angles. In 'real time', slow motion, super-slow motion and still frame. The impatient batsmen playing wild, Sunday-league hoiks, the ill-disciplined bowlers shirking responsibility, the hapless novices knowing not which way to turn or sway. When the new, young wicketkeeper Chris Read bobbed under a ball from Chris Cairns which looped over his head and bowled him, the *Sun*'s headline was 'Who's a Silly Ducker?'

Worst of all, I had to try and explain it all. But as the series wore on, it was better to celebrate the zest and determination of the New Zealand players and draw a veil over England. They'd totally lost the plot. They sacrificed the series 2–1 and ignominiously sank to the bottom of the Wisden league of Test nations, for the first time ever. England gave cricket to the rest of the world and now, effectively, the rest of the world had run off with it.

This spurred the usual outbreak of mawkish humour. The *Sun* front page was 'In memoriam of English cricket 1744–1999' and featured a set of stumps on fire in a mock-up of the creation of the Ashes in 1882. On Radio 4's *I'm sorry I haven't a clue*, Tim Brooke-Taylor was asked what were the eleven best British jokes he knew. 'The England cricket team,' he said, without hesitation.

After the series, there were the predictable demands to find a match-winning fast bowler or a leg spinner or the new Botham, alongside the clamour for an Australian style cricket academy. Yet people seemed to forget that we've produced few really fast bowlers and even fewer leg spinners, and there is, of course, only one Ian Botham.

There still seemed to be this obsession to look abroad for the solution to our woes, to try and import the assets of other successful cultures. I suddenly saw a parallel with my own previous situation. I had fondly believed that the quality of life and love was better overseas, and that's where I'd gone to find it. In fact, I'd discovered a niche and a wife in my own back yard.

Now, excuse me being serious for a minute, but perhaps England ought to be following the same tack. We shouldn't be searching abroad for 'ourselves', we're not like *them*. From my two decades of yakking and trekking round the world, I could see that we weren't flamboyant like the West Indians or as daring as the Pakistanis, or super-drilled like the South Africans, and we didn't have the brash, clenched-jaw ruthlessness and flair of the Australians. We didn't share these countries' bright, light outdoorsiness.

What we should be doing is refining our own strengths. We're canny, durable cricketers going stoically about our business. Like the British army, we're dependable, ballsy, good in a crisis; calmly confident of overcoming a superior force with an orderly, diligent approach and some courage. The English play with common sense and unflappable determination. Unbridled passion is reserved for the fourth Friday after Lent and Spanish hotels.

Our typical batsmen – men like Hutton, Barrington,

Boycott, Atherton – wore opposing bowlers down with their spirit and cussed resilience. Our typical bowlers are nagging medium pacers like Bedser, Cartwright and Fraser. They're persistent with their line and their length and their dry wit: 'Want a bell in it mate?' or 'That plank will last you a few years,' when a hapless batsman keeps playing and missing.

Under bold, shrewd captains (Illingworth, Greig, Brearley) England *was* greater than the sum of its parts. Players expressed their individuality. In the seventies we won fifty per cent more Tests than we lost (W33 L21). Ten years of West Indian shelling and another ten of Australian sniping has totally eroded our self-belief. We're numbed by inhibition and the mission-less, petrified world of county cricket. We've forgotten who we are and what we're good at. In the nineties we'd fielded eighty-six different players at Test level under generally dour leaders. Individualism tended to be swallowed up by a manager/captain's monoculture. The statistics from the previous generation have been reversed: we've lost fifty per cent more games than we've won (W26 L43).

People say English cricket's had its last rites. That all you can see is the rusting stern about to plunge into the depths. It's unnecessarily morbid. There's still bags of talent and enthusiasm, Test matches are sold out and junior cricket in many places is thriving. I saw several impromptu kids matches going on simultaneously in my local park last summer. The game is not in its last throes. It's just dead in our heads.

With a bit of ingenuity, the damage could be repaired. Sprinkle the core values – the dogged determination and the dry wit – with the element of surprise. Experiment, take a risk, outsmart 'em. Indulge the mavericks, tolerate the non-conformists, encourage the oddballs (Nasser Hussain looks as if he might have the right idea). If nothing's happening on the field, borrow the Monty Python mantra: 'And now for something completely different.'

Smitten

'Something completely different.' Not a bad epithet for London. It's a city where there's rarely a dull moment and always something unexpected round the next corner. It constantly surprises you. Everything's mixed up abstractly, it's a total hybrid. Standing beneath the (stationary) Millennium Wheel just before the New Year, it suddenly dawned on me that my life had come full circle. After almost two decades of wanderlust, rummaging through many of the world's hotspots and fleshpots, The Girl had literally turned up on my doorstep. So had The Place.

I'd met my wife, Tanya at home. She was stylish, sexy, sophisticated, unpredictable and diverse. I was feeling the same way about London. Its elegance was emerging, its moodiness kept you on your toes, it pouted and smouldered, it was a whole world in one city. If I wanted an African tribal head-dress, or Sri Lankan papaya or a bar full of Australians, I could find them all in Kensington. Within walking distance of our house there were twenty-nine different types of cuisine, and in Great Windmill Street, you could get a chicken rendang – my favourite dish – as authentic as any in Kuala Lumpur. You were spoilt for choice. Nineties London was electric and eclectic. There was a constant *frisson* of excitement. Even the weather seemed to have got warmer.

I hadn't found anywhere to match it. Australia's cities are too hot (Melbourne was 43°C for a month in 1997; the sun felt as if it was burning through you) and the people are too smug and narcissistic and identi-kit, like the characters in *Neighbours*. New Zealand, as a place, was too isolated, West

Indies too repetitive and expensive, India too crowded. South Africa was too unstable and humourless.

You can have all the sunshine and seascapes that you like, and a bevy of beautiful women, but if you can't have a laugh it all gets a bit tedious. Take the piss out of an Australian and he gets the shits. Umbrage is his middle name. You can't have a joke with a South African because they don't get it, or with an Indian because they laugh at everything (or nothing), or with a New Zealander because they are the joke. And as for West Indians . . . well it's probably not the greatest idea taking the piss out of people who are bigger and stronger and run considerably faster than you can.

English comedy was booming. It was there on street corners, in pubs and at motorway service stations, never mind all over the TV. The depth and self-deprecation of English humour is both our social strength and our sporting weakness. If someone gets too big for his boots, we cut him down to size (what the Aussies call our 'tall poppy syndrome'). No one's on a pedestal for long. It keeps our feet on the ground, helps us retain our perspectives.

My perspective is this. England is one of the most liberal, tolerant countries on earth. London is its mainspring. With energy and confidence and creativity it has become one of the most vibrant cities in the world. It doesn't force artists to conform or Marxists to shut up or cricketers to 'bool seydweys'. It resonates and tolerates and indulges. There are no holds barred. It's a limitless smorgasbord of art and lit and music and cool bars and exotic restaurants and pub comics, and the women aren't all leathery from too much sun.

OK, so the nearest decent beaches to London are two hours' drive away, but, let's face it, that's about the time it takes to find a parking spot near Bondi. And in every London borough there are leafy, green parks where you can do most of the stuff you do on a beach, and you don't get sand in everything. I actually find it quite a relief being outside in summer without having to daub every bit of exposed flesh in factor 30, and I've grown to appreciate the English seasons and snug winter clothes. I can even stand the rain. And if the weather's crap and England have lost another Test series at home or abroad and depression sets in, there's always 'Secrets', the lap dancing club at the end of my road . . .

'London is not a pleasant place,' Henry James wrote in 1870, 'it is not agreeable, or easy, or exempt from reproach. It is only magnificent.' Nothing's changed. Except my opinion. London has totally seduced me. London is the DW I've been looking for all these years.

The Score

People		Parks*		Cricket		Caught (wives)		Total
9½	+	8	+	4	×	2		= 43

*beach substitute

I was in a Soho bar one night just before the millennium when a stunning girl walked in. She was about twenty-four, very slim, with a pale complexion, huge brown eyes and lustrous curly hair cascading over her shoulders. Not entirely of sound mind, I approached her and said, 'You're beautiful, but you're too thin. Eat some food.' Without hesitation she said, 'You're ugly, you're bald. Grow some hair.'

They'll have to try harder than that to make me want to leave again.

Final Scores

	P		B		C		Ct		Total
Sri Lanka	5	+	6	+	7	×	1	=	18
Zimbabwe	5	+	0	+	5	×	2	=	20
South Africa –									
Pretoria	–2	+	0	+	5	×	1	=	3
Durban	6	+	5	+	6	×	1	=	17
New Zealand –									
Auckland	8	+	8	+	4	×	2	=	40
Australia – Perth	2	+	7	+	8	×	2	=	34
Australia – Sydney	5	+	9	+	6	×	2	=	40
India	6	+	3	+	8	×	1	=	17
West Indies	7	+	8	+	9	×	1	=	24
Pakistan	3	+	1	+	8			=	12
England – London	9½	+	8	+	4	×	2	=	43